# THE SECOND WORLD WAR IN FICTION

*Further titles in preparation*

# THE SECOND WORLD WAR IN FICTION

### Edited by Holger Klein
#### with John Flower and Eric Homberger

**MACMILLAN**

*First published 1984 by*
THE MACMILLAN PRESS LTD
*London and Basingstoke*
*Companies and representatives*
*throughout the world*

ISBN 0 333 25964 5

*Filmsetting by Vantage Photosetting Co Ltd*
*Eastleigh and London*
*Printed in Hong Kong*

# Contents

# Preface

The literature of the Second World War – and especially fiction – has been largely neglected by critics, if not by readers. This book, in some ways a successor to *The First World War in Fiction*,* is the first major critical contribution on the subject within an international framework. The earlier volume presented full analyses of individual novels. The scale of the Second World War as well as the mass and diversity of fiction produced during and after the war years suggested the need for a different approach. Thus this volume offers fairly detailed survey essays on the fiction of five principal nations involved in the war, together with a short contribution on Japan. Given the particular historical, political and literary situation in each country, uniformity of treatment is neither possible nor even desirable.

Soon we shall be as far removed in time from the Second World War as Tolstoy was from Napoleon's Russian campaign when he wrote *War and Peace*. No work of comparable stature has as yet appeared; but there is a vast amount of writing, from ephemeral, popular stories and thrillers to journalistic narratives and to works of great scope, seriousness and complexity. The ways in which literature has recreated the war in the various countries represent important facets of modern history and contemporary consciousness. The time has come to take stock of this literature, to analyse it and to reflect on its implications.

J.F., E.H., H.K.

---

*ed. by Holger Klein (Macmillan, 1976).

# Notes on the Contributors

**Alan Bance** is Professor of German at the University of Keele. He is the author of *The German Novel, 1945–1960* and *Theodor Fontane: the Major Novels*, and has edited *Weimar Germany: Writers and Politics*.

**Ray Davison** is lecturer in modern French literature in the Department of French and Italian at Exeter University. He has published work on the impact of Dostoevsky on Albert Camus, and he has made a number of contributions to the Exeter Tapes series. He is at present working on an edition of Simone de Beauvoir's *Une Mort très douce*.

**John Flower** is Professor of French at the University of Exeter. He is the author of *France Today; Intention and Achievement: an Essay on the Novels of François Mauriac; Roger Vailland: the Man and his Masks; Literature and Politics in Modern France; Literature and the Left in France*. He is also editor of the *Journal of European Studies*.

**Harry Guest** is a poet and novelist. He was British Council Lecturer in English Language and Literature at Yokohama National University from 1966 to 1972. With his wife Lynn Guest and Kajima Shôzô he produced *Post-War Japanese Poetry* for Penguin in 1972 and has recently edited the Japanese section of the *Elek Book of Oriental Verse* and also published a new book of his own poems, entitled *Lost and Found*. He is currently Head of Modern Languages at Exeter School and also teaches Japanese at Exeter University.

**Eric Homberger** is lecturer in the School of English and American Studies at the University of East Anglia, Norwich. He is the author of *Ezra Pound: the Critical Heritage; The Art of the Real: Poetry in England and America since 1939* and *'How I became a Socialist': American Writers and the Socialist Party, 1901–1919* (forthcoming).

viii

**Holger Klein** is Senior Lecturer in the School of Modern Languages and European History at the University of East Anglia. He is the author of a study of English Renaissance poetry, a translation into German of Wycherley's *The Country Wife*, and a translation and commentary on Shakespeare's *Hamlet*. He edited *Gerstenberg English Reprints* and *The First World War in Fiction* (Macmillan, 1976).

**Don Piper** is Lecturer in the Department of Russian Studies at the University of Manchester, and author of a study of the Soviet novelist, Veniamin Kaverin, *V.A. Kaverin: a Soviet Writer's Response to the Problem of Commitment*.

# 1 Britain

## Holger Klein

Having read the "war books" so far published, Tom Harrisson in December 1941 talked of a "cataract of tripe"[1] which he surveyed, identifying a few interesting wavelets here and there. In 1943 Granville Hicks found that "some moderately good books have been written about the war" while stressing that "Literature, as everyone knows, cannot be expected to flourish in wartime."[2] The difficulties of sustained writing in Britain during the war were great and have been vividly illustrated in Robert Hewison's *Under Siege* (1977). In 1941 they prompted a group, including Cyril Connolly, George Orwell and Stephen Spender to issue a manifesto demanding an officially recognised category of "war writers" who should (in parallel to "war artists" or "war correspondents") be given "the necessary facilities for writing their books".[3] For better or worse this plea went unheeded and, taking stock in 1946, Alec Waugh and Spender ruefully recalled all the unfavourable conditions.[4]

In the same year Vernon Mallinson postulated, rather more briskly, "Nothing written in England since 1939 gives the slightest indication that this World War, however cataclysmic, has produced or is likely to produce anything immediately significant."[5] Surveying *The Novel 1945–1950* in 1951, P.H. Newby made favourable mention of four novelists, particularly Alex Comfort (for a work actually published in 1944), but joined earlier voices in noting the absence of any "good English novel" to "paint the horrors of war".[6] He explained this by the nature of total war in which (as opposed to the First World War) civilians suffered as much or more than soldiers, and suggested also that perhaps "war experience is a handicap in writing about the war ..". Yet he held out hope, arguing that the "process of gestation" was still going on. In 1956 John T. Frederick combined both arguments; with reference to the time-lag with which "some of the most important novels of the First World War" appeared, he surmised "major novels of World War II may be just around the corner, chronologically speaking".[7] They were not, if we trust Frederick R. Karl as *A Reader's Guide* (1961).[8]

And there the matter rests, apparently. Apart from its partial inclusion in Mary Cadogan and Patricia Craig's *Women and Children First* (1979) the subject as such has by and large been left to a couple of German and (peripherally) American theses,[9] discussions of individual authors who (as e.g. Anthony Powell and Evelyn Waugh) attract attention in a wider literary framework, finally to reviews following the appearance of new works and prefaces to occasional reprints.

War drama from, say, J.B. Priestley's *Desert Highway* to Ian McEwen's *The Imitation Game*, is still awaiting intensive treatment. Poetry had not fared much better until Vernon Scannell's *Not Without Glory* (1976). Scannell remarks on "the way in which the Great War has become a powerful myth while the Second World War, to a succeeding generation, has never been other than a historical event ...".[10] Indeed the stream of fresh literature particularly fiction, about 1914–18 is astonishing. Among the factors contributing to this mythic quality Scannell stresses the inexperienced and unjaundiced attitudes prevailing in 1914, the relative remoteness of the actual fighting, and the preponderance as well as the largely static nature of the Western Front, which facilitated its transformation into a "fixed imaginative landscape".[11]

On the part of Britain the Second World War was, as A.J.P Taylor put it in 1975, "that very rare thing – a just war".[12] Opposing at last the aggressions of the tyrannical and barbarous National Socialist German state could leave little sense of tragic i.e. unnecessary and futile waste such as hangs over the Great War and informs much of its literature. On the other hand, there was no "innocence" (Philip Larkin)[13] to be lost. People knew, or thought they knew, what a war with modern weapons involved and what comes out of it. Not surprisingly there was no enthusiasm, nothing resembling the euphoric war hysteria of August 1914. Instead, there was resigned resolution. In an exercise of "Mass Observation" carried out before the German attack on Poland, only 2 per cent of those questioned were glad at the prospect of war; 34 per cent still agreed that "anything was better than a war"; 9 per cent had no definite view. A majority, 55 per

nt , assented directly or indirectly to the proposition that "we
ight to get it over with".[14]

This war proved, overall, anything but static. It was also more
tensely global and much more diversified than the First. With
ascist Italy and Imperialist Japan as further enemies, no single
heatre" of war held for very long a position of unique impor-
nce. Furthermore, other arms besides the infantry, and the
her Services besides the Army had an incomparably more active
·le than in 1914–18. Finally, while in the Dominions and in
dia the war remained (just about) *ante* or *ad portas*, large parts of
e Empire were scenes of destructive combat, and in Britain the
opulation was directly affected by aerial attacks. Civilians have
iffered from war throughout the ages. This time, however, as
aylor says, "The distinction between Front and Home almost
sappeared under the impact of indiscriminate bombing." These
ctors may, at least for a time, have helped to inhibit the growth
a large literary myth. As time passed, certainly some smaller
yths seem to have arisen.

Mythical or not, and whatever Hicks meant by "flourishing",
as literature has definitely been booming. Harrisson's
cataract" of forty years ago has become a floodlike river. And the
ipply shows no signs of dwindling. A step to the nearest bookstall
usually enough to procure the latest comics in *The War Picture
ibrary* (more than 1600 numbers so far) or in *Commando: War
tories in Pictures* (more than 1300 numbers). Halfway between
omic and book one finds Marcus Allgood's *D-Day Dawson*
977), "The Hero of Battle Picture Library". Indeed as far as
iortish and fairly stereotyped novels are concerned, the tide was
sing in the 1970s. In 1973, Charles Whiting set *The Destroyers* on
eir devastating path, in 1974 Klaus Netzen unleashed *The
illers* around John Standish (a combination of Campion, Bond,
id The Man from ORGY) while Leslie McManus launched
*hurchill's Vixens*; 1976 saw the first of Joe Hunter's books on the
inpalatable) feats of "Major Harrison" and his *Attack Force*.
ompared to these, earlier series like those of *Biggles* and W.E.
ihns's additional ones (*Worrals* and *King of the Commandos*)[15] or
ennis Wheatley's *Gregory Sallust* stories (covering his stupend-
is activities from 1939–45) appear as it were hand-made, fairly
urdy and homely, though they are as easy to read and as
redictable.

Nor is this recent rash confined to secret agent and commando-type stuff. Whereas with John Fuller's *Desert Glory* (1960) Spencer & Co's "World War II Series" of independent and solid stories had reached 91 numbers, the 1970s witnessed a proliferation of specialised one-author series. In 1976 David Williams started *Tank*, in 1978 Matthew Holden *Squadron*, ". . . the riveting series of aerial combat adventures", joining Frederick E. Smith's bulkier *633 Squadron* (1956) with its sequels. All these have a long way to go before nearing *The J.E. MacDonnell Sea Adventure Library* which already in 1968 numbered around 80 volumes. Moreover, there are book versions, assured of mass consumption, made after television series – notably the three-volume Ashton Saga of John Finch's Granada production *A Family at War:* Vol. 1 (Kathleen Barker) appearing in 1970, Vol. 2 (Jonathan Powell, with some very effective writing) in 1971, Vol. 3 (Roy Russell) in 1972. Another example is William Buchanan's *Pathfinder Squadron* (1972) after the Toledo series.[16]

"Tripe"? – most things mentioned so far would be called that by many. The term would be unjust to Fuller, and Finch's wartime panorama deserves a better name. And what shall one call authors like John Harris or Douglas Reeman who turn out, nearly year by year (something little known in the literature of the Great War) self-contained, solid, interesting and on the whole competently written novels? Hardly "great" in the sense applying to Dickens or Scott. Pondering "Prospects for the English Novel" in 1949, V.S. Pritchett claimed that "the gulf between the intelligent novels and the popular pulp has become wider than it has ever been".[17] Only a thorough history of the novel since 1939 could help decide on that. Meanwhile Pritchett's term is useful. Leaving aside "greatness", always best used for the past, one must insist that there are good and very good novels of the Second World War. A vast distance lies between *D-Day Dawson* and *The Cruel Sea*; but the "gulf" is filled with works many of which may well be described as "moderately good" (Hicks) or as "intelligent" novels. The whole gamut needs to be taken into account. What "tripe" is read by vast numbers of people cannot be a matter of indifference. Moreover the excellence of certain works is often best seen by comparison with thematically or structurally similar ones. And the strong appeal of the war as a subject in contemporary fiction is noteworthy in itself.

In a literary field so vast (and largely uncharted) as to make one doubt the possibility of ever reading half the relevant books drastic limitation might seem to commend itself, perhaps by region (e.g. Europe, the Far East) or by period (e.g. the war years, the seventies) or by Service (Army, RN, RAF). But such restrictions would entail losses in perspective outweighing the advantages. Moreover, the field itself, "war fiction", is by no means easily definable, and even if it were, discussing it in isolation would entail grave impoverishment, indeed distortion of the horizon. There is, indicated by Harrison's term "war books" (continuing a critical tradition arising from the Great War) much closely related prose literature, often excellent and representing a challenge to fiction. In view of these circumstances and the scope here available, a mainly exploratory and theoretical approach seems preferable at present. Thus the survey offers an inquiry into what *war* fiction may encompass with regard to the Second World War; a consideration of the general condition of war *fiction*; a review of the thematic context followed by a typological review of war fiction according to a fundamental aspect of structure and, by way of a sample, a look at a quality-linked aspect; finally, some reflections arising from factors of chronology.

The narrowest compass of war fiction would be, following Oldsey (note 9), "Aspects of Combat", concentrating on the fictional representation of battle and its effects on men. This, while feasible, would segregate one aspect of the war experience and preclude many important avenues of investigation. It would also tend to overlay features of reality: "combat" in this war was not so clear-cut. Riding on a bus through London, Rowe, the central character in Graham Greene's *The Ministry of Fear* (1943) reflects:

> Knightsbridge and Sloane Street were not at war, but Chelsea was, and Battersea was in the front line. It was an odd front line that twisted like the track of a hurricane and left patches of peace.

This is just one among many contemporary impressions of what Taylor later characterised as the near-merging of between Front and Home – a corollary of total warfare that could only be sustained as *The People's War* (Angus Calder, 1969).

John T. Frederick confines himself to "books of fiction that deal

primarily with the experience of men and women in the armed
services during the war" (see note 7). This would seem to afford
sufficient scope, but the problems of such a formula need to be
explored. Cecil Lewis's *Pathfinders* (1943) e.g. deals "primarily"
with the past lives of a Wellington bomber crew as reflected upon
in turn during a flight to Kiel. Leslie Kark's *Red Rain* (1945)
proceeds analoguously with a Lancaster and Munich. Both books
have essential affinities with Rex Warner's *Why Was I Killed?*
(1943), a (non-realist) composite portrait of British society which
remains outside Frederick's terms as the characters (except
perhaps the dead soldier) are not "in the armed services". Yet
such works cannot be dissociated from the subject, however one
defines it.

Considering the receiving end of air warfare, can one really
draw a firm line separating "fighters" on the ground like those
portrayed in William Sansom's "The Wall" (1941) or "Building
Alive" (1946), Henry Green's *Caught* (1943), Nicholas Monsarrat's *Heavy Rescue* (1947) from those figuring e.g. in Hammond
Innes's *Attack Alarm* (1941) which aims, "Within the framework
of a thriller" at giving "some idea of the atmosphere of a fighter
station during the Blitz"?

Furthermore, given a war that *was* partly fought "unconven-
tionally" by spies, agents, small groups of saboteurs and raiders,
often in co-operation with resistance movements in enemy-
occupied territory, a war moreover of ideologies, cutting to some
extent across nationalities, "thrillers" are hard to reject as part of
war fiction. And there is no difference of principle between those
fighting this kind of war at home and those doing it abroad –
between, on the one hand, Nicholas Blake's (Cecil Day Lewis's)
*The Smiler with the Knife* (1939), Michael Innes's (J.I.M.
Stewart's) *The Secret Vanguard* (1940), Margery Allingham's
*Traitor's Purse* (1941), Agatha Christie's *N or M?* (1941), Somerset
Maugham's *The Hour before the Dawn* (1942), Greene's *Ministry of
Fear* (weaving rings round many "professionals"), Priestley's
*Blackout in Gretley* (1943) and, on the other hand, books like
Wheatley's *V for Vengeance* (1942), Walker Taylor's *Spylight*
(1943), Johns' *Gimlet Goes Again* (1944), Nevil Shute's *Most Secret*
(1945), Alistair Maclean's *Where Eagles Dare* (1967), Leslie
Thomas's (splendid) *Ormerod's Landing* (1978) and Harris's *The
Fox From His Lair* (1978); to take two novels with the same
intended assassination victim: between Geoffrey Household's

(just pre-war) *Rogue Male* (1939) and Heinz Kunz's *The Führer must die!* (1959) or, juxtaposing two novels by the same author, between Peter Leslie's *The Bombers* (1972) and *Killer Corps* (1971).

An intriguing case in this connection is Duff Cooper's *Operation Heartbreak* (1950), peculiarly linked to a documented incident. To divert German attention from the planned Allied invasion of Sicily (July 1943), Naval Intelligence ingeniously fabricated official letters pointing to Greece, and put them on the body of a dead British officer with a likewise fabricated identity, whose body was floated off the Spanish coast in April 1943. The German intelligence network functioned well, as expected; the deception came off.[18] What (clothed in decorous camouflage) Cooper does is to invent a life-story for the man who posthumously served his country in this bizarre fashion. He makes no thriller of it nor a combat story. The dull, disappointing career of Captain Willie Maryngton is a poignant portrait of an increasingly frustrated Simple Soul. It is moreover an ambivalent view of military and clubland Britain before and during the war as well as a (likewise unhappy) love story. That touches on another direction in which the subject's delimitation is problematic.

A "love interest" is, quite naturally, frequent in war fiction, and practically *de rigueur* in the thriller variety (of late, often juicily explicit) as well as essential to the type of romance Rachel Anderson treats under "The Relentless Lava of War" (1974). There are again many gradations. In many novels love and war are equally central, e.g. Dan Billany's superb *The Trap* (1943; publ. 1950), Lionel Shapiro's *The Sixth of June* (1955) and J.L. Carr's *A Season in Sinji* (1967); or, from complementary points of view: Dan Brennan's *Never Too Young* (1944; the pilot's) and Sarah Patterson's *The Distant Summer* (1976; the girl's). In other novels love is linked to the action but subordinate, as in Antony Trew's *Kleber's Convoy* (1974). In still others the war serves as background, with varying degrees of intensity: from Robert Grant's *A Clutch of Caution* (1975), unfolding the doomed love between a Conscientious Objector and a fighter ace's wife (literally) beneath the Battle of Britain sky, to the twisted passions Beryl Bainbridge sets against a less concrete backcloth of war in *The Dressmaker* (1974). Structurally viewed, there are besides stories of continuous co-presence others focussing on love and war in "blocks". Very sharply sequential is Eric Lambert's hard-bitten *The Veterans* (1954); an inverse sequence is found in Morris

West's *The Second Victory* (1958), won in the first phase of occupation in Austria. This romance also illustrates the problem of
deciding at what point the war ends for fiction: the novel opens
with the last killing of a British soldier in those parts and seems to
lead away from the war (as does, definitely, Priestley's *Three Men
in New Suits*, 1945); yet the war is, very concretely, omnipresent in
the book.

A different block structure occurs in novels where the war
action frames love, very strongly in Richard Mason's *The Wind
Cannot Read* (1947); Michael Quinn's harrowing participation in
two Burma campaigns encloses the pathetic story of the love
between him and "Miss Wei", the Japanese instructress. Alexander Fullerton's *A Wren Called Smith* (1957), complicated by a
fictional present frame, demonstrates the deceptiveness of appearances: despite the brief and gory war action this romp is in
essence a "lonely island" adventure equally feasible with other
circumstances to the key situation. In Monsarrat's *Leave Cancelled*
(1945) on the contrary, the war as action is only there as past and
threatening future to the consummate moment of love; but it is
vital. So it is in Alexander Baron's *There's No Home* (1950),
explicitly introduced with the words: "This is not a story of war
but of one of those brief interludes in war when the almost-
forgotten rhythms of normal living are permitted to emerge
again...". The scene is Catania, at the beginning exhausted
troops arrive for a rest, at the end they move forward again. Yet
this "interlude" is inseparable from what surrounds it. The war
impinges continually and forcefully, as in the ambulance incident
witnessed by the Sergeant and his love.

With the exception of West's books all these works technically
fit into Frederick's formula. It remains to probe it once more, with
the emphasis not on the active "fighting" of all sorts that could be
subsumed under Greene's "front line", but in a more general
conspectus. Before the Germans conceived the wobbly "Festung
Europa", people in Britain had come to think of themselves as
living in a "Fortress": ever since the "colossal military disaster"
(Churchill, 4 June 1940)[19] in France. Hewison's title *Under Siege*
recalls this concept. An early, widely disseminated instance of its
use is found in Priestley's BBC-*Postscript* of 23 June 1940.[20]

If one grants the image validity, one may reasonably argue that
other defenders of the garrison must be considered alongside
those in uniform as depicted, say, in Gerald Kersh's (pyrotechnic)

recreation of training in the Guards, *They Die with their Boots Clean* (1942), Alun Lewis's *The Last Inspection* (1943), Ernest Raymond's Home Guard novel *The Corporal of the Guards* (1943),[21] Howard Clewes's brilliant *Dead Ground* (1945) or Powell's three war novels within his long sequence: *The Valley of Bones* (1964), *The Soldier's Art* (1966) and *The Military Philosophers* (1968). An Army existence like that of Nick Jenkins involves no fighting,[22] and he personally encounters less danger than Sammy Rice, the weapons research scientist of Nigel Balchin's *The Small Back Room* (1943). From there one is lead to the factory people in Priestley's *Daylight on Saturday* (1943) or Monica Dickens's *The Fancy* (1944) and beyond them to all individuals whom fiction shows experiencing the war. One might begin with Jan Struther's *Mrs. Miniver* (1939, 1942) who in the autumn of 1939 felt "they weren't back to normal, and never would be" and continue with Evelyn Waugh's blithe cad Seal of *Put Out More Flags* (1942), L.P. Hartley's massive egotist Casson in the village struggle around *The Boat* (1949; equally massive), Ursula Bloom's gushing *Jenny WREN* (1944), the blighted and twisted existences of Elizabeth Bowen's *The Demon Lover and other Stories* who embody a general feeling of insecurity, strain, abnormality and distortion that she acutely analysed in her "Author's Postscript" (October 1944), the staunch back-bencher Merriwell of Raymond's *Our Last Member* (1972), Henry Williamson's embittered Phillip Maddison, out of tune with his countrymen also in the last volumes of *A Chronicle of Ancient Sunlight*,[23] Summers, the ex-soldier repatriated to the fortress with a peg leg and a bruised soul in Henry Green's *Back* (1946),[24] to end with Joanna, one of Muriel Spark's *Girls of Slender Means* (1963) who is killed when a house collapses through the explosion of a buried bomb in July 1945 – still during the war, but long after the fortress had been re-inforced, had broken out, had stormed and liberated what was not so much another "fortress" ("Festung") but, as Joseph Kessel termed it in 1943, "a prison":[25] France, and many other prisons besides.

A renunciation of the wider canvas to which these lines, indicated both by reality and fiction would lead, is very difficult to defend in theoretical terms. It can be upheld in practical terms, of course. All the more since a good portion of the picture has already been analysed by Cadogan and Craig, looking at "the experience of women and children in the two major wars of the twentieth century, as presented ... in fiction". They also contribute a delimiting formula not quite congruent with Frederick's: Following a suggestion by Bowen they insist on a distinction between a "wartime" and a "*war* novel".[26] By "war" novels they probably mean "combat" novels (like Oldsey) and subsume everything else under "wartime". Clearly, there exists again a gliding scale of emphasis shift, as also with yet another, perhaps more adequate distinction: "wartime" designating fiction set in the war as environment, "war" designating fiction in which the war is a major subject. While keeping the wider conspectus in mind and emphasising its basic unity, it seems indicated here to complement in some measure the work of Cadogan and Craig by concentrating on soldiers in fiction about the Second World War. A second practical advantage of this restriction is that it allows inquiries particularly dependent on a rough comparability of materials.

On balance it appears defensible to pass over most British novels dealing with the war from the enemy side, such as Errol Brathwaite's *An Affair of Men* (1961), Earl Gray's *No Survivors* (1974) and Spencer Dunmore's *Ace* (1981). This whole area, interesting and significant in itself, warrants separate discussion. Nor are other countries lacking in this – Albert Maltz's *The Cross and the Arrow* (1944) is an American example, Chapter 3 discusses Alfred Andersch's *Winterspelt* (1974) as a German analogue.

On the other hand books like Comfort's *The Power House*, Newby's favourite, which depicts the French side 1939–41, or C.S. Forester's *The Good Shepherd* (1955), centred on the captain of an American escort destroyer, are close to the British experience and therefore directly relevant. The same applies to Pierre Boulle's *The Bridge on the River Kwai* (1952; transl. 1954). Nor could one do without Brennan's novels about the war in the air (even if he had not himself served with the RAF until 1943). They are essential to the subject.

So are the numerous contributions from the Dominions who stood by Britain in the hour of need – as a popular ANZAC song good-naturedly put it: "There'll always be an England/While Australia will be there."[27] It would be feasible and in some ways desirable to discuss these books in separate groups. However, these countries' war efforts were closely intertwined with Britain's; thousands of volunteers served in the British Forces[28] (including thousands from Eire whose official neutrality one finds as resented in fiction as it was in fact), and in many if not most campaigns entire units from the various Forces were involved jointly.[29] So there is something to be said for discussing the literary reflections of this situation intermingled with the British. The only alternative in our present context would be to leave them out altogether – and that could not be justified.

As it takes its subject matter from a historical event – really a vast conglomerate of events – it is not surprising that most fiction dealing with the Second World War is realist. Briefly to characterise successful realist fiction we may adopt Harrisson's (incidental) definition of literature, "the reconstruction and arrangement of life" as verisimilitude of plot and life-likeness of characters and environment. Furthermore, as in all fiction, unity and intensity which, notwithstanding old and new blurring devices (*ars est celare artem*) we recognise, on reflection, as properties not of life, of reality, but of the aesthetic experience. Unity derives mainly from "rearrangement". Intensity derives mainly from the language. Without a use of words apt to evoke whatever impression the author wants to communicate, the whole falls flat; the touchstone of literary quality is, ultimately, style. It goes nearly without saying that a long and continuous tradition in this kind of fiction has conditioned many readers to accept and appreciate variations and partial deviations from this set of conventions.

In war fiction, one limit of realism is transgressed by the speculative projection of what might have happened, if it contradicts the generally known course of history. No buttressing by possibility and probability or historical scholarship avails in this case. Kenneth Macksey's *Invasion: The German Invasion of England, July 1940* (1980) has a peculiar air of unreality, fictitiousness about it.[30] This is brought out even more when one contrasts it e.g. with Netzen's second *Killers* volume, called *The Winston Churchill Murder* (1974) and Jack Higgins's vastly superior *The Eagle has landed* (1975), both thrillers about (imagined) unsuccessful attempts to silence "That Voice", as Vere Hodgson described it on 8 May 1945, "which had steered us from our darkest hours to the daylight of deliverance."[31]

The effect of realism is not eroded in such novels but by others, straining the conventions in different directions: that of snobbish whimsicality as exhibited by Curzio Malaparte (esp. in *La Pelle*,

1949, transl. *The Skin* 1952) or in that of Sven Hassell's monotonous Grand Guignol manner (e.g. *Monte Cassino,* 1969). Of both traits there is little evidence in British war fiction, while a third type, veering towards romantic melodrama (beyond West) is present. Take Jerrard Tickell's *Appointment with Venus* (1951). The general situation and mood on "Armorel" (presumably modelled on Sark) answers well enough the early phase as described in Alan and Mary Seaton Wood's *Islands in Danger* (1955), itself subtitled "The fantastic story of the German occupation of the Channel Islands 1940–1945". There is no impossibility and perhaps not overmuch improbability about the idea of commandos taking a priceless pedigree cow plus calf off the island, linked to the destruction of the latest German E-boat. Yet the realist potential of the story, including humour, is drenched and eventually drowned by soft-soap sentimental eyewash.

Whatever its weaknesses, Tickell's book can serve to point out the general relationship between war fiction and war-as-history. The fundamental principle is that fiction does not show the historical event *qua* event but *qua* impact, depicting the collective experience through the actions and sufferings of individuals.[32] This emerges as clearly, to take weightier examples, from a comparison of Monsarrat's *The Cruel Sea* (1951) with Donald MacIntyre's *The Battle of the Atlantic* (1961). It likewise becomes evident from comparing analogues to Finch's *A Family at War* such as the early (and very solid) *The Corbells at War* (1943) by R.H. Mottram[33] and, on the other hand, Arthur Marwick's *The Home Front: The British and World War II* (1976), perhaps flavoured with a taste of Rayne Minns's *Bombers and Mash: The Domestic Front 1939–45* (1980).

A corollary principle is also illustrated by these novels: war fiction has to be highly selective with regard to the war as event. Williamson devoted five long novels to recreating Britain in the Great War[34] – and even that "covered", itself selectively, only the Western Front and the situation at home. No one else tried anything near that scale of representation. In the case of the Second World War such an undertaking becomes even less feasible. James Aldridge furnishes an example. He showed what can be done within a limited range in *Signed With Their Honour* (1942), a remarkable novel of the (disastrous) Greek campaign. On the other hand, *Of Many Men* (1946), read as another piece of

realist fiction, is unconvincing. The war is not effectively depicted
in the series of episodes (from Finland 1939/40 via Norway,
Dunkirk etc. to the Russians' crossing the Oder 1945) which
Wolfe witnesses as an unaccountably present and accepted observer. And while John Quayle, the Gladiator pilot, is a convincing character in his own right *and* a suitable reflector for situations
and events in the earlier book, Wolfe is not just "a man in the
shadows" (cover) but a pale, floating shadow himself. The book
acquires interest and importance only if read as showing the
reaction to the war on the part of a (thinly embodied) Communist
mind. By contrast, Waugh's *Sword of Honour* Trilogy: *Men at Arms*
(1952), *Officers and Gentlemen* (1955) and *Unconditional Surrender*
(1961) manages, though renouncing the direct witnessing of most
war action and shaping an unrepresentative outline, to create not
only a coherent and credible (though grotesque) story but in some
ways an image of the war beyond the (quaintly elitist) horizon of
Guy Crouchback, the central character. And even its pedestrian
pendant, Powell's trilogy of war novels within *A Dance to the Music
of Time*, though it shows no campaigning at all, achieves something in that direction.

   Most war fiction is less ambitious and, far from trying to trace,
by fictional reflection, the war as a whole, operates with more
confined objects. A common scale can be gauged if one relates
Reeman's *The Pride and the Anguish* (1968), centred on an officer of
a British gunboat based at Singapore, successively with Noel
Barber's *Sinister Twilight: The Fall of Singapore* (1968), then Paul
Kennedy's *Pacific Onslaught: 7th Dec. 1941/7th Feb. 1943* (1972),
finally Taylor's or any other History of the Second World War.
Generally, both restrictions of scope and of focus are required for
the depiction of the war *qua* impact. If the novelist chooses a
"panoramic" method, the restriction of action will be more severe
– a very high point being reached by Len Deighton's *Bomber*
(1970), comprehensively re-constructing a single RAF raid over
Germany. If an "existential" method is chosen, the restriction of
focus will be more stringent, often to a single consciousness. A
good example, in Frank Kermode's view "probably the best
English novel to come out of the Second World War" is David
Piper's *Trial by Battle* (1959)[35] tracing the inner development of a
subaltern as he moves from his Indian garrison to his death in the
Malayan jungle. There are many different modes of balancing the

two factors. An example of fairly extreme restriction of both (broadly comparable and arguably as good as Piper's novel) is Francis Clifford's *A Battle is Fought to be Won* (1960).

Selectivity, though a prerequisite to unity and intensity, is of course not the only important criterion. Apart from aspects of versimilitude and life-likeness as well as style, there always remains the issue of what one may describe as "Welthaltigkeit": what, if anything, is being concentrated – what of life and human substance the author integrates into his chosen frame. This question can be asked of all fiction, thinking of Joyce's *Ulysses* as a most glorious achievement in "concentration". But the direct relationship of war fiction to specific world events gives the question a particular slant; the 6 June 1944 is in this respect in a category different from the 16 June 1904.

"Reconstruction" (even by the historian) involves interpretation; "rearrangement of life" in fiction is not only ineluctably but prominently interpretation. It already informs the very choice of characters and action, and permeates the whole work – whether or not authorial comment is added. This interpretative character of fiction (probably more than the laws of libel) accounts for the fact that in war novels, though a link to historical events is established and frequently elaborated, historical personages: famous leaders and commanders tend not to be at the centre but mostly appear, if at all, as marginal or background figures, often mere props to realism. A novelist's characters fulfil specific functions within the overall fabric of his fiction, and the more central a character's role, the more it needs shaping according to the meanings the action is given, not to the reality it reflects.

Also imaginary admirals, air marshalls and generals are rare and usually marginal. There are Brigadiers who play important roles in fiction and are developed as visualisable people, notably Waugh's Ritchie-Hook and Robert Henriques's Hatherley-Cooke in *Red Over Green* (1956), but also Heathfield and Tallemach in Harris's *Swordpoint* (1980). But few if any central characters get beyond the rank of naval captain, group captain or colonel. Two reasons immediately suggest themselves: firstly, the necessary malleability of a character as set out above decreases in inverse ratio to the rising weight not only of documented but also of logically required official circumstantiality. And secondly, while such a swift-moving kind of warfare brought top ranks often close to the situation of other soldiers, their function was still to plan, organise and command others to fight. A necessary role, but it sets them apart.

No doubt there is a human problem: "the burden of ultimate responsibility" or perhaps "the tragedy of high command". War fiction, while not poor in relevant comments or even short scenes (often as sympathetic, sometimes condemnatory side-glances) has not often taken it up.[36] The reason is perhaps that such figures are difficult to endow with representativeness, a quality essential – notwithstanding many a hero's pronounced individuality and uncommonness of circumstances – to the relevance and appeal of modern fiction. On the other hand it is noticeable that few British war novels have central characters taken from the vast majority of "members of the armed services" like able seamen, stokers, mechanics, gunners, drivers, cooks; even private infantrymen are not as often the hero as one might expect. And while it is obvious that captains, tank commanders and pilots had a more directly "interesting" war, the same does not apply to the infantry, to paratroopers or marines. The main explanation is perhaps that a certain measure of responsibility for others, scope for decision-taking and freedom of movement such as enjoyed by NCOs (whose share as fictional heroes is much larger in Second than in First World War fiction) and particularly officers makes widely relevant fictionalisation easier. It would however appear that the number of war novels centred on private soldiers has been rising since the later 1960s.

Interpretation in war fiction can go beyond the extent entailed in a recreation of actual or representative events. Few novels entirely lack comment on the war, many reflect on the conditions obtaining before it started, on contemporary society, the enemy and the post-war future. Others show a strong interest in analysing aspects of the human condition. Laurie Andrews describes *Tattered Battalion* (1957) as "an attempt to portray the reactions of certain types of men to a certain set of circumstances" (Author's Note). More frequently this is implied, in Clewes's *The Unforgiven* (1947), Charles Morgan's *The River Line* (1949), D.A. Rayner's *The Enemy Below* (1956), William Allister's *A Handful of Rice* (1961) or Stephen Ashton's *The Pitiless Sky* (1979). Usually, it seems, novels in which this interest dominates present their characters in circumstances of far-reaching or total isolation. Thus the spotlight falls naturally on a confined group. A prime instance is James Clavell's *King Rat* (1963), which, besides being "terrifyingly exiting" (Ian Fleming on the cover) could be called a study of man as captive animal. Rex Warner's allegorical *The Aerodrome*, pre-dating the war but inseparable from it and (over-) enthusiastically praised both by Harrisson on its appearance (1941) and much later by Angus Wilson[37] works on the same principle. It is perhaps most valuable as a study of the Fascist leader mentality, complementing as it were Priestley's *Postscript*-sketch of the Fascist follower (23 June 1940), but necessarily more impressive on account of the scope and manner afforded by fiction.

Great scope is not always required for such studies, as one sees in Laurens van der Post's *A Bar of Shadow* (1954) which reconstructs, skilfully disjointed, in Sergeant Hara the mentality of a Japanese prison tyrant/torturer. There emerges an unforgettable portrait; it matches closely personality traits of at least one case presented in Lord Russell's survey.[38] Nor is seclusion the only method – Deighton's series of chilling vignettes entitled *Declarations of War* (1973) might be termed studies of man as military animal.

Like that of the First World War, fiction of the Second World War is embedded in other prose literature: histories, biographies and autobiographies detailing not what could be true, but what is true in the sense that it can be documented as fact or vouched for by specific persons. This is an immediate, likewise immense context to our subject, meriting close consideration. In the war, fiction shares with other literature a general subject as dramatic – or traumatic, as exciting, in many respects as hair-raising as anything a writer could conceive.

No surprise therefore that in accounts of *all* kinds expressions abound that are taken from other high-tension areas of human experience, especially from the theatre, competitive sports, and gambling. Stages are set, curtains rise and fall, first or last acts of dramas are played out; leaders put in appearances, make gestures and give speeches, they make moves, they take risks, outwit their opponents, play trump cards; grounds are prepared, ships race to destinations, planes are downed, guns score hits, strongpoints are knocked out; units reach start lines, others are handicapped or trapped, reserves are thrown in, enemies will be hit for six, aces come and go; there are good and bad shows, rules get broken, eventually one side wins and the other loses, is beaten.

The analogies are wider than such arbitrary culling of stock phrases reveals. Not only do these other genres share the subject matter and the medium of prose, the mould in which they are cast basically corresponds to the adventure story, from the brief tale to the epic. There are not infrequently narrative experiments in war fiction, such as mixing of forms, shifts of perspective, the occasional *tour de force* like Brennan's systematic "you" in *Never Too Young*, probably a spin-off from the last pages of Hemingway's *A Farewell to Arms* (1929) and best known through *Second Thoughts* by Michel Butor (*La Modification*, 1957, transl. 1958). In non-fictional war writings one usually finds a consistent third-person (omniscient) narrator for histories and biographies, or a consistent first-person narrator for fixed-perspective histories like Alan Moorehead's *African Trilogy* (1944) as well as for memoirs, reminiscences and autobiographies (often adding something like omniscience in the form of hindsight enjoyed by the narrating as opposed to the experiencing "I"). By and large, however, even stretching the notion of experiments, these two main possibilities account for the bulk of war fiction as well. Regarding style, war fiction has famous rivals. And good writing in non-fictional prose is broadly based.

That does not turn such works into novels. Nor are these considerations intended to deny differences in rationale, approach, objectives and methods as well as presentation between what might comprehensively be called "historical" as opposed to fictional war writing. That would in principle be absurd. In practice, the distance is not consistently wide. On the one side of a "no-man's land" many war novels incorporate textbook-type summaries, some use procedures recalling the documentary. And quite a few novels are not only based on personal experience (that is frequent) but amount to slightly modified autobiographies. On the other side, a variety of historical writings addressed to a wide readership either show similarities to fiction by their general cut, or they employ, for divers reasons, devices of arrangement and animation well-tried in fiction.[39] Looking at some examples (with films occasionally serving as analogues to novels) not only brings some of the related material to mind as interesting and valuable in itself, but also helps to delineate further the contours of our field.

From earlier arguments we may deduce where to look in

event-centred accounts: not at histories of the war, of whole theatres and campaigns, but accounts of specific actions – battles, operations, raids – or units. And even at that level the scope of action embraced and the given perspective determine the distance to analogy with fiction. We find affinities not (despite the title) in Richard Hough's *The Hunting of Force Z* (1963) but in Forester's *Hunting the Bismarck* (1959) which must in fact count as fictionalisation; not in Brian Connell's *Return of the Tiger* (1960) nor C.E. Lucas Phillips's *The Raiders of Arakan* (1971) but in W. Stanley Moss's *Ill Met by Moonlight* (1950); far less in Michael Calvert's Chindits book *Prisoners of Hope* (1952) and *The Grey Goose of Arnhem* by Leo Heapes (1976) than in K.W. Cooper's *The Little Men* (1973) and Louis Hagen's *Arnhem Lift* (1945). An instance of conversion across the divide highlights one fundamental difference: Paul Brickhill's *The Dam Busters* (1951) is a fine and full account of 617 Squadron, encompassing much more than the title operation. The *Dam Busters* film (1954)[40] concentrates on this most famous exploit and structures the story to lead up to it. This kind of patterning underlies, too, Smith's novels about *633 Squadron*.

Passing to person-centred stories, potentially close to much fiction, one observes that scope can still sharply differentiate in cases where a great number of people are presented in equal or comparable focus. Examples are John Dominy's Heydekrug book *The Sergeant Escapers* (1974) and P.R. Reid's *The Latter Days at Colditz* (1953), to a lesser extent his famous *The Colditz Story* (1952), and Giles Romilly's and Michael Alexander's *Hostages at Colditz* (1954). The success both of the *Colditz* film (1954) and the BBC/Universal television series (1972) rested particularly on the selection and balancing out of the cast.

A far-reaching similarity to fiction is effected by different methods and in a smaller format in the collection "Authentic Stories of the RAF Escaping Society", written and published by Brickhill as *Escape – or Die* (1952). These are colourful narratives, told (except the last) in the third person, focussing on the drama of a single – character, one is tempted to say, but they are actual persons, each tale is headed by a biographical note into which, as it were, the bones of fact have been pressed, leaving the narrative itself freer to recreate the experience. The effect is particularly striking in contrast to E.C.R. Baker's *The Fighter Aces of the RAF* (1962) which, apart from a few dramatised flashes, gives straight accounts of article length. The contrast is even stronger between the pieces H.E. Bates published as "Flying Officer X" (particularly the title story of *How Sleep the Brave and Other Stories*, 1943) and the "authentic" incidents retold by David Masters in *So Few* (1941).

An especially relevant half-way house in this connection is Kessel's *Army of Shadows* (cf. note 25). He introduces his moving account with the words: "There is no propaganda in this book and there is no fiction. No detail has been forced, and none has been invented." And he continues:

It is not that a novel or a poem is less true, less vivid than an account of authentic happenings. I rather believe the contrary. But we are living in the midst of horrors, surrounded by bloodshed. I have felt neither the right nor the strength to go beyond the simplicity of the chronicle, the humility of the document.

Circumstances forced Kessel to fiction-like procedures. In order to protect the Resistance workers whose terrible struggle he depicts, he had to invent names, departicularise localities, switch incidents and people, modify appearance, etc. Above all he had to recreate life in this vast "prison" through its impact on a few people – in order to engage his readership. The book has simplicity (so has much modern writing); it may have in spirit the "humility of the document", and one readily believes its documentary authenticity; the point is, it is *not written* as a document. One honours Kessel's motives in eschewing full assimilation. Yet even as it stands, the collection is organised as a sequence, Gerbier is close to functioning as a central consciousness; this world of shadows looks akin to the many special worlds we enter when reading fiction. The burden of establishing the character of the book (discussed from a different angle in Chapter 2) falls heavily on the Preface.

Full-size biography, though it has a given focus, tends to stay remoter from fiction, probably because many real-life structures are less analogous to those of fictional appeal than incident/event structures; Brickhill's Bader-book *Reach for the Sky* (1954) as opposed to the (easily convertible) biography of Orde Wingate, *Gideon Goes to War* by Leonard Mosley (1955) or to R.J. Minney's *Carve Her Name with Pride* (1956), the heroic life-story of Violette Szabo successfully telescoped in Daniel Angel's film (1957). And again a centrally important position in the war itself would necesitate more radical restructuring for fiction, as one sees from biographies like Moorehead's *Montgomery* (1958) – to say nothing of Churchill[41] – as opposed to Vincent Brome's account of "Pat O'Leary"/Dr. Albert Guérisse's sufferings in *The Way Back* (1957) which is a near-equivalent to a novel.

Some biographies of famous soldiers conspicuously vary the usual procedure in that genre. Thus in Russell Braddon's *Cheshire VC* (1954) the pivotal experience (watching the atom bomb hit Nagasaki, 9 August 1945) is placed first and thereby dominates the otherwise sequential presentation. Less successful is R.T. Bickers's interspersion of "from within" perspectives – logically closed to the biographer unless it be in the form of diaries etc. An excellent demonstration of this principle is the fictitious biography James Balfour chose as the form of his black-humour novel *The Glory Boy* (1961). In Bickers's *Ginger Lacey Fighter Pilot* (1962) the "from within" stretches are accompanied by stylistic variations (notably once more Hemingway's "you"), making them jar even more. Partial fictionalisation and biographical portraying are not easily integrated unless special circumstances obtain, as in the account of Sir Basil Embry's escape (1940), written down by Anthony Richardson in the third person under the wrily connotative title *Wingless Victory* (1950) based on lengthy sessions with the Air Marshall held nearly ten years after the Wing Commander's spectacular adventure took place.

Turning from this autobiography written by someone else and another transitional case, an autobiography written in collaboration: C.F. Rawnesly and Robert Wright, *Night Fighter* (1957; very full and good) to straight autobiographical writings, we can respectfully bypass Montgomery's *Memoirs* (1958) or Sir Francis de Guingand's *Operation Victory* (1947) and Sir John Kennedy's *The Business of War* (1957). Competent and vastly interesting, such works necessarily contribute to the presentation of the war as event. For "My War" books that depict it in analogy to fiction through impact, we have to move much further down the hierarchy and, usually, away from the headquarters to the sphere of, say, Cooper and his *Little Men* or Stephen Bagnall and his part in *The Attack* (1947). Most of all, move "inwards" to where we may expect to share intimately and directly another being's thoughts, feelings, moods, reactions to events – however overlaid, unconsciously organised and stylised they may have become in retrospect, as Roy Pascal demonstrates.[42] What can only be guesswork in biography, or rational if empathetic outside assessment (and irritates if presented otherwise in that genre) comes naturally to the fore in autobiography; in fiction of course it has long by convention been accepted and is most highly valued. Most autobiographical accounts by soldiers stick very closely to events and are widely valued for that; but the "from within" perspective does represent a significant point of contact with fiction – if the author permits it.

Probably the most important example of one who does not is Spike Milligan. You cannot move much lower in rank and further away from GHQ than to Gunner Milligan. Yet few books can be more remote from fiction than his ingenious series of reminiscences begun with *Adolf Hitler: My Part in His Downfall* (1971), continued with *"Rommel?" "Gunner Who?"* (1974), *Monty: His Part in My Victory* (1976) and *Mussolini: His Part in My Downfall* (1978).[43] Milligan shows impact alright, as we follow him and his friends in D Battery, 56th Heavy Regiment, RA, on their accurately charted journey from training to Algeria, onto Tunis, and up into Italy. Not only, however, is he reconstructing and documenting "Our War", the experiences of a spirited band of brothers; he also leaves the reader politely outside – by means of the irrepressible Goon Show humour and by montage. There is an array of alienation devices like sketches, flashed-in "Milli-News", "Hitlergrams" etc., climaxing in *"Rommel?"* where the precious contemporary snapshots of other volumes (bearing captions many a *Private Eye* might envy) are replaced by photographs from earlier wars. Milligan's Saga is a work of art *sui generis*. Its documentary value should not be overlooked, nor the underlying seriousness: amidst all the clowning there comes across affection for his fellow-soldiers low and higher, conviction that Britain had to fight this war, modest pride at having been there, and humble wonder at having survived. The distance from fiction can perhaps best be gauged by reference to a likewise humorous work whose hero, Lt. Ernest Goodbody (inhabiting a fictional space between Donald Jack's Bandy and Hašek's Švejk) roughly covers the same ground: Patrick Ryan's novel *How I Won the War* (1963).

Unfortunately Keith Douglas's *Alamein to Zem Zem* (1943/44; publ. 1946) remained a (substantial) fragment. He fell in Normandy (1944), and it is impossible to judge in what way he would finally have rounded it off and revised it.[44] Even so, it forms an

important and interesting complement to his poetry. Its spirit
corresponds perhaps most often to the last stanza of "Gallantry"

> But the bullets cried with laughter,
> the shells were overcome with mirth,
> plunging their heads in steel and earth –
> (the air commented in a whisper).[45]

Richard Hillary, who was also killed (on a re-training flight,
1943), was able to complete *The Last Enemy* (1942), and this book
is truly outstanding. One of its qualities is its likeness to a novel in
the sense that intermeshed with external events (and no work of
fiction has quite matched Hillary's intensity in depicting the
Battle of Britain) there is an inner development which is completed at the close. The book resembles in this respect John
Brophy's *Immortal Sergeant* (1942). The course of the inner process
is different, indeed opposed in the two works: Colin Spence, a
sensitive writer, grows (very fast) through hardship and battle,
inspired by his mortal but immortal Sergeant Kelly, into "a man
at last", meaning the kind of hard, tough and experienced fighter
Brophy (and others) felt Britain had not enough of at the time
among those with leadership potential. Richard Hillary, a gifted
but careless and lazy exponent of Britain's *jeunesse dorée* who,
rallying his innate strength, had easily (like so many) turned into
an accomplished fighter pilot, develops through suffering that
cracked, as it were, his shell of insouciant hardness, into a
different kind of man: a writer whose public is "Humanity". As in
Proust, the stage reached at the end is the starting point of the
book one has just put down. There is a "Lost Generation"[46] also of
the Second World War, and Hillary as well as Douglas figure
prominently in it, along with Sidney Keyes, Alun Lewis and
others.

Between the positions indicated by Milligan and Hillary there
is a host of interesting, substantial and often well-written volumes
that many readers may turn to in lieu of fiction, others as
complementary equivalents: Books such as Braddon's *The Naked
Island* (1952) and Ernest Gordon's *Miracle on the River Kwai*
(1963), both very effectively starting *medias in res*, followed by
flashbacks; and both, incidentally, revealing (as does Allister's
*Handful of Rice*) the relative "harmlessness" of prisoners' conditions achieved by downscaling and side-tracking, that makes

Boulle's *Bridge* so attractive, the book itself as well as the film (1957). Or Leonard Cheshire's *Bomber Pilot* (1943), closing flushed with the (apparent) breakthrough-success of the thousand-bomber raid on Cologne (May 1942), and Pierre Clostermann's *The Big Show* (1951), a gripping and perceptive diary, pithy even in translation. Or *The Tartan Pimpernel* (1952) by Donald Caskie, the doughty Minister of the Scots Kirk in Paris, and Sir Eric Lang's *Return to St. Valéry* (1974). Both recount special cases but are near enough the natural pattern of escape stories; freedom/fighting – capture – prison life – escape – clandestine existence – freedom, as exemplified in Richard Pape's *Boldness be my Friend* (1953)[47] or, without epilogue, and thus even more shaped, George Millar's absorbing *Horned Pigeon* (1947) and W.B. Thomas's *Dare to be Free* (1951). Against the background of this basic structure one can look across at Bates's *Fair Stood the Wind for France* (1944). The novel lacks the prison life phase (as Embry's account) and the capture itself. Also, it is group-centred, and introduces both romance and tragedy. So does Morgan's *River Line*, a much more complex novel where the tragedy is doubly internalised and moreover presented on two time levels, the past interacting with the present. Yet even in Morgan the underlying pattern is still perceptible. Some works give only half the cycle, starting with the prison life, e.g. *I Walked Alone* (1940; publ. 1950) by the Earl of Cardigan, and Eric Williams's famous *The Wooden Horse* (1949).

This book reaches another borderline between autobiography and fiction. Where truth is reconstructed (instead of verisimilitude being constructed) and presented to the reader in vivid detail of incident and dialogue, there arises the issue of a credibility gap. Many war autobiographers show awareness of it. Clostermann stresses he has not retouched his diary, Millar the prodigious retentiveness of his memory, etc., and generally there is little reason to demur. Guy Gibson takes a different line in his attempt to "illustrate", in a zesty personal narrative, conspicuously framed by the account of the Dam Buster mission (16/17 May, 1943) "the growth of Bomber Command" (Foreword and Dedication). And he pleads: "But I hope that living people who have served with me will forgive me if I have left them out, or worse, put words into their mouths which they have never said. A memory is a short thing, and flak never does it much good." He wants, in *Enemy Coast Ahead* (1944; publ. 1946) to adhere to what

passed, and probably gets very near. Where Gibson had slight
doubts, Michael Nelson – if we are to believe him – had no
qualms, disposing of the problem in quite another spirit:

> I have changed some names [not his own] to avoid giving
> offence. All the events described are based on truth but some-
> times I have removed them from their true background and
> telescoped them in time, because army life is boring, and this
> seemed the only way to make this book readable.

The procedure reminds of Kessel's, but the motivation could not
be more different. Or the result, a vastly amusing book with a hero
who is a literary cousin – on the RASC side – of Ryan's Lt.
Goodbody, however one interprets Nelson's "Author's Note" to
*Captain Blossom* (1973).

Williams is much terser. His "Author's Note" states: "For
various reasons I wrote *The Wooden Horse* in the third person and
used fictitious names for my real characters." Whatever made
him adopt the third-person autobiography (as distinct from
disguising names, which is easily explained), a well-established
form brought to eminence in English letters this century by Sean
O'Casey, the book is exceptionally unified and intensive. Had
Williams set out to write one of *the* escape novels of this war, he
could scarcely have done better, and the handling would presumably not have been much different. In general, the *données* of
escape stories place them close to fiction. For a characteristic
difference between the two genres in Second World War literature an example from another field of experience seems apter.
Andrew Wilson is quite explicit in *Flame Thrower* (1956):

> I believe that my feelings and experiences were not very
> different from those of many other young officers... For this
> reason, and because of a feeling of detachment which comes
> from describing what happened eleven years ago, I have found
> it easier to write in the third person (Author's Note).

The first part of Wilson's statement finds parallels e.g. in Clostermann ("change the dates and a few minor details and it is a record
of the daily life of a fighter pilot" – modest, but correct in
principle) and Nelson ("All men who have been in the Services
will find parallels with their own experience in *Captain Blossom*");

back cover) and reinforces, from a specific angle, the representativeness-argument advanced earlier on. The second part helps to round off our present concern. One may fitly compare Wilson's account with a (likewise modest) novel, Peter Elstob's *Warriors for the Working Day* (1960). That also arose from personal experience, and activity as well as scope are roughly similar (tanks from before the Normandy invasion to the last phase of the war in the West). *Flame Thrower*, the "detached" autobiographical account, has no other structure than that imposed by the circumstances of war on the individual, whose course we follow from the passing-out parade at Sandhurst (Feb. 1943) to the celebration of VE-Day (8 May 1945) in Oldenburg. "Wilson knew that it was over. It ended for different people at different times, and for him it had ended at the end." In *Warriors* the central theme: the relentless strain of fighting and the limits of the individual's endurance, emerges forcefully from the overlapping succession of tank commanders: Donovan (already worn out), Brook (the complete cycle), Sanderstead and Page (in full swing) and Bentley (just shaping up). Such autonomous patterning is a fundamental method by which war fiction generates meaning. And it can best be achieved where the author feels free, beyond reconstructing reality, to rearrange it.

Novels and stories of the Second World War show a great variety of structural traits. They can be grouped under certain aspects, and some of them overlap, others correlate. But there is no one "formula" particularly promising, nor can the tangled mass of phenomena be reduced to a neat system. Arguably the most fundamental aspect of structure is the positioning of the action in war fiction within the overall action of the war. As such it has an unlimited fund of examples. While identifying recurrent positionings as notional types one can point to especially interesting realisations and explore some links to other factors.

One type, apparently not too numerous, and clearly a post-war phenomenon, may be described as frontal and comprehensive animation of a specific historical event. If the event is "small" in historical terms, an incident really, this animation can be nearly continuous while presenting visualisable people and details of action, as James Leasor does in *The Sea Wolves* (1978; the Goa affair, March 1943). The moment such an event is "larger" and more complex, choices need to be made. Thus Forester's *Hunting the Bismarck* sacrifices nearly everything for an outline of the action itself. Rapidly moving locations and perspectives, he synoptically unrolls the entire breathtaking episode from the Bismarck's leaving Gdynia to her destruction in the Atlantic on 27 May 1941. What he achieves is a skilful but sketchy dramatisation of a page in a textbook, with only fleeting impressions of people – mainly Admiral Lütjens (over-optimistic) and Captain Lindemann (more cautious). He does not forget the small people: there is a Dusty on the Suffolk, a Nobby on the Hood, a Ginger on the Ark Royal. But they and many others, named and unnamed, are mere functions in the big chase. As fiction, this remains rudimentary.

Quite the opposite happens in *Ride out the Storm* (1973) by Harris, perhaps the most significant achievement so far within this type. Harris opts for representative particularisation. Here again we have a synoptic and chronological reconstruction, this time of Dunkirk, from 26 May to 2 June 1940. The book may have been inspired by Cornelius Ryan's D-Day epic *The Longest Day* (1959), but the technique developed is different still. Embedded in the historical panorama and the activities of the people organising the operation, about a score of characters come firmly into view, chosen from all parties, while the stories of about a dozen are consistently told. Instead of evanescent Dusties we meet real characters like Sieveright, the ex-scout and ex-clerk (who manages, always dutifully, to pass through the entire campaign without firing a shot), the upright Gow, lance corporal in the Guards (who could have walked straight out of Kersh's barracks and, while death spares him on that occasion, certainly fights with his "boots clean"), and Private Noble (the shifty commercial genius who is more influenced by Gow than he cares to admit). The panorama entails, particularly at first, some heavy-handed transitions, and Harris needs a lot of coincidence to achieve contact between his main characters (wildly different in every respect, even nationality, and clearly of representative value). As the massive tale gets under way, the machinery creaks less and less, and as the perimeter contracts, any and every coincidence becomes credible. The fate of these people, all essentially "anonymous", unimportant to history, fills the bulk of the book. Its subject is of decisive importance to the British war experience; thus some further considerations are due. *Ride out the Storm* appeared late, long after the event and many other books about it. The breadth of vision, the method, the balance of characters and attitudes, all aspire to a fictional *summa* of Dunkirk. The subject is a most rewarding one for such an undertaking, because it can be celebratory. For a national epopee, the folly of Greece and Crete, the shambles of Hong Kong, the shame of Singapore cannot be balanced by rehearsing the numerous individual acts of heroism and generous sacrifice. With Dunkirk even the weaknesses of some and the stupidity of others can be absorbed in the collective glory.

Literary reaction was not undivided: the same year 1941 saw the publication of David Rame's ecstatic prose hymn *The Sun Shall Greet Them* and of Eric Knight's *This Above All* whose hero, getting through, decides to desert (accidental death at home preventing the issue from developing). A wonderful light is, incidentally, thrown on the civilisation then at stake by the fact that such a book was published and moreover proved a great success.[48] Without doubt however, Rame came nearer to catching the general mood. And he is by no means extreme. Churchill sternly reminded the House and the country (while offering gratitude for this "miracle of deliverance" to those who made it possible): "We must be careful not to assign to this the attributes of a victory. Wars are not won by evacuations" (4 June 1940). A timely warning, reactions tended to veer that way; there was much belabouring of *Henry V*. Immediately convincing for the Battle of Britain, the evocation of Agincourt for Dunkirk seems a paradox – yet not entirely so. In his *Postscript* of 5 June 1940, Priestley put it like this:

We have gone sadly wrong like this before; and here and now we must resolve never, never to do it again. Another such blunder may *not* be forgiven us.

But having admitted this much, let's do ourselves the justice of admitting too that this Dunkirk affair was also very English . . . in the way in which, when apparently all was lost, so much was gloriously retrieved. Bright honour was almost "plucked from the moon".[49] What began as a miserable blunder, a catalogue of misfortunes and miscalculations, ended as an epic of gallantry.

With variations, and often in less glowing terms, this image of Dunkirk has persisted. It underlies even so deliberately downbeat and stark a recreation as Elleston Trevor's *The Big Pick-Up* (1955). And it still governs the sober, realistic yet grand and forceful projection by Harris. That ends as it has to end. The scene is the Channel. Horndorff, a captured German officer, fails to comprehend:

> 'You English are mad', he exploded. 'How can you laugh when you have just lost a battle?'
> Connybeare shrugged, apparently unmoved at the thought of defeat. 'Long practice', he said, 'We always lose 'em'.
> Hatton grinned. 'Everybody expects us to', he added.
> Noble had swung the boat on to course again ... 'Except one', he said. 'The one that counts. The last one'.

This finale is not the easy product of hindsight, but an animation of the conviction prevailing at the time and shaped in war literature again and again.

Returning to the aspect of positioning, Rame's and Trevor's Dunkirk books are examples of a second and more frequent type: oblique and limited dramatisation of a specific event. In *The Sun Shall Greet Them* the evacuation is recreated from the perspective of Brandon, a middle-aged gentleman whose anxiety for Britain drives him to volunteer for the small boats.[50] In *The Big Pick-Up* Dunkirk is experienced by a group of soldiers around the stout Corporal Binns. Harris uses this oblique method too, but the multiplicity of individual fates and perspectives amounts, aided by the general framework of observations, to a full panorama. On the other hand, his *Swordpoint* (Monte Cassino; miles better than Williams's *Tank 2, Fortress Eagle*, 1977) and his *Take or Destroy* (1976; El Alamein) clearly demonstrate this type, as well as George Greenfield's *Desert Episode* (1946; also Alamein) and Reeman's *The Pride and the Anguish* and *Strike from the Sea* (1978; again Malaya/Singapore). More openly in the form of animated history is Leasor's *Green Beach* (1975), concentrating on the radar expert vital for one Object (out of 16) of Operation Jubilee, the Dieppe Raid (August 1942), while David Walker's *Operation Amsterdam* (1974) is as fully fictionalised a "true story" as *Sea Wolves*.

These examples are tied to their particular historic occasions.

Where this link is relaxed, a third type emerges: stories merely tacked on to such events. Rarely like Cooper's *Operation Heartbreak*, usually as thrilling adventures such as Maclean's *The Guns of Navarone* (1957; tailend of the Greek campaign), Gordon Landsborough's *Patrol to Benghazi* (1959; tenuous assertion of a link to Alamein), Leslie's *Killer Corps* (marginally connected with the Allied landings in North Africa, Nov. 1942), Smith's original *633 Squadron* (based on attempts to bomb the heavy water plant at Rjukan in Norway, 1943) or Harris's *The Fox from his Lair* (spy chase ending on D-Day and D+1 in Normandy), though this book verges on the second type, a real impression of the Invasion being conveyed.

With further loosening of the link we get as a fourth type: adventure stories pure and simple, set in some phase and location of the war, like Maclean's *Force 10 from Navarone* (1968; a weakish sequel), Whiting's second *Destroyers* volume, *Operation Stalag* (1974; lurid) or Max Catto's excellent *Murphy's War* (1969). This type of story is most frequent in the form of sea adventures, cf. besides Catto, Fullerton's *The Waiting Game* (1974; the Arctic), Reeman's *Go in and sink!* (1973; the Mediterranean), or Brian Callison's gripping *A Flock of Ships* (1970; South Atlantic) as well as lesser successors like his *Trapp's War* (1974; around Malta), also many of MacDonnel's books. Why the sea? Thousands of ships *were* ploughing the waters, many of them independently. And seafaring matter has an age-old appeal to island populations.[51] Furthermore, a ship's company is an ordered and secluded unit of which a concrete impression can be quickly conveyed. And, as *The Waiting Game*, even more *Go in and sink!* illustrate, a ship's voyage (half or full turn) has a given, very satisfactory overall structure. Reviewing the *Dam Busters* film, Lodge (note 40) proposes the medieval Quest as an underlying pattern. Dunmore's *Bomb Run* (1971) offers a better example, but even with ships, for which more pertinent fiction exists, the analogy is at best tenuous, if stimulating.

Reeman's *Go in and sink!* and Dunmore's *Bomb Run* represent transitions to a quite numerous fifth type in which a certain area of war experience is condensed into an imaginary episode, constructed and told in such a way as to represent that experience's essential features. This is what Brophy aimed at with his desert action in *Immortal Sergeant*; another example is Fred Majdalany's *Patrol*, a very successful novel (1953; the 1973 edn claims 1 million copies sold). The same features characterise Andrews's *The Patrol* (1956; Burma) and his *Tattered Battalion* as well as Clifford's *A Battle is Fought to be Won*, Ronald Adams's two fighter station novels, *Readiness at Dawn* (1941) and *We Rendezvous at Ten* (1942), Bates's "How Sleep the Brave"; Dunmore's *Final Approach* has some affinities to this type. Here again, the sea seems particularly rich: from Monsarrat's *HMS Marlborough Will Enter Harbour* (1947) to Forester's intense *Good Shepherd*, Rayner's *The Enemy Below* and of course Maclean's *HMS Ulysses* (1955) which far exceeds an imaginative reshaping of PQ 17 (June/July 1942). Its masterly concentration of the Arctic convoy experience is even more striking when compared to "intelligent" successors like Trew's *Kleber's Convoy*.

In one sense, Clewes's *Dead Ground* also belongs to the 'quintessential episode' type. However, the brilliantly modulated incident in the mine-begirt, sleepy East Coast town is only the basis for a near-allegorical, ideological parable. There rages a multiple battle of wills, the most important being that between the military and establishment mind as represented by the Adjutant, against on the one hand, obstinate individualism represented by Thwaite, the superannuated, baulked old sea-captain, and on the other hand against the creative, humanitarian and revolutionary artistic soul as represented by Private Elwes and expounded, in his defence, by the company commander. The establishment "wins" after a fashion: Thwaite sails into the minefield, Elwes lands in the glasshouse. The spiritual and moral victory is theirs, the future being vested in Elwes. The whole is no pamphlet, but a wry and sober story, enacted rather than told; a rare achievement of fiction. The affinity to socio-philosophical and political analyses like Lewis's *Pathfinders*, Kark's *Red Rain* and Warner's *Why Was I Killed?* is more immediately obvious in *Captain Smith and Company* (1943) by Robert Henriques. There a sparsely adumbrated commando raid to Norway serves as focal point for a retrospect on some lives, representative of Britain with its values and problems. This work is multi-generic, the interspersed poetry continues the argument on a different level; an experiment possibly inspired by David Jones's *In Parenthesis* (1937). These novels, a small group necessarily, involuntarily remind of Saint-Exupéry's *Flight to Arras* (*Pilote de guerre*, 1942); but they are all group-centred, fictionalised, and (except in Clewes) show less concrete integration of action and speculative thought. This type seems largely confined to the war years.

A seventh type of positioning is very frequent: here a small group, or an individual within a group, is followed through a longer stretch of time, often whole campaigns. The characters are not shown in the moment of crisis only, into which may be drawn (as in much drama, especially by Racine and Ibsen) what led to it, but pass through a sequence of experiences and often change under their impact. Simultaneously a considerable portion of the war becomes visible from the particular perspective chosen. As opposed to the "adventure story" and "quintessential episode" types there is no firm and relatively isolated group and no closed action, complete within itself. Instead, the central characters directly participate in a larger movement of action within which they are, strictly speaking, dispensable (a contact point with types one and two). Reeman's *A Prayer for the Ship* (1958) and Brophy's morale-boosting commando plus society romance *Spearhead* (1943) are transitional examples, Aldridge's *Signed with their Honour* a central one. His (weaker) partisan action on Crete, *The Sea Eagle* (1944) and Thomas Keneally's story of war with the Yugoslav partisans, *A Season in Purgatory* (1976) belong here, as opposed to Maclean's *Force 10*; so does Fuller's *Desert Glory* as opposed to Greenfield's *Desert Episode* let alone Landsborough's *Patrol to Benghazi*.

This large and strong type (for which the sea seems to furnish fewer examples) is particularly suitable for following various others, subordinate aspects which suggest closer comparisons and instructive contrasts. The quality of Piper's *Trial by Battle* is brought out even more when seen alongside an intelligent novel like Andrews's *Of Lesser Renown* (1958; Burma). Thematic and other similarities connect Trevor's *Squadron Airborne* (1955) and Brennan's more sophisticated *The Sky Remembers* (1977). And both contain apt pointers to reasons why Holden's *(Squadron) Sons of the Morning* is less "riveting" than advertised. This sequence of aerial combat and ground interludes from May 1940 to the first defence of London against the Blitz remains unimpressive because it lacks a central organising principle. Also, the few constant figures – mainly Perowne and Joe Caton – gain little profile and are moreover swamped by a continuous flux of other pilots. This comparison reinforces the reality–versus–artefact argument: losses in the Battle of Britain and indeed the entire air war were horrendous (the statistical average reveals Clostermann's 462 missions as another "miracle"). The coming and going in Holden's book thus corresponds to the tragic world of fact, but its straight transposition into fiction proves self-defeating.

A strong contrast (with important general consequences) separates large numbers of novels within this type when one looks at the distribution of action in the sense of fighting. Many novels show iterative or on-going battle action, especially Trevor's *Squadron Airborne* and Elstob's *Warriors*, also Ronald Kemp's *No Time To Die* (1954; tanks), John Watson's bomber tragedy *Johnny Kinsman* (1955) as well as, more pointedly patterned towards a climax, MacDonnell's (harmless) *Gimme the Boats!* (1953), Fuller's (jubilant) *Desert Glory*, Ashton's *The Pitiless Sky* and Guthrie Wilson's *Brave Company* (1951; using the "flying start" technique of Remarque's *All Quiet on the Western Front* and Frederic Manning's *Her Privates We*, 1929). In other novels, long periods of preparation or different concerns *end* in violent action, thus Baron's famous *From the City, from the Plough* (1948), Lambert's *The Veterans*, Henriques's *Red Over Green*, Shapiro's *The Sixth of June* and David Holbrook's *Flesh Wounds* (1966); occasionally they continue long beyond it, as Kemp's book, or Billany's penetrating *The Trap* (closely based on his life).[52] A further structural trait, more difficult to determine, is the centrality of focus: either on the group, as in Andrews, Baron, Elstob and Wilson, or on a principal character, as in Billany, Brennan, Holbrook, Kemp and Piper. Often of course the two are balanced.

Very strong focusing on a single character obtains in an eighth type in which the individual's position is, while superficially tied up with the war, paramount and essentially independent – or develops away from it. In one sense, Catto's Murphy belongs here in that he overshoots the war, extending it when everyone stops relieved, to persecute his vendetta against a German U-boat up the Congo. A clearer example is Carr's *A Season in Sinji* whose protagonist, Flanders, conducts – partly with and for his friend Wakerly – an unremitting feud against Turton, an officer and rival. Bill Cooper, *The Third Man at Berezna Bridge* by Geoff Parnell (1973) fights, beside the official war, his lonely underdog's battle against society for a kind of life. One might say the same about Bracken in John Chancellor's (less well-written) *Mario's War* (first publ. 1971 as *The Train with Misty Windows*), but what this accidental deserter adds in sexual stamina he lacks in convincing cause, such as animates, on quite a different level both conceptually and in execution, the deserters Clive Briggs of Knight's *This Above All* and Oliver Knight in P.H. Newby's *The Retreat* (1953). In the latter (another "atypical" Dunkirk reaction) the chaos of war is intensively paralleled in the chaos of private existence.[53]

Oliver Knight is eventually, completing the story of *A Step to Silence*, retrieved from chaos and despair. No such inner recuperation is possible in Walter Baxter's *Look Down in Mercy* (1951). In one way, the novel impresses as a powerful Burma novel of type seven. What it centrally shows is the disintegration of one man, Captain Tony Kent. He starts out like many clean-shaven young officers. But his movement is inexorably away from his world, in which he was a fairly privileged, comfortably married man of average qualities. Under the impact of war he multiply transgresses the rules and taboos of his class and profession – drunk but coldly deflowering a tipsy Eurasian nurse, warmly seducing his batman, neglecting his duties in battle, giving (after he has watched some of his men being horribly butchered by their Japanese captors to make him talk) the enemy the desired information, thus saving his own life, finally murdering a soldier who divines his homosexual relationship. By Baxter's arrangement of the plot and cut of the other characters, Kent could get away with all this – if he were able to live with his self as he now knows it. Yet he can neither forget nor change but lingers on, dying a spiritual death during physical convalescence. The war is shown as a school of egoism, and there is horrifying violence all round. With the murder of his potential blackmailer, however, Kent has transgressed not just against class and profession, but humanity. While the juxtaposition of this private crime and the gigantic collective crime remains for the reader to ponder, Kent cannot go back, but jumps out of a high window, the war, the world altogether. He does not ask for mercy. Yet who would withhold compassion? As in the "philosophical" novel type, the constituent criterion here is more one of content than of form.

By a different criterion, Parnell's *Third Man at Berezna Bridge* and Chancellor's *Mario's War* also belong to a ninth type, necessarily dating after 1945: novels whose action spans the entire war period, or nearly so. This is also the case e.g. in Ryan's *How I Won the War* and Nelson's *Captain Blossom*, likewise stories concentrating heavily on an individual but moving along with the war, not divorced from or away from it. There is no attempt in these books at depicting the war as such; instead they describe "The War of X" as fictional, in Ryan's and Nelson's case also formal, equivalents of the survivor's autobiography. It seems noteworthy that implied rebellion and bland humour should be their respective keynotes, and that they date long after the war. All three traits are found in Balfour's *The Glory Boy* – really a (pre-*If* public school boys') group portrait, with more telescoping to balance the widened focus, conceptually blending protest and humour in sub-acid to savage satire. Given a writer of the calibre evinced in the Greek campaign book, the disjointed episodes in Aldridge's *Of Many Men* could have grown to memorable full-length pieces. The result might have been a composite history of the Second World War in fiction of nearly Balzacian dimensions, and presumably better overall than Harris's and Reeman's collections that seem to be heading that way. In 1946 however, Aldridge was after something else – a rapid purview.

In *The Cruel Sea* Monsarrat works in the opposite way. The book, a "true story" (Before the Curtain) in the sense of truth Kessel assigns to fiction, concentrates on one continuous battle, that against the U-boats to protect Britain's lifeline, the North Atlantic convoys. It also forms a prime example of the campaign type novel; but it exceeds it in scope. This battle is recreated stage by stage from November 1939 until May 1945, from the beginnings to the moment when the enemy submarines, preying monsters of the deep, so long only felt as an oppressive, omnipresent threat, experienced in their destructive manifestations, hunted as blips, audible shadows, and glimpsed on rare occasions in the form of torn and charred remains, at long last surface to surrender and are shepherded to harbour where their teeth are drawn. Building on Monsarrat's own experience and earlier sketches[54] the novel presents this enormous battle through the experiences of two successive escort corvettes; it achieves coherence and density by focusing, within the larger framework, on two characters, Captain Ericson and Lt. Lockhart, with many more crew members firmly delineated. Quite apart from its other qualities, *The Cruel Sea* exemplifies in rare clarity how war fiction aiming at representativeness can successfully operate on a large scale.

Monsarrat restricts himself to one particular front, a constant portion of the periphery, as it were, achieving concreteness there while conveying the overall movement of the war only by intermittent and indirect reflection. Shapiro's *The Sixth of June*, covering the stretch from 1941 to 1944, has the potential of showing more from a near-centre perspective: that of a junior American staff officer. But nothing much comes of this because Shapiro's different concern: illustrating the contact and clash of two cultures (American and British) as personified mainly in the triangle Brad Parker – Valerie Russell – The Hon. John Wynter (commando officer). Mere existence, however, as a soldier placed like Parker (London – Algiers – again London) through these years yields some relevant impressions.

The same may be said of the much larger canvas formed by Powell's war novels. Especially *The Valley of Bones* with its depiction of Army life in the raw at company and battalion level is intensely executed. The overall note of ironic detachment (Nick starts his war with a concrete embodiment of the theatre metaphor) increases steadily; and as he moves to staff jobs in the following two novels, narrative density lessens. Furthermore, dramatic tension is progressively diverted to issues of no great import, though this image of British society at war is still held back, by its very subject matter as it were, from the parochial, vulgar and dull irrelevancy prevailing in the next volume of Powell's *roman fleuve*, *Temporary Kings* (1973). The basic analogies to Waugh are remarkable: comparable main social setting, correspondingly wide scope, the three-volume format, even the phasing (to 1940, then to 1941, lastly the remaining years until 1945). There is detachment in Waugh too, though of a less grey and grim kind. And of course, Powell's hero experiences no fighting action at all. Both sequences are palpably imbued with a spirit of disgust nursed by the less palatable aspects of war society as well as by the war's aftermath and the Cold War (something not usual in our field); thus they include in their large social conspectus figures foreshadowing all degrees of defection from Burgess to Blunt.

The contrasts are equally remarkable, from the central figures (Nick Jenkins is a sounding board rather than a character) to the polish of language. Rather than pursuing this comparison, some traits of Waugh's work may be used to round off our present concerns. In principle, the balance of wider panorama and central focus does enable Waugh to reflect the general movement of events; and his solution of keeping Guy Crouchback mainly in Britain but also getting him to various fronts abroad could have enhanced this quality. Yet in fact it does little of the kind. The patterning is extremely strong and autonomous: these rare forays occur towards the end of each volume. Moreover, they underscore the meaning Waugh wants to generate: futility. Selection of incident was obviously necessary. The choice of the Dakar failure (September 1940) in *Men at Arms*, followed by the catastrophe of Crete (May 1941) is extreme but defensible. These military fiascos are however not balanced by anything in *Unconditional Surrender* but are on the contrary continued by the miscarried "show piece" attack in Yugoslavia (imaginary; summer 1944) in which Ritchie-Hook is killed. *Unconditional Surrender* stretches further, as to Britain's early military muddles and incompetence are added moral duplicity and powerlessness to influence any-thing, made concrete by the example of the Balkans and mir-rored on the personal level in Guy's frustrated attempt to help the Kanyis.

Novelists as well as dramatists place emphases by what they *show*. Waugh cleverly makes Guy himself reflect on the disap-pointing nature of his share in the fighting;[55] but that does not relativise it. Dakar, Crete and the Croatian forest are the only such scenes the reader witnesses, and the arrangement is, after all, the author's. *Sword of Honour* is deliberately unrepresentative of the war as event. So is Guy as a character, so are the "Halber-diers" and "Hookforce" as units. Again this is reflected on in the novel itself,[56] and it is likewise the author's choice. In determining his central figure and the world in which he principally moves Waugh renounced wide representativeness from the start. His choices could not result in anything but a tragic Quixotiade combined with a concave mirror image of the war. Guy's world is not far from that evoked in the Dedication to *Put Out More Flags* and already diagnosed as dead by Ford Madox Ford in *Parade's End* (1924–8).[57] Kilbannock's pointer must be expanded in one respect: Guy's world is not primarily defined by class as such but by attitudes, values, and ways. The main story in *Sword of Honour* is that world's interaction with the world at large and the forces now dominating it – an interaction concluding with defeat on terms of "Unconditional Surrender". Amidst this defeat, indeed throughout the three novels and the war, Guy achieves one solitary act of lasting validity: accepting Virginia's child by Trimmer as his son.

The "concavity" of the war image has endless funny effects. And their pervasive superimposition on the bleak and tragic tenor is a stroke of genius. Waugh impishly puts his best skills to the creation of absurd characters (besides the immortal Hook and Apthorpe there is a whole gallery of minor ones) and of comic scenes (e.g. the interview with "Chatty" Corner and Trimmer's raid). They make the work sparkle, render it eminently readable. *Sword of Honour* is not an adequate fictional representation of the war, but nor are other books on this scale, and the theoretical indications are that none can be. One may disagree with Waugh's general outlook, analysis and reaction to the times, yet be struck by the justness of numerous observations, the penetration of many social pointers, as well as delight in the effective writing. There is no need to *share* (though one should perceive) a great clown's melancholy in order to enjoy, and benefit from, his performance. *Sword of Honour* remains the most substantial exponent of its type so far, and generally among the best books in the field.

Value judgments, with which this essay has not been sparing, are subjective; comprehensive analyses including style, which might vindicate such judgments, cannot figure in a survey, only indications. One aspect of quality, not specifically mentioned among the criteria since it lacks general application, is sufficiently frequent to warrant discussion.

In most fiction of the Second as of the First World War soldiers are not only pitted against the enemy. Usually there are additional "enemies" or, put more abstractly, resistance factors. The mud of the Western Front is the most famous example, in a wider sense the climate and weather – heat, cold, rain, snow, wind – and conditions generally – dirt, lack of sleep, fatigue, hunger, thirst. A different kind is pressure from immediate superiors (like staff sergeant MacAllcane in Holbrook's *Flesh Wounds*); far more often this sort of "enemy" is higher up and further away. There is resentment against the rear and particularly the staffs also in Second World War fiction (see Aldridge's *I Wish He Would Not Die*, 1957, Ashton's *The Pitiless Sky*, Balfour's *The Glory Boy*, Harris's *Swordpoint*, Majdalany's *Patrol*, Maclean's *HMS Ulysses*, Reeman's *The Pride and the Anguish*; but cf. also Quinn's sober reflections in Mason[58] and Harris's "Author's Note" to *Swordpoint*); it may be somewhat less than in fiction of the Great War, and certainly the resentment against those at home is rarer –

a corollary of total war. Thirdly, such resistance may be internal: most of all fear and, as numerous British war novels present it (including at first Baxter) the "fear of being afraid". Lastly there are hostile environments, much more frequently important in fiction of this war than the First; the Desert, the Jungle, the Arctic. The Air appears mostly as a liberating and exhilarating element to pilots (rear gunners feel differently), allowing fulfilment of the Daedalian dream. Sometimes however, this element does become inimical (e.g. the cumulo nimbus episode in *The Pitiless Sky*). The Sea, on the other hand, is usually a terrible enemy; Monsarrat goes further: " . . . the only villain [is] the cruel sea itself".

Such additional resistance factors may be called concomitant, as they arise directly and naturally from the subject matter. Some concrete impression of them seems demanded, especially in realist war fiction. Only when their depiction reaches as it were excess level, when these factors assume large proportions and important functions in a novel, a distinct kind of quality emerges, as in Greenfield's *Desert Episode*, Baxter's *Look Down in Mercy*, Andrews' *The Patrol*, Gerard Bell's *Side Show* (1953), Bates' "How Sleep the Brave", Dunmore's *Final Approach*, Catto's *Murphy's War*, Callison's *A Flock of Ships* and *The Cruel Sea* of Monsarrat, and other works.

There is another type of additional resistance factors not necessarily given with the subject and unexpected. One may call them spontaneous. They are usually vested in specific figures or states of mind. This can be a question of special plot elements such as Redman captaining against the German Hans with whom he has personal ties, in *Kleber's Convoy* by Trew, or an interest like the rabbit breeding in Dickens's *The Fancy*. More impressive is something like the uneasy co-existence in George Krause, Forester's *Good Shepherd*, of the man as captain desperate to do his job well and the man as product of a God-fearing Bible education. This leads (within an enthralling battle against the enemy and the sea) to continual juxtapositions like this:

'Steady on course two-six-seven, sir'.
'Very well'.
Wait for it. They that wait upon the Lord shall renew their strength.
'Sonar reports indications confused'.
'Very well'.

Another example is Kate in Henriques's *Red Over Green*. She is a gratefully registered exception to the grey-eyed, graceful and pliant or dark-haired graceful and pliant women that abound in war fiction. She is more, however: partly due to her speech mannerisms (mainly "one" for "I") she is one of the women in this fiction that one remembers. Most of all she is a *force* (as opposed to an important character like Shapiro's Valerie) dominating the book (as Powell's violent Pamela might have been in a smaller, less complex framework). Similarly Holl in Piper's *Trial by Battle* is not only an unusual figure, one of the exceptions to the procession of tall, firm, cultured but energetic, personable officers. He is an embodiment of practically all things Alan Mart has been educated to dislike and despise but to which he has to adapt. In the final, horrific encounter (comparable to Piggy's with *The Lord of the Flies*) Holl, the distorted black corpse atop the wrecked carrier is an embodiment of War. In Clifford's *A Battle is Fought to be Won* the shadowy and mostly silent figure of the Subedar, Nay Dun, fulfils the role of father/king/god for young Tony Gilling, the willing but inexperienced Lt. (or "Knight", cf. Motto). During the nightmarish retreat in Burma, Gilling fights two battles; besides the one against the enemy that for the esteem of Nay Dun. It is the latter battle that he wins, though he will never know it. Applying this criterion, one might perhaps view Guy Crouchback's outdated and impracticable ideals as such a factor. There are good war novels operating without either high-level concomitant or spontaneous additional resistance. Nevertheless, in trying to establish why a particular book does strike as good, a look for this is often rewarding.


Some specific developments through time have been considered where this seemed called for, but in the main our treatment was systematic rather than chronological. One main justification for this is the constancy of historical perception. It has been recognised that mistakes were made, chances missed, that necessity enforced problematic steps, that also on the Allied side atrocities were committed. Moreover, this proved again no "war to end war"; if anything, the danger left behind was greater, while Britain's influence was smaller after 1945 than after 1918. But granted all this, the basic necessity and justness of fighting this war has not been, and is unlikely to be, widely in dispute. One finds broad agreement between a minimal formula like that of Cecil Day Lewis, 1943: "Defend the bad against the worse"[59] and a maximal one like Taylor's of 1975: "As the war proceeded, the anti-German coalition came to stand for the simple cause of humanity."

Systematic treatment is also indicated since there are no fundamental changes of outlook in war fiction either. Nor has it developed in many major respects (as far as a limited reading shows). The general constancy of reaction may be demonstrated in various ways. One is a look across at historical studies where they overlap. The pictures drawn by John Ellis in the chapter "Attitudes" of *The Sharp End of War* (1980)[60] is based more on testimonies, reminiscences and documents than on fiction, but corresponds roughly to that arising from our material. Stolid pertinacity and realistic scepticism prevail over enthusiasm for the war and faith in grand war aims. The dictators are viewed with contempt, the superiority of the British over all kinds of *Herrenvolk* is undoubted. One finds hatred and disgust concerning Hitler's Germany and the atrocities it committed, as well as those of the Japanese. On the other hand, hatred of the enemy soldiers is rare except in the sense that they represent a threat to one's friends' and one's own life, and must consequently be eliminated. Most soldiers were afraid, but somehow battled on. Bloodthirst was rare (save in the immediate heat of fighting), so were feelings of heroism. Staffs were unloved, the need for discipline basically accepted. Group cohesion was high, comradeship very strong. The dead have not been forgotten. There remained a certain pride at having stood through the worst. One might perhaps go further: Miles Tripp (a witness Ellis does not use) sought out his old companions after the war and states: "Nearly all the crew looked back on the days of operational flying, without qualification, as good times."[61] That is what Corporal Hadfield in Wilson's *Brave Company* prophesies to his men; but in the novel the idea is undercut by death overtaking him and most of the squad. In general, fiction seems more emphatic in differentiating the image of the enemy – less with the Italians and the Japanese (but cf. Allister and Mason) than with the Germans of whom one meets many others besides the sadistic Nazi and the puffed Junker. And fiction seems to pay more attention to the criticism of British society before and during the war as well as to the contemplation of "What are we fighting for?" (though Carr's Flanders ridicules this) linked to brief visions of the future, many of which are not incompatible with Orwell's *The Lion and the Unicorn* (1941). Two fundamental aspects stand out most clearly of all. The one is a mostly likeable image of the British soldier. There is no lack of narrow-minded, stupid, nasty, selfish and mad or weak individuals; but on the whole, there emerges a great deal of common decency and kindliness, of loyalty, fortitude and good-humouredness. Secondly, there is no advocacy or glorification of War as such; on the contrary, it appears in this fiction as loathly and terrible, something mankind should not be subjected to.

Two specific aspects may further illustrate the overall constancy. One is quality. Harrisson simply wrote too early, quality rarely mushrooms. He may moreover just have missed Knight's *This Above All*. However, critics who could not see anything really weighty and significant in war fiction by 1946 and 1956 would have been unlikely to have seen it by 1966 or 1976. The issue remains one of outlook and standards, and models from which they are derived. A completely different aspect is social orientation. This was a People's war, agreed. Now the People/people at the time were overwhelmingly working and lowest lower middle class in a traditional sense. Yet war novels asserting this majority's outlook (as opposed to including characters from it) have so far been a small minority. Notable examples are spread over the decades: Parnell's *Third Man* (1973: cf. also his *A Day is 26 Hours*, 1974), Catto's *Murphy's War* (1969), Carr's *A Season in Sinji* (1967), Watson's *Johnny Kinsman* (1955), Monsarrat's *Heavy Rescue* (1947) and Billany's *The Trap* (1943; publ. 1950). For this scarcity there are socio-historical reasons, no doubt; but beyond them a different kind of phenomenon may be at work, one connected with mood. With more examples to hand, a chronological approach could investigate this further and possibly reveal a gradual change.

The most constant feature of British fiction about the Second World War is in any case the great diversity of attitudes and reactions. This is not the paradox it sounds. There was variety from the beginning (as opposed to fiction during the Great War), and this has persisted. Knight's Clive Briggs will not fight again (1941), Pelham, the doctor in Keneally's *Season in Purgatory* (1976) turns pacifist, we are told he would later become an Aldermaston marcher. The more frequent change was the other way round:

pacifists renouncing their creed in the face of the Nazi menace, e.g. young Hubert of Mottram's *The Corbells at War* (1943), the noble Lionel Fallaize of Tickell's *Appointment with Venus* (1951) and Paul Grimmer in Holbrook's *Flesh Wounds* (1966). For Paul this became easier with the German attack on Russia (June 1941), and in that reaction he is more usual than Waugh's Guy to whom the Russian connection signified the demise of his crusading ideals. One extreme example may help to drive home this vital point of diversity. Towards the end of Comfort's *Power House* the reader follows the stream-of-consciousness of Claus, an old slave labourer. A brief extract must suffice:

> Your natural kindness is canalised to swell the massacre. You set out to save your fatherland and find yourself butchering Jews. You set out to save the Jews and find yourself butchering civilians in crowded cities. There is only one responsibility – to the individual who lies under your own feet. To the weak, your fellow.
>
> The weak do a great deal – every woman who hides a deserter, every clerk who doesn't scrutinize a pass, every worker who bungles a fuse saves somebody's life for a while.

This aggressive *refus*, this militant pacifism is not a result of Dunkirk shock as some may have experienced it. Neither is it the result of disillusionment at Britain's decline or of despair engendered by the constant threat of nuclear annihilation. Of all unlikely years, this was published in 1944. That very fact could again be used against its tenor, but that is beside the present point.

Having re-emphasised the uses of a mainly systematic and synchronous approach one must add that eventually it will have to be complemented by a chronological one. Towards this, some impressions may be sketched. At the technical level, the form of a fictional frame present enclosing a past, so promisingly employed by the "philosophical" type (except Clewes) but also by Morgan's *River Line* (1949) does not seem to have been used for much substantial later war fiction; exceptions are Van der Post's *Bar of Shadow* and Dunmore's *Final Approach* (spanning much more than this war). By contrast, the use of alternating own-side/enemy-side perspective (hardly known in Great War fiction) has significantly developed. Not a device to be expected during the war itself, it seems to have been used in America (Heym's *The Crusaders*,

Shaw's *The Young Lions*) sooner than in Britain. Rayner (*The Enemy Below*, 1956) and Forester (*Hunting the Bismarck*, 1959) are early examples, followed by MacDonnell's *Hunter-Killer* (1968), Deighton's *Bomber* (1970), Dunmore's *Bomb Run* (1971), Harris's *Ride Out the Storm* (1973) and Trew's *Kleber's Convoy* (1974), mostly important examples. This method, clearly indicated for panoramic presentation, has more than technical import: events and people involved in them are perceived in quite a different light. Hardy's poem "The Twain" is an instructive analogue. Rather than fatalism, however, a greatly enhanced appreciation of the exigencies in which people find themselves at "the sharp end of war" can be generated in this way, helping to increase the desire for non-Clausewitz diplomacy.

Turning to morally problematic issues of the war as waged by Britain, Comfort's novel contains seminal points for a fictional exploration of two. In both it runs counter to prevailing opinion in its own period. The first is the question of instigating and aiding violent (as opposed to obstructive) resistance in occupied France, as e.g. Walker Taylor's *Spylight* (1943) exultantly praises it. This question does not seem to have been taken up as yet, unless it be subliminally in Thomas's *Ormerod's Landing* (1978). Secondly the strategic bombing of Germany. This question is complicated by the Blitz and the V1/V2 offensive (and one remembers Guernica, Warsaw, Rotterdam). Complicated also by the horrendous human sacrifice of air crews. No doubt the terrible "cost-effect" equation was not made lightly. And there was widespread conviction that it was right – one reads this not only in Cheshire's and Gibson's accounts (1943; 1944, publ. 1946) but also in Lewis's *Pathfinders* (1943). As became even clearer after the war, the equation was not correct, though A.J.P. Taylor perhaps over-states the case against it.[62] And this issue has been taken up in at least one major work, not surprisingly long after the war: Deighton's *Bomber* (1970). This is a remarkable book in many respects (especially social perception). The aspect relevant here is central to it and built on proven possibility: a pathfinder mishap not dissimilar to one mentioned by Gibson.[63] To explore in fiction is not necessarily to condemn, as Baxter's title and book show. It is to create awareness of an individual or collective human problem – one way in which war fiction can enrich and deepen retrospective perception of the war, thereby making a valid contribution to present-day and future consciousness.

Chronology may also lead to other considerations. Late person-

al memories of the Great War kept appearing into the seventies.
In this respect, no end is yet in sight for the Second World War.
Nevertheless, one may surmise that the majority of works based
on some form of participation in the events have already appeared
(with perceptible "bulges" in the 1950s and 1970s). And their
tenor in human terms is apt to evoke respect, admiration and
affection for those generations. Assuming that the bulk of future
publications will, apart from historical writings, within a decade
or so consist of fiction by people younger than the war generations, there are two tendencies of a possibly alarming nature. The
one is the apparent pandering to instincts of brutality, indeed
sadism, in recent series like Hunter's *Attack Force*, Netzen's *Killers*
and Whiting's *Destroyers*. The other is the provision of a vicarious
experience of strong physical 'action' in publications like the *War
Picture Library*, Holden's *Squadron*, Williams's *Tank* etc. One could
argue that this may not be much more harmful than the provision
of vicarious sharing in the glamorous lives of the rich and famous,
and that the instincts they cater for are equally ineradicable.[64] Yet
a certain unease arises at the prospect of more fiction (to say
nothing of comics) failing to stress the sordidness, horror and
inhumanity of war – something that comes across powerfully in
the vast majority of war fiction as a basic "message" conveyed
independently of the solid conviction that this particular war had
to be waged and of presenting some specific figures to whom, as
individuals, the war offered occasions for acts of courage, mag-
nanimity and even self-fulfilment. Bell's *Side Show* epitomises the
co-existence of these aspects as it has so far dominated. His Major
Hogan is a case of personal salvation through command in battle.
Yet he can reflect:

> And that's what you looked like when you were dead – when
> you died the noble death on the field of battle; a ridiculous,
> oafish, bloody and dusty mess, sprawled in the dirt like a
> discarded rag doll in the gutter of a slum street; small and
> physically repellent and stinking, like a rabbit crushed by a
> lorry on a country road, like the rubbish thrown out from the
> back of a vast butcher's shop. And that's all you were, really.
> Rubbish – in a vast butcher's shop; the sweepings of war. And
> you looked like that, no matter how important you were.

One balance, war fiction has not blurred this fundamental one
among war's many faces, and newer tendencies in that direction

seem fairly contained. Moreover, recent publications of First World War fiction encourage one to expect many substantial novels yet about the Second World War.

More generally still, the fact that this war as a period should exert such a strong pull in Britain must provoke reflection. Among the speculative reasons for this attraction are widespread disappointment with the post-war decades, the renewed experience of economic failure and social strife, this time accompanied by a staggeringly rapid fall from world power. And one may surmise that there exists a broadly based nostalgia, not so much perhaps for the days of Empire themselves as for the days when people in Britain, though reeling under the realisation of just how much had been done amiss, though ferociously besieged and in deadly jeopardy, did pull together. Few would pretend that the nation was metamorphosed overnight into a host of selfless angels. The high-society satire e.g. of Waugh's *Put Out More Flags* (and later Hartley's *Boat*) as well as the sober portrait of the workforce at Canning Kyle's in Monica Dicken's *Fancy* (1944) are sharp reminders of some persisting realities. But a great move towards serving the common weal seems undeniable. It is most effectively (because unemphatically and indirectly) conveyed e.g. in Henry Green's *Loving* (1945), set on an English-owned estate in Eire. Raunce, the sneaking butler, is easily one of the most unprepossessing characters in modern fiction. And the whole intricate web of weird meanness and petty intrigue seems far from the war, let alone from heroism. Yet "Raunce's Complaint", as becomes gradually clear, is precisely his skulking in safety. His unease, his ridiculous ailments stem from that. He knows what awaits him at home, yet in the end he goes. There is multiple irony in the close: "The next day Raunce and Edith left without a word of warning. Over in England they were married and lived happily ever after." There are fairly good grounds to suspect a nostalgic feeling for the sense of national purpose and united effort that did seem to augur well for any future and at any rate, transformed weakness into temporary strength, made Dunkirk possible and enabled the country to withstand Hitler's Blitz.

The early war poster "*Your* Courage *Your* Cheerfulness *Your* Resolution WILL BRING US VICTORY" was inept, indeed could sound provocative at a time (1940) when, as Holbrook's Grimmer reminds his girl friend, there were still one million unemployed (*Flesh Wounds*). But there was courage, there was resolution, and even some cheerfulness – a particularly instructive contemporary witness is an outsider like Ernie Pyle.[65] These qualities did not bring victory in the sense that Britain won 'the last battle' but in the sense that Priestley's "common folk" (*Postscripts*, Preface) stuck to their guns – real and dummy ones – in the face of awful odds and of further disastrous defeats after Dunkirk, until help was at hand. Until the aggressors overreached themselves, aligning with Britain such powerful economic and military potential as would eventually crush them. There is no myth about that: nostalgia for this period can also be based on the fact that Britain did fulfil a historic mission of universal import.

If there exists such nostalgia in any of these senses or in still others, it could be made productive. And a chronological review points to the beginnings: in the war years themselves and those immediately following there appeared literature (war fiction prominently included) full of constructive impulses, blending social awareness, a sense of responsibility and need for reforms, general good-will and the assertion of communal identity. The warnings contained in this literature are equally strong. As an example encapsulating the mood even before the greatest emergencies, a letter in *Mrs. Miniver* (1942 edn) dated 25 September 1939 may serve to summarise both aspects:

> I wonder whether it's too much to hope that afterwards, when all the horrors are over, we shall be able to conjure up again the feelings of these first few weeks, and somehow rebuild our peace-time world so as to preserve everything of war which is worth preserving.... So write all the letters you can, Susan, please... and keep all the ones you get, and put down somewhere, too, everything you see or hear which will help later on to recapture the spirit of this tragic, marvellous, and eye-opening time: so that, having recaptured it, we can use it for better ends. We may not, of course, ever get the chance: but if we do, and once more fail to act upon it, I feel pretty sure we shan't be given another one.

# 2 France

### John Flower and Ray Davison

In May 1940 the German army broke through the eastern defences of France near Sedan and moved rapidly westwards to capture Amiens and Arras: within a month it advanced to Paris, entering the capital on 14 June. On 17 June Philippe Pétain called for a ceasefire, on 25 June the armistice between the two countries was signed and Pétain replaced Paul Reynaud as head of the national administration. For France the war – what became known as the "drôle de guerre", the phoney war – was officially over, but within approximately one month what was to prove perhaps the most deeply humiliating and internally divisive episode in French history had begun.[1]

Despite sharing the ultimate victory of the allied forces France had, twenty-five years earlier, been brutally ravaged by war. Massive expanses of the countryside had been laid waste and the male population decimated. The strident jingoism of some writers and intellectuals like Barrès or Benjamin and of much of the national press during the immediate pre-war period and the first year or so of fighting was gradually replaced by grim accounts of the truth and by an increasing number of openly anti-war statements. Most of the novels published during the 1916–18 period were of this kind, with Barbusse's *Le Feu* (1916) and Dorgelès's *Les Croix de bois* (1919 but written 1916) being perhaps the best known and most influential. And in the following two decades French novels which, like Giono's *Le Grand Troupeau* (1934), dealt wholly or in part with the war continued, like most (though not all) works throughout Europe, to be written in similar vein. But during this same period a new threat to European if not world peace began to appear in the form of Fascism. In France many writers and intellectuals responded not only by participating in international pacifist groups but also by producing works in which Fascist activities were openly discredited and attacked –

Nizan's *Le Cheval de Troie* (1934), Aragon's *Les Cloches de Bâle* (1934), Malraux's *Le Temps du mépris* (1935) or Cassou's *Les Massacres de Paris* (1936) to name but four. Yet Fascism was not without its admirers and practitioners in France, a fact which had already been witnessed by the growth in the late 1920s of *ligues* like *Le Faisceau* or *Jeunesses Patriotes*, by the activities of journals and newspapers like the *Action Française, Gringoire* and later *Je suis partout*, and by the various works of writers like Brasillach, Châteaubriant and Drieu la Rochelle – even though their attitudes spring essentially from different origins. Furthermore, as Pascal Ory has shown, Germany was, by the early 1930s, already preparing the way for its expansionist policy by encouraging a number of cultural links with France which included lavishly paid lecture tours of Germany and highly remunerative translations of French works.[2] Just as the Soviet Union exerted considerable fascination for many on the political left – those who became fellow travellers – so too did Hitler's Germany seduce others. The accounts which both Drieu and Brasillach give of their visits to Nuremberg illustrate this well, while the personal appeal of the Führer himself is summed up by the much more mystical Châteaubriant: "If with one hand Hitler salutes the people in that way which has become so well-known, with his other he faithfully clasps the hand of God."[3] By 1939 and the outbreak of war therefore there was in France, an important if relatively small body of support for Germany, and not only for her cultural but for her social and political values as well. Invasion this time was to amount to more than physical subjugation.

That the Germans expected their attack on the Maginot line to meet with such little resistance is inconceivable. The capitulation of the French army resulted, as is well known, in the massive flight (*exode*) of a terrified and impotent civilian population towards the south. It is impossible to estimate the total number of people involved, but figures of up to ten million have been claimed and the biblical overtones of *exode* are apt; this was indeed the flight of a nation. Harrassed by German troops and even attacked from the air, people took with them what they could: motor vehicles, petrol, bicycles and even prams were at a premium; rivalries and antagonisms between local residents and the migrating hordes developed; families were separated; the rout was complete. In the circumstances it is not surprising therefore that the armistice should have been accepted, as it was, with such enthusiasm by a large percentage of the population for many of whom, it should not be forgotten, memories of 1914–18 were also still vivid and painful. Some of course interpreted Pétain's action as an astute way of buying time thus enabling France to regather her forces for counterattack. But some, less ready to capitulate on any terms, set out for North Africa or London and began from an early date to organise the Free French. Some went to Switzerland or, like Bernanos, to South America.

Although in these early months the idea of resistance as a positive response to the German presence was not being widely canvassed, the division between those who accepted and collaborated and those who came increasingly to reject the new state of affairs here had its roots. De Gaulle, already involved in diplomatic duties between France and Britain, established himself in London and by late 1940 was recognised by the British government as leader of the Free French. As a counter to Pétain and the armistice, he appealed in three broadcasts on 18, 19 and 22 June for a concerted, collective effort by his countrymen in the name of honour, discipline and the spirit of resistance: "The flame of Resistance must and will not be extinguished." Regular broadcasts followed but developments were inevitably slow. With the return of prisoners of war, with the realisation during the early months of the occupation that German soldiers were not behaving in the barbaric way they had expected, the number of people ready to obey such authoritarian commands was relatively few. Indeed, as Beynon John has pointed out, de Gaulle's expectations at this time were somewhat unreal.[4] Some months would pass before the resistance movement emerged as what Malraux in a de Gaulle-like phrase called "a mobilisation of French energy".[5]

With the first killings of German soldiers and the beginnings of reprisals in the winter of 1940–41, however, the situation began to change. Two other factors were also particularly important. First was the German invasion of the Soviet Union in June 1941. The French Communist Party (PCF), outlawed since 1939 on account of its support for the Nazi–Soviet pact, could now reverse its position of non-involvement with a clear conscience and re-emerged to play a vital co-ordinating role in a national struggle against the oppressor. Indeed so much did Communists come to dominate resistance activities that at the Liberation in 1944 the efforts of many others were sometimes overlooked – a fact which was politically much to the Party's advantage. The second was the invasion by the Germans of the southern zone in November 1942 in response to allied landings in North Africa. Pétain's refusal at this juncture to leave France and lead a national revival from Algeria was seen by those not already so persuaded to be final evidence for his complete acceptance of Nazi policies. The enemy was no longer merely the occupying German forces but all those who supported Pétain, the Vichy government and its openly collaborationist policies. The division between "the two Frances – one heroic, the other treacherous"[6] here has its roots. Such a picture is obviously both simplistic and dangerous. So too is one which considers these few years, during which private and personal issues were inextricably linked with political and collective ones, to be a neat, self-contained period in the history of France. Pierre Seghers warns against this in the Introduction to his anthology of Resistance poetry: "For me and for plenty of others the ashes are still – and will always remain – hot, whether they are those of people in my family or of murdered friends. . . . This history is still very much alive, red with blood that spurts out at your face."[7]

The reverberations of this period were many and what we attempt in this chapter is to show how they were reflected in the fictional works written contemporaneously and in those produced later.

Although in the southern zone writers and intellectuals continued for some time to enjoy relative freedom, the German presence in the north had its effect almost at once. Supplies of paper (reduced by 1943 to one tenth of the amount available in 1938), ink and print were strictly controlled. Censorship too was imposed in various ways; in July 1940 the Propaganda-Abteilung[8] was established to keep a careful watch over the press, radio, cinema and publishing houses, and in October 1940 "la liste Otto" was issued. This, so called after the German cultural ambassador Otto Abetz, contained the names of about 700 Jewish writers and of Germans (including Mann, Zweig and Remarque) whose works expressed open hostility to the Third Reich. There was also some attempt to limit translations of English works and to encourage those of German novels instead. But by the summer of 1941, novels by Edgar Rice Burroughs, Agatha Christie, Kipling, Mazo de la Roche and even Jack London (*Smoke and Shorty* as *La Fièvre de l'or*) and John Steinbeck (*In Dubious Battle* as *En un combat douteux*) had appeared and even by 1942, when the situation had very considerably worsened, with all manuscripts having to be officially checked by the authorities, works of fiction still came from the presses in some quantity. During the first week of February 1942 for example over forty titles (including those of translations) were published and during the second week of April, sixty. The picture which is often conveyed of a highly restrictive German presence is one which probably needs to be modified therefore. Similarly the questions not just of censorship but of activities of a number of major publishers like Grasset, Denoël, Gallimard, Albin Michel, and Plon might also be examined to a greater degree than they have been so far, and with some profit.[9] Grasset for example willingly acceded to the German cultural policy, Denoël (publisher of Céline and Rebatet as well as of some left-wing authors) accepted the investment of German capital. Yet Gallimard, who continued to publish the work of Drieu la Rochelle, was singled out by the Vichy government as early as 1940 for having been at least in part responsible for the decadence which, it was claimed, characterised the Third Republic: "French literature from 1909 to 1939 has been controlled by a corrupt team headed by that arch-criminal, Gallimard ... Gide and Corydon, Breton, the peddlar of ectoplasm; Aragon, the archbishop of *Ce Soir*; Naville, the anarchist banker; Eluard, that rotten fruit; Péret the slanderer; and all those other monomaniacs, drug-addicts and habitués of clinics — that's what the Gallimard team is. Destroyer of the intellect, the young of France spit you out, Gallimard."[10]

Issues and developments of this kind have either been neglected by or omitted altogether from general accounts and surveys of French literature written during and dealing with the 1940–4 period. Instead it has become almost traditional to focus attention on events and attitudes as they developed after 1940–41 and on writing which reflected and encouraged resistance: the poetry of Aragon, Eluard, Seghers and Cassou for example, plays like Sartre's *Les Mouches* or Anouilh's *Antigone*, the short stories and *nouvelles* published from 1942 onwards (the first, Vercors' *Le Silence de la mer* appeared in February) by the clandestine Editions de Minuit. Although almost entirely ignored by literary histories of this period, there was quite a body of prose fiction published between 1940 and 1942 which took the events of the invasion as its subject. Many of these novels are near-documentary in character, at best thinly disguised reminiscences or journalistic accounts of personal experience and, as with the earliest novels of the First World War, it is arguable that having been written so close to events it was virtually impossible to be otherwise. Their pattern tends to be predictably the same – incredulity that France (and the Maginot line in particular) should be so vulnerable, growing awareness and acceptance of the reality of the situation, an account of the invasion and *exode*, and a recognition that the nation has deserved its fate usually tempered in the closing pages by a statement of belief in the ultimate re-emergence of a new, spiritually purer and victorious France. In most of these works there is little that can have given the German authorities very much concern; moreover to allow their publication could be interpreted as an indication of the new administration's tolerant attitude. Some were temporarily withdrawn and only allowed to reappear in censored form, notably Noël's *La Guerre des avant-postes* (1940) and Dorgelès's *Retour au front* (1940). But the cuts made in these were more, it seems, for reasons of the factual information which they contained than for others of propaganda or subversion. Otherwise novels appeared quite regularly in this period dealing with various aspects of the fighting on ground, sea or in the air, according to the authors' personal experience – Dartey's *Après la Nuit* (1940), Chamson's *Quatre mois. Carnet d'un officier de liaison* (1940), Roques' *Le Sang de nos fautes* (1941), Mégret's *Jacques* (1941), Baroncelli's *26 Hommes* (1941), Balbaud's *Cette Drôle de Guerre* (1941), Jamet's *Carnet de déroute* (1942), Masson's *Ligne Maginot, bastion inutile* (1942) to name but a few. Not all were published in France. Balbaud's very pro-British work, for example, was produced by Oxford University Press; Victor Pozner's *Deuil en 24 heures* (1942) by Brentano in New York. In both cases publication abroad was advisable not so much because of any specifically anti-German statements which they contained but because of their open criticism both of Pétain's collaborationist policy together with his anti-British attitude, and of the sheer inefficiency of the French authorities in 1940. In terms of structure, style and treatment of their subject, however, neither is unusual. They also share with the others a reluctance to dwell on the brutality and violence of war which we find in Barbusse's *Le Feu* and other novels of the First World War. Descriptions of military activities, of ruined buildings or of medical provisions are often muted and distanced as though impersonally observed, and the thoughts and attitudes of the ordinary soldiers who were directly involved in the fighting are rarely recorded. *Deuil en 24 heures* does, however, achieve rather more than most.

Pozner's novel describes events from the invasion to the armistice, concentrating on a number of carefully defined individuals, each offering a representative point of view: in particular Caillol, a lorry driver, and his immediate superior officer Cardin, a colonel, are contrasted one with the other. Caillol is casual, brave and generous; Carvin is officious, at times supercilious and blindly acccepts government propaganda which he reformulates in clichés: "obliged by circumstances to abandon Paris. But we have not given up the struggle".

Pozner directs much criticism at the incompetence and self-centredness of those "in command". Carvin's immediate responsibility is to ensure that certain papers relating to military supplies do not fall into German hands, and on arrival in Toulouse he instructs Caillol and his fellow soldiers to burn them. Only then do they discover that many of the papers are of no military value whatsoever, often relating to the nineteenth century or to the 1914–18 war. Incompetence and unreadiness are evident elsewhere as well. Unfinished tanks are sent to attempt to stem the German advance; retreating soldiers are issued with rifles which prove to be virtually unusable since they have been assembled from incompatible pieces. By the end of the novel Pozner's authorial comments are also more in evidence. The general chaos of the *exode* and the almost total breakdown in military discipline are clearly stated: "From one minute to another, the town gradually filled up with soldiers. They prowled around food shops ready to beg or to steal as they felt like it. None of them saluted the officers." Like many others the novel closes with a token statement of hope and of conviction that France will one day re-emerge victorious; it also offers through Carvin the standard excuse offered by the authorities that the Third Republic is to be blamed for the present circumstances: "The Germans were working... while we listened to a Minister for Leisure." But Pozner's position is rather different. While he may share this view to some extent, the real point he is making is that the present authorities have shown themselves to be incompetent, spineless and concerned only for their own safety. Real hope for the future lies with Caillol and his colleagues.

The kind of criticism made by Pozner and others was not shared, however, by all. One writer, Jacques Benoist-Méchin in *La Moisson de 40* (1941), a novel based on his own personal experience, describes the concerted attempt by thousands of prisoners to join with their German captors in an effort to save an important harvest. The suggestion that a common interest between the two sides exists is explicit and the book expresses unambiguous support for Pétain and his policies. And Benoist-Méchin was not unusual in his attitude. The belief that Pétain's action might ensure that France would be spared the kind of damage and suffering caused by the 1914–18 war was also expressed – and in some cases forcefully – by a number of prominent writers and intellectuals. Some, like Montherlant or Mohrt, went further, seeing the invasion as an opportunity for France to find a positive and virile alternative to an effete, decadent society, what Montherlant described in *Le Solstice de juin* (1941) as "twenty years of not giving a damn and feebleness". Many of these people were subsequently accused of collaboration, and in some cases – that of Brasillach for example – were tried and executed once the war had finished. For others the consequences were less severe though the scorn and viciousness with which people like Jouhandeau or Montherlant were attacked after the Liberation were no less extreme.

Montherlant had already made his attitude to war clear in his early novel *Le Songe* (1922). Now in a variety of texts – most of them collected together as *Le Solstice de juin* – he showed himself to be a supporter of, if not a spokesman for, the Vichy government. But his position was to some degree idiosyncratic. Aloofness and isolation were vital to him and he claimed, in a way that was not so very different from Sartre's, that the very abnormality of present circumstances could in fact be beneficial to the creative artist. (One of the interesting statistical facts to emerge from this period is that, according to sales and library records, more books were being read than before.)[11] Mohrt, whose later novel *Le Répit* (1945) with its triple focus of sex, religion and war, reminds us of Drieu's *La Comédie de Charleroi* or parts of *Gilles*, regarded Germany in a different way again; for him (like Drieu) Germany brought the chance of spiritual and physical rejuvenation. Although he produced no novel early in the war, his essay *Les Intellectuels devant la défaite de 1870, 71* (1942) unequivocally illustrates this view. In an analysis of nineteenth-century French writers, Mohrt highlights strengths and weaknesses which he considers equally relevant to an understanding of pre-war France. Hugo and Michelet are directly attacked for their encouragement of democratic trends; and About for his inability after 1871 "to recognise his mistakes and to come round to political good sense". Renan and Veuillot, however, are praised for their willingness to abandon the principles of 1789, while finally Gobineau, whose aristocratic spirit and belief in hierarchy and inequality make him "one of the last real representatives of that cosmopolitan spirit which spread through France at the time of a 'French Europe'", is offered as a model of political and moral good sense. Never afraid to draw the parallels between 1871 and 1940, Mohrt was clearly yet another who believed that defeat was the inevitable consequence of the French way of life under the Third Republic.

Similar views were expressed by some novelists albeit in a rather more muted form, an appeal being made instead for a recognition of and return to the values of an older, rural, religious and conservative France. Two writers who belong to this category are René Benjamin with *Le Printemps tragique* (1940) and Pierre Benoit. In 1915 Benjamin's novel *Gaspard* depicted war as an adventure and as such was a contribution to the attempt to keep a nationalist spirit alive at a time when it was considered important to do so. *Le Printemps tragique* is equally nationalistic in tone and message though it is not, as Benjamin's critics would claim, a book which positively advocates collaboration. Rather it is a novel expressing regret at what has been lost.

The novel takes the form of an account by the narrator who has (significantly) left Paris to recuperate from illness in the Loire valley. There he stays with a farming family (the Courvalain) whose son has already joined the army and is fighting in Belgium. (He is later reported killed.) Through his contact with the local doctor the narrator/author meets two people whose values gradually emerge as being those of which he approves. The first is Le Meunier, an eccentric, eighty year old aristocratic figure, who in a moment of passion marries a young local peasant girl. He believes he has discovered in her a primitive force which he can harness in the last years of his life, but exhausts himself sexually and dies, symbolically, on the day the Germans enter Paris. His wife is subsequently seen to offer hospitality to German officers and unquestionably meets with Benjamin's disapproval. Although in a sense Le Meunier has been misguided and has failed, his analysis of the present situation is similar to the one offered by the Vichy government: "for some time now the French have given up their principles, their laws and their beliefs and have continued to go backwards, ill and moribund, in spite of various demagogues who spoke day and night in order to put them to sleep and make them believe in health".

The second character is Fiamma, the doctor's wife, who is also a passionate, forceful and strikingly independent figure. Her castigation of pre-war society and of the present attitudes of the French is violent. A visit which she and the narrator pay to Tours (Chapter VI, "La Débâcle") prompts a long outburst against what she too considers to have been years of decadence.

'– Did you know Tours twenty years ago?' she asked. 'I was a little girl, but I can remember it well. We were already decadent. . . . As things got rapidly worse around 1930 you'd see people taking it easy in cars as if they were at home. What a state of affairs. In 1938 they went about in bathing costumes. They only had to see a café and they'd stop and drink themselves sick. A book shop and they'd buy some filthy book – a new one came out every day. . . . Tours was like any other town with its cinemas and its people who were spoiled, ill-mannered, worthless. . . . People simply didn't have any standards.'

By the end of the novel refugees are pouring through the Loire valley; one, a young Parisian girl, spends several days with the Courvalain family. Benjamin presents her as a typical product of modern society: "She was dolled up just like all of them from the big towns – artificially pretty, too thin and completely out of place in the naturalness of her new situation." She in turn is followed by a group of retreating soldiers who, in spite of the efforts of one officer, are ill-organised and without guidance. In the final chapter (where Pozner criticises French authorities) Benjamin re-affirms what he regards as true values: "France must respect its peasants!"; "a warrior spirit and a willingness to start again is essential!"; "If she wants to go on living, France must turn to spiritual values again."

Such statements as these from one whose admiration for Pétain bordered on worship – see, for example, his two essays *Le Maréchal et son peuple* (1941) and *Le Grand Homme seul* (1943) – are not surprising. One of the interesting features of *Le Printemps tragique* is that it offers them without resorting to a form of allegory. No less than Pozner or Balbaud, Benjamin takes and describes contemporaneous events for his basic material. Pierre Benoit, whose position and sympathies were similar, does not. In novels like *Lunegarde* (1942) and *Seigneur, j'ai tout vu* (1943) both of which basically advocate a restoration of the kinds of values which we find in Benjamin's work, Benoit turns to earlier periods: 1939–30 for the former, 1920 for the latter. Their substance therefore is clearly different. Allusions to Germany are few. Lunegarde himself, "this solitary old man", may invite comparison with Pétain, and Aude in the second novel ("I'd rather leave than share our home with a foreigner") may suggest positive response to the Occupation, but such features are not sufficiently emphasised for the novels to be considered as statements of a preferred political position.

In some ways similar to the works of these writers (and for which his political sympathies were on occasions also subsequently questioned) are those of Marcel Aymé. Published by Gallimard, it seems they were either sufficiently enigmatic or too urbane and witty to fall foul of the censors. His novel *La Vouivre* (1943) is the story of the destructive effect which the appearance of the legendary serpent-woman with her priceless ruby has on a rural community in the Franche-Comté. For most of the time *La Vouivre* reads like a novel by Giono or Bosco, but the implications are serious, as different members of the local population either suffer violent death or fail to resist – or even comprehend – the significance of what is happening to them. Only in the closing pages, when it is clear that there is no limit to the serpent-woman's violence, does it begin to emerge that the novel may be rather more than a piece of dark rural fantasy.

In his short stories, however, and in *Le Passe-muraille* (1943) in particular, Aymé's position and intentions, while not overtly political, are much clearer. Here allusion and allegory are tempered by pointed satire. In the title story, for example, that of a man who, when he takes the wrong medicine, loses his ability to walk through walls and is finally trapped inside one, Aymé clearly aims at those who readily make the most of present circumstances. In "Le Proverbe" the infallibility of authority is questioned, in "Le Percepteur d'épouses" the gullibility of bourgeois society is ridiculed and in "La Carte" the need for measurable productivity and usefulness. (Those who fail to meet required standards officially die for a certain number of days each month – Jews more than most!) Finally in what is perhaps the best known, "En attendant", Aymé depicts a queue of fourteen people. Each in turn is described or expresses a point of view – a young woman whose husband has been taken to Germany, a prostitute, a Jew, a child who has lost his family's bread coupons, for example. While an awareness of contemporary circumstances is indubitably vital for the full implications of these stories to be seen, Aymé's point is clear. His is a call not so much for a restoration of past standards any more than it is one for an open attack on the occupying forces. Instead it is for a reassessment by his country-men of their own values and priorities since a future will, ultimate-ly, have to be faced: "When the Germans have gone, there will be some accounts to settle" ("En attendant", *Le Passe-muraille*, p. 257).

Aymé was right of course, but such statements can hardly have given the German authorities particular cause for alarm in 1943. Indeed it is fair to say that during the first two and even three years of invasion and occupation there is no evidence that either the German presence or the Vichy government was directly challenged by anything contained in imaginative literature. At the most charges of incompetence and lack of foresight were levelled against the last governments of the Third Republic – hardly something to give the Germans cause for anxiety. Encour-agement and appeals for national revival were also too vague and incidental to be of much influence and, as we have seen, most of the novels of this period either offered a near factual account of the events of 1940 or, where they indulged in any form of political statement, reflected what a large percentage of the population felt.

It was not long before circumstances began to change. The war was over. France had emerged defeated and occupied, and what calls for resistance there were came in the early months from abroad. But this was only a beginning; increasing repression, the inauguration of the Service du Travail Obligatoire, the persecu-tion of Jews and Communists, and the viciousness of reprisals in response to the growing incidence of resistance activities all served to make people begin to realise what a Nazi regime could mean. Again it is important to remember that the picture of the years up to the Liberation can, retrospectively, be distorted. There were still many ordinary people who were not unduly (if at all) disturbed by the occupying forces; there were others who clearly continued to believe that France had to be purged of her past sins or that the political future of Europe (and of France within Europe) could lie only in some kind of federal system with Germany as a guiding power. But there were others who refused to accept Nazi domination, and it was from these that what is generally recognised as the truly representative literature of France during this period came.

Given the circumstances it is not surprising that this writing, inspired by the spirit of resistance, should differ from literature which dealt with the war in England, America or Germany. One reason for this was, as Sartre pertinently remarked in "Paris sous l'Occupation", that there was no clearly defined, separate enemy to be fired at as in a conventional war: "The idea of an enemy is only really clear if the enemy is separated from us by a wall of fire."

As a result, while some resistance writing like the story "F.T.P." in Edith Thomas' *Contes d'Auxois* contains accounts of armed attacks, the emphasis generally is far more on covert activities and on "spiritual" resistance. Proclamations of patriotism to be found throughout the literature of other nations during the war tend to be replaced by a wider appeal to duty and to a need above all to preserve human dignity in the face of what Bernanos called the forces of paganism. For the French the war – or the fight against the occupying forces – is not a matter for the military alone but for the nation as a whole. Nazism is not a target to be shot at but a disease to be treated with clinical efficiency. Gabriel Marcel in his preface to Camille Mayran's *Larmes et lumière à Oradour* (1952) captures the idea perfectly when he writes: "to be effective – spiritually effective that is – revolt must not be based on hate – it must be like the attitude of a doctor struggling against leprosy".

As the Nazi grip tightened it became increasingly difficult and indeed highly dangerous to write in a way in which words, effectively, were to be weapons. Paradoxically, the very artificiality of the situation created (as again Sartre and Jean Starobinsky have remarked) an impression at least of a kind of freedom. Starobinsky in 1943 remarked that "time is out of joint" and saw in such circumstances an opportunity for national revitalization.

Within weeks of the armistice a number of intellectuals and writers began to voice their own resistance in what was to become an ever-increasing wave of pamphlets and reviews. In the north these were often roneocopied on poor-quality paper and distributed by hand; clandestinity was essential. In the south, at least before November 1942, conditions allowed for a more normal production. Many of the publications were inevitably short-lived: *L'Arc, Pantagruel, En Captivité, Résistance.* Others continued until and sometimes beyond the Liberation, their message clearly indicated by their title – *Défense de la France, L'Université libre, Libération* in the north; *Combat, Temps nouveau, Franc-Tireur* in the south. At first "literary resistance" found expression in poetry, and a number of reviews in the unoccupied zone quickly established themselves as important outlets: René Tavernier's *Confluences*, Pierre Seghers' *Poésie* and Max-Pol Fouchet's *Fontaine* in Algeria. The advantages of poetry over prose were several: it used less print and paper, it could be memorised and transmitted orally and above all by its normally dense qualities it could carry meaning which, not being instantly obvious to the German or Vichy authorities, was symbolically resistant.

This new conception of writing was developed in particular by the group of writers and intellectuals associated with the Front National pour la Liberté et l'Indépendance de la France. (There was also vigorous support for the spirit of resistance given by a number of writers already in self-imposed exile – Bernanos and Supervielle in South America or Béguin in Switzerland for example.) Established in 1941, this association evolved largely due to the efforts of Jacques Decour, former editor of *Commune*, who also had a scheme for a specifically literary group, the Comité National d'Ecrivains. On Aragon's advice he contacted Jean Paulhan and together with Jacques Debû-Bridel, Guéhenno and others planned a newspaper to be called *Les Lettres Françaises*. Decour was arrested in February 1942 (and shot in May) and the paper's first appearance was delayed until September. Its message remained unchanged however: "LES LETTRES FRANÇAISES will be our weapon and by its publication we, as writers, mean to play our full part in the struggle to the death in which the French nation is engaged in order to be free from her oppressors."

During the next two years the paper – largely the work of Claude Morgan – welcomed contributions from, amongst others, Eluard, Aragon, Sartre and Mauriac. In April 1944, in the second of two articles, Sartre crystallised the essence of resistance literature: "to write is to claim freedom for all men". But like other resistance papers, *Les Lettres Françaises* was first and foremost a call to action and not, despite the publication of several poems, a literary journal. Aware of this, several people associated with the paper hoped to provide an opportunity for writers to express their feelings through literary works. At first it was thought that another clandestine paper, *La Pensée Libre*, would meet this aim, but, discovered by the Nazis, it was suppressed before such plans could be realised. As a direct result, however, the Editions de Minuit were born.

The story of this dangerous and difficult enterprise has been told by various people and notably by Debû-Bridel.[12] Between 1942 and the Liberation of Paris in August 1944, forty-three manuscripts actually written in France were received. A few were passed to the Swiss publisher Les Trois Collines, some remained unprinted and others appeared after the Liberation. Even so thirty-four texts – short stories, poems, essays, recollections and extracts from private diaries – were published in the small format, high-quality volumes of which the first, Vercors' *Le Silence de la mer* (originally intended for *La Pensée Libre*) became the most celebrated and almost a symbol of the whole enterprise.

Unquestionably the most noticeable quality of the prose fiction to appear under the Editions de Minuit imprint is that of detachment and dignity. Konrad Bieber considers this to be a reaction against the overt patriotism of some of the early writing of the 1914–18 war,[13] but just as much it results from a nice awareness on the part of the authors of the current climate. Through 1942 and into 1943 the oppressive measures of the occupying forces and the capitulation of the Vichy administration gave every indication that France would eventually be totally overcome. The temptation to acknowledge this as inevitable was strong and for many irresistible, but Vercors and others thought differently. They saw the need to take stock of themselves and of their situation, to be seen to do so and thereby to act as an example to others. This tone is perfectly set by *Le Silence de la mer*. Like many of his fellow resistance writers Vercors had a fundamental belief in humanity which he saw threatened not simply by the policies of the occupying forces (though these were bad enough) but by Nazism as a faith which shaped a person's being and attitude to others. Quite deliberately therefore he gives the German in his story a name which is both vaguely aristocratic and French – von Ebrennac. Like Barrès's Frédéric Asmus in *Colette Baudoche* (1909), von Ebrennac is both intellectually and emotionally in sympathy with France and French culture; he regrets his country's behaviour and is at odds with his fellow Germans. Moreover his feelings for the narrator's niece (and hers for him) are clear. But for all his qualities he *believes* in the eventual collapse of France and must be resisted. She forces herself to remain silent in his presence therefore until he finally leaves at which point her only word is "adieu" – the acknowledgement of his presence which he has sought for so long, but also a final and absolute rejection. Throughout the story the French couple are passive, but there is strength in their passivity and in particular in the young girl who on more than one occasion is an inspiration for and example to her uncle.

This presentation of individual Germans as decent human beings we find as well in Edith Thomas' "Le Tilleul" (*Contes d'Auxois*) where a young German soldier is openly anti-Nazi: "We have been beaten" said Hans. "We have been beaten since 30 January 1933." A character in Pierre Bost's *Haute Fourche* makes the same point in a different way: "In any case, I don't detest the Germans. It's not very intelligent to say that." This third example is in fact quite significant since, written relatively late in the war (probably in late 1943 or 1944), it suggests that although in reality the possibility of there being a "civilised German" had for most people disappeared, a sense of balance was still considered important. When, in these stories, the Nazi presence is openly attacked, the result is usually caricature though it never reaches the extremes of the kind to be found, for example, in the post-Liberation *Les Lettres Françaises*. In Thomas' "L'Arrestation" or in Aveline's *Le Temps mort* the interrogation scenes (Chapters 2 and 11) are typical and, in the second case, acknowledged as such: "the closely cropped hair, steel-rimmed glasses and white flabby double-chin, the jacket which was too tight to hold in all that fat, the chubby hands, folded on his stomach – the perfect caricature of the learned professor. The judge's attitude towards him was servile". But while descriptions of Nazis may be relatively few, their presence and influence are acknowledged in other, indirect ways. In "Les Moules et le professeur" (*Contes d'Auxois*) they can afford to offer higher wages for a *femme de ménage*; in *Les Amants d'Avignon* compartments on trains are reserved for them while the French travel in crowded and uncomfortable conditions. In the same story the capture of a resistance worker is recorded as a matter of fact: "There had been a struggle . . . there was blood on the walls. They took him away in a Gestapo car which was waiting down below. There's nothing odd about it."

As much if not more scorn and hostility are reserved for collaborators – in "La Relève" or "Veillée" (*Contes d'Auxois*), *Le Temps mort* and in particular Vercors' *Marche à l'étoile*. But whereas anti-Nazi feeling appears to be absolute and uniform, attitudes towards collaborators can be coloured by political sympathies. Like the other Minuit writers, for example, Elsa Triolet sees true patriotism as being exemplified by the actions of ordinary people, but for her it is particularly the strength of those who share her Communist faith: "After the war we shall have to take account of them, we shan't be able to govern the country without the martyrs' party" ("le parti des fusillés"). But beyond the political dimension of patriotism and a sense of duty these writers all underline the dignity and the spirit of France. It is not by chance, for example, that in "F.T.P." (*Contes d'Auxois*) resistance messages are carried inside a copy of the *Chanson de Roland*.[14] But this kind of national heroism is not to be expressed by any ostentatious display of courage. The self-denying attitude of the niece in *Le Silence de la mer* is repeated in more extreme circumstances by Céline in *Le Temps mort* just "one of the hundreds of women who are never seen who are in prison, theatened with all kinds of things and who go on singing". The emphasis on the supportive role and strength of women is factually accurate in the context of a diminishing male population. Whether in the apparently insignificant queuing episode in "Les Moules et le professeur", or in the parts played by Anne in "L'Arrestation" (*Contes d'Auxois*) or by Juliette Noël in *Les Amants d'Avignon*, the message remains the same.

From Moscow the Russian novelist and critic Ilya Ehrenburg (whose own novel *The Fall of Paris* [1941] gives an interesting and graphic account of life in the capital during the 1930s) accused French writers of not being sufficiently angry in their attitude to the Occupation. It is likely, however, that a more violent reaction could have been seen as the predictable and perhaps hysterical outcry of a minority group. What is striking about most of this resistance writing – and to a large extent this is true of the poetry as well – is not just the absence of violent content but the casual,

everyday and at times almost muted quality of the style. All of the
Minuit stories contain enough detail to be "real" for the reader:
the circumstances of Juliette Noël's life, the interior of the house in
*Le Silence de la mer*, the settings of the various tales in *Contes
d'Auxois*. Dialogue too plays a dominant role in the narrative of
most of them; private reflection (*Le Temps mort* and *Le Silence de la
mer*) is effective and both syntax and the use of image are kept at a
simple level. In *Le Temps mort*, for example, Aveline's sentences
are usually short with *et* as the principal conjunction; in *Le Silence
de la mer* Vercors manages to create an impression of repetition, of
suspension and thereby both of suffering and expectancy. One
important consequence of this is that certain images, references or
allusions are thrown into significant relief – the opacity and pale
quality of the narrator's niece in *Le Silence de la mer* or the value of
the peasant and the countryside in *Les Amants d'Avignon*, "Veillée"
or "Les Evadés" (*Contes d'Auxois*).

As with any writing which aims essentially to encourage people
to become aware of the plight of others and to break out of what
Vercors in *Le Songe* calls "this filthy isolation", the danger of
authorial intrusion to interpret attitudes and events for us or to
direct our attention is considerable. Perhaps aware of this, Aveline and Vercors, by the very fact that they resort to a first person
narrative, create a perspective within which little or no ambiguity
is permitted. But almost inevitably some intrusion occurs. When
Charles, who has been tortured by the Gestapo, appears before
Céline in *Le Temps mort*, Aveline underlines her (and therefore
our) admiration for him: "And he appeared to be bigger and
stronger than ever." This is less a commentary than an emphasis,
a technique to which all the authors resort at some stage. Elsa
Triolet, however, whose Communist sympathies can, as we have
already noted, influence her writing, and Edith Thomas are more
willing to ensure that certain points are made. The latter's *Contes
d'Auxois* illustrate this both in the development from one story to
another as well as in specific instances. From the opening "Les
Moules et le professeur" with its emphasis on resignation but
dawning awareness of the need to respond positively (Monsieur
Pocelet, we should note, works on Virgil's *Aeneid*) through accounts of resistance, collaboration and increasing atrocities,
Thomas guides us to the final story in which revenge is beginning
to be exacted. And in addition to this conscious structural pattern,
we also find that she openly intervenes in a variety of ways: she

interprets characters' thoughts for us, ensures that the significance of the French countryside is not lost and, most obviously of all, resorts in the final "F.T.P." to a presentation of her six characters in the inflated language of a roll of honour. Louis is one of them: "And here we have Louis, the leather worker, who is here so that he can be with the workers and peasants of the USSR who are free now and know what they are fighting for and why they are dying for it."

In Part Four of Pierre Courtade's last novel, *La Place rouge* (1961), the main character Simon Bordes arrives in occupied Paris from the southern zone. His luggage is searched and the police discover various books including Malraux's *La Lutte avec l'ange* (never, of course, completed). One officer remarks: "Between you and me, I wonder why books are forbidden. Do you know anyone who has changed his mind because of a book? That's not what makes people change their mind." The question is a nice one and Courtade who himself participated in and wrote a novel, *Elseneur* (1949) and short stories, *Les Circonstances* (1954) about the Resistance, never found a satisfactory answer to it. Nor indeed, in spite of the debate which the issue has aroused generally, has anyone else. Yet in the context of the period 1940–44 there can be no doubt that writing did play its part in promoting a certain attitude, that words were in a sense weapons. The message which Jean Cassou neatly summarises as "carry on and you will be saved"[15] was heard by many. For the writers, too, participation in the struggle in this way gave them a sense of dignity which was otherwise threatened. André Chamson's reaction was one shared by many: "Being a writer was what saved me and allowed me not to despair."[16]

With the Liberation and restoration of national security, the writer's choice to use the war as subject matter for his work becomes much more complex and is related to wide-ranging considerations about meaning and intention. Of course it would be wrong to claim that the Resistance writer's immediate objective of freedom necessarily restricts his work to its historical context and thereby limits its value to a contribution to the war effort and to the records of war. However, the post-Liberation writer is not subject to the pressures of war nor is he using his work against an occupying enemy. The Resistance writer created against a background of uncertainty and danger; whatever hope or encouragement his work expressed, he could not know for certain how the war would end, whether France would regain its sovereignty nor even if he would live to see victory. The security and relief provided by the Liberation alters the context of the writer's work and the potential meanings of his choices: he is writing about the war because he finds it a suitable subject matter for his purposes, he is not fighting the war. The post-Liberation writer can, if he so chooses, forget about the war entirely, for it is suddenly part of history and if he does decide to write about it, he can do so without fear. In other words, post-Liberation literature about the war is necessarily rooted in preoccupations and interests which transcend the Resistance writer's aim of ridding France of her enemies. As Sartre had already recognised in his article in *Les Lettres Françaises*, the literature of Resistance is part of Resistance, but post-Liberation literature of war is much more obviously part of literature.[17]

If the literature of Resistance is unified in a general sense by the fight for freedom, it is not at all easy to detect and claim a common aim among post-Liberation writers in their treatment of the war. To be sure, many works are commemorative or written to ensure that certain events are not forgotten – acts of heroism and self-sacrifice, acts of barbarism, experiences of disorientation and fear.[18] Many are concerned in one way or another with the piecing together and description of an event found overwhelming and confusing, in an endeavour to use literary structures to reassert coherence and direction to life. The war may appear as an extreme situation, precipitating, against a background of death and danger, moral problems and conflicts which are always part of existence but may not be posed with the same intensity and in such stark relief in times of peace. In turn the war may stimulate the literary imagination to present it as something of a nightmare, particularly in terms of the concentration camps and images of suffering to which it exposed people, or as a basic metaphor of the human condition, a vehicle for the exploration of existence and the articulation of a metaphysic. The dramatic, the tragic, the melodramatic and the comic are all possible responses to war, for it does not in itself call forth any particular response. With certain writers the war presents an opportunity to analyse difficult questions about the relationship between lived experience and literary narrations of them and associated debates about the fictional aspects of history and the historical aspects of fiction.[19] Does an event that has occurred necessarily mean that it is realistic when committed to words? Does actual experience of an event grant a privileged position and insight when it comes to writing about it? What do we mean by an event, or a fact? Such theoretical problems, nowadays fairly fashionable, are posed both consciously and unconsciously in many works and confront the reader with complicated issues when it comes to the description and classification of post-Liberation literature of war: mémoires, souvenirs, souvenirs romancés, carnets de route, carnets de vol, journal, roman, récit, témoignage, chronique, histoire, all such descriptions tend to come under pressure as a result of the war and of the literature to which it gives rise.

Variety of approach, intention and technique combine to produce a very diverse literature of war, particularly between 1945 and 1950, and it is largely biographically based. If we add to this variety the fact that participation in the war is not a precondition of writing about it or that any writer can, if he so decides, turn to the war as the material for his work and that in a sense the war is never over, problems of classification become even more obscure. An author like Patrick Modiano is a useful example. Modiano was born in 1947 and grew up in the shadow of the war. His first published novels: *La Place de l'étoile* (1968), *La Ronde de nuit* (1969) and *Les Boulevards de ceinture* (1972), evoke the atmosphere of Occupation and Resistance. *La Ronde de nuit* in particular presents a somewhat gripping account of the activities of a young man who works simultaneously for the French Gestapo and a Resistance group, Les Chevaliers de l'Ombre. The work is set in Paris and it contains an account of the *exode* and a description of the Resistance activities of a group of ex-war prisoners against the Germans, collaborators and black-market speculators. The writing reflects the doubts, muddled values and confused aspirations of the protagonist as he lives his double life and divided loyalties. As the novel progresses, one senses that the historical setting is a pretext for the analysis of the dilemma of youth in post-war society.

For Modiano, who did not witness the war, the war evidently is not over, and it is worth noting that the author's interest in the war was sufficient to make him contribute to Louis Malle's *Lacombe Lucien*. Modiano's use of the war, his recreation of the

Occupation and Resistance from the supposedly non-privileged viewpoint of the outsider raise a biographical paradox which really haunts all literature but seems especially to haunt literature of the war: it does not appear to be necessary to have lived through the war to write about it convincingly, nor does the fact of participation automatically guarantee an effective literary transposition. This is an obvious point but one which is easily overlooked in discussions about literary realism. Maurice Rieuneau in his book *Guerre et révolution dans le roman français 1919–1939* (1974) notes that between 1915 and 1930, 304 books were published directly inspired by the war and written mostly by active or passive participants using "le vécu" (lived experience) or the "fait d'histoire" (historical episode) as a departure point. Nevertheless, he is the first to admit (p. 212) that Jules Romains' *Verdun* is an outstanding work, although the author is not writing a "témoignage" and was not a privileged observer of the events narrated. As a further point, one might also retain the view of George Steiner who feels that the greatest novel to appear in France in the immediate post-war period is Rebatet's *Les Deux Etendards* (1950). Rebatet lived through the war and indeed was fortunate not to share Brasillach's fate, but for all his involvement with the period, *Les Deux Etendards* is set in the pre-war period 1920–27 and the experience of war is not evident even in a transposed way.[20] The war cannot thus be said to be a privileged nor even necessary subject for the post-war writer. It is simply a possible subject among others, capable of use for a wide variety of purposes.[21]

1945 witnessed the publication of Joseph Kessel's *L'Armée des ombres* and Romain Gary's *L'Education européenne*. Both writers had been active in the Resistance, and Kessel had flown with the RAF. In fact Kessel's book had been published in English as early as 1944 but not until France looked safe did the work appear in French. Although in several respects these are very much Resistance works, the authors' preoccupations are beginning to widen, particularly in the case of Gary.

Both writers may be seen as examples of individuals who, whatever their dislike of war, find it stimulating and respond to its dramas and emotions and get a sense of enhanced existence from participation in it.

Kessel was already known in 1945 for his literary work on the First World War,[22] based on his experience and knowledge of the heroism of its fighter pilots of whom he was one. He is forty years old by the time of the second war. In a tersely worded Préface to *L'Armée des ombres*, he claims emphatically that his work has "the simplicity of the chronicle and the humility of the document". The work is neither fiction, nor propaganda, he states, but a collection of authentic episodes and experiences, put together in a rather haphazard way. His aim is to give a true and accurate picture of "the national hero", the Resistance fighter, not the professional soldier but the ordinary people of France opposed to Pétain and actively involved in the restoration of national sovereignty.[23] What follows the preface is a rather episodic picaresque narrative evoking the Resistance activity of Gerbier and a number of fellow resisters. The work begins one year after the armistice with Pétain described as "a disgusting old man" ("un vieillard immonde"), Resistance as "the sap of freedom" and England as "the only centre of hope and human warmth". Sometimes events are narrated in the third person, sometimes through Gerbier's notes. Gerbier is used to string together a multitude of Resistance experiences, stripped to their bare essentials. Gerbier's activities take him to a prison camp originally meant for German prisoners of the French, to Gibraltar, to London and elsewhere. Beset by fears of capture, of torture and of reprisals; having to kill without much idea in the first place of how to do it (for we are not dealing with a professional soldier); uncertain as to who can be trusted and preoccupied with what to do about unmasked "mouchards" (informers) and former helpers now known to the Germans, Gerbier's life is made to reflect the great abundance of situations, anecdotes, emotional and moral contradictions thrown up by the war and occupation. Kessel is attracted to action, has an eye for conflicting emotions, and likes swift and simple narrative. He also is given to a rather romanticised view of the energy and individual resourcefulness which war experiences can generate.

The really paradoxical feature of *L'Armée des ombres*, however, is its strange lack of power to convince, despite the interest of many individual elements. When Gerbier is finally captured and is awaiting execution, he meditates à la Malraux on death. However, a miraculous escape, just as he is about to be shot, is engineered by other resisters. One of these is a woman called

Mathilde, who later has to be killed by her associates after she falls
vulnerable to Nazi threats to harm her daughter. The leader of the
group, Saint-Luc, figures in the text in idealised terms, always
maintaining a saint-like serenity and belief in the cause. Elements
such as these may all well have been true, but presented as they
are in a concentration of episodes to show as many sides as
possible of the experience of Resistance, much of their effect is lost.
A certain sentimentality also weakens the text. Kessel, writing too
close to events and under the influence of considerable emotion, is
a good example of the way authentic experience of war does not
necessarily produce convincing literature on the subject. Real
events are not in themselves realistic – this is a question of the
aesthetic of realism.

Both Maurice Druon's *La Dernière Brigade* (1946) with its
glorification of a few model soldiers during the fall of France, and
Romain Gary's *Education européenne*, are comparable to *L'Armée des
ombres* in their effects on the reader. The latter work traces through
an abundance of episodes the lives of a group of Polish resistance
fighters in the forests near Wilno at the time of the battle of
Stalingrad. As with Kessel, the narrative is episodic, but rich in
incident and full of emotion generated by deprivation, insecurity,
sudden death and moral conflict. In addition Gary's work is
overlaid with preoccupations about suffering and violence. The
protagonist Janek is a highly charged idealist and a great lover of
Chopin. He is simultaneously moved by the courage, heroism and
camaraderie of his associates and confused by the necessity of
violence. He finds it hard to accept that men are capable both of
Resistance and Nazism and that war intensifies love and friendship at the same time as cold, hunger and brutality. A further
interesting dimension of the work is provided by the character
Dobrenski who is composing a book on their experiences, entitled
*Les Environs de Stalingrad* whose subject will be the discovery of
solidarity in war. Despite its readability, Gary's work, like Kessel's, is marred by a degree of sentimentality and rhetoric – Janek,
for example, is rendered almost unconscious by emotion when
listening to Chopin, so responsive to beauty has the ugliness of
war rendered him.[24] Thirty-five years later and distant from the
events, Gary wrote a more impressive work, *Les Cerfs-volants*,
dealing with the Occupation (discussed in a later section).

Michel Mohrt's *Le Répit*[25] (1945) shows us another author who
finds in war stimulation, at least if one is to judge by the

protagonist of his book, Lucien Coggan. The work is presented as
a novel and describes Lucien's experiences during the "drôle de
guerre". A former law student now mobilised, Lucien has to leave
his native Brittany and go to Saint-Damiens in the Alps where he
becomes "chef de la section d'éclaireurs skieurs". The novel is
structured through the twin perspectives of third-person narrative and Lucien's diary of events. Lucien awaits the possibility of
war with a degree of anxiety but it also offers adventure, a new
world of strong sensations, excitement and a sense of existence
enhanced by the risk of death. Amid references to Stendhal,
Lucien expresses the wish to escape from the "médiocre" (which
could mean the Third Republic, Republicanism, the bourgeoisie
or just peacetime existence) and explore the epic and mythical
dimensions of war. War excites him sexually as well, and elements
of Malraux, Standhal and Drieu La Rochelle combine in a
bastardised form in Lucien to give a picture of war and action as
superior to the comforts of secure, peaceful life. Other sections of
*Le Répit* describe phases of the soldiers' lives, their daily man-
oeuvres and duties, Lucien's sense of solidarity with his men and
doubts about his capacity to lead them. The frustration of the
soldier, desirous of action, but feeling isolated from the centres of
activity is another significant theme. Lucien feels the war will also
destroy liberal capitalism and generate great reforms (he had
supported the Popular Front) but it is really individual fulfilment
that rests uppermost in his mind. War is life intensified in terms of
adventure, dream, sex and beauty. Sadly, the novel ends with the
defeat of France, a defeat which Lucien would have found un-
thinkable, bringing as it does to an abrupt end the wishful
thinking of his youth.

A rather different picture of war emerges from works like Roger
Nimier, *Les Epées* (1948), *Le Hussard bleu* (1950), Georges Mag-
nane, *Où l'herbe ne pousse plus* (1952), an account of the Oradour
massacre, and Robert Merle, *Weekend à Zuydcoote* (1949). Solitude,
desperation and disorientation are generated by a world of violence and destruction where human values seem remote. Merle's
work takes place during the evacuation of Dunkirk. Maillat, a
former English teacher and now a sergeant, tries to secure passage
on a British ship. He succeeds but the ship is damaged by an
enemy attack and Maillat has to stay. The narrative pace is slow
and gives rise to a feeling of purposelessness and distraction in a
world characterised by unreality and nightmare (for a discussion

of similar themes in German literature see Chapter 3). In the course of his weekend wanderings, Maillat discovers a young girl being raped by two Frenchmen who have lost all sense of humanity in the outbreak of war. Maillat fights and kills both of them but then suddenly finds himself violently making love to the girl. Both Maillat and the girl have become infected by violence: he feels he has raped her and that she has enjoyed it. They cannot escape the dehumanising effects of war. The novel ends with both dying in an air attack as they struggle but fail to make some sense of their contact with each other, other than through violence. Their failure points to the death of hope and the destruction of the normal life of France. War, for Merle, is loss of meaning mingled with fascination at the ugliness and brutality of death.

Action in the air is the central concern of two writers, both fighter pilots working with the RAF, Algerian-born Jules Roy and Pierre Clostermann, perhaps the most distinguished French pilot of the war.[26] Roy is best known for *La Vallée heureuse* (1946) and *Retour de l'enfer* (1951), the former an autobiographically based "récit" of Roy's bombing missions in the Ruhr valley, the latter a series of "souvenirs romancés" of other continental missions of the author. Neither work has the descriptive power and pace of Clostermann's *Le Grand cirque* (1948) or the later *Feux du ciel* (1951). Both writers possess the skill to use their experiences and to recreate them in a convincing and exciting manner. Clostermann's work poses more explicitly the question of whether such works can be classified as fiction. Clostermann, for example, describes *Le Grand cirque* (see also Chapter 1) as the "recollections of a fighter pilot in the RAF" and claims it to be a "reportage". He asks the reader not to look for a literary work yet admits that the "reportage" is selective and structured to maximise its readability. His intentions are both documentary and commemorative although the information was collected in the first place so that, in the event of his death, his parents would have some record of his experiences in action and of the beauty and glory of life in the airforce. *Le Grand cirque* comes complete with photographs and various appendices on a number of operations and on the organisation of the RAF and the LUFTWAFFE. However, by skilful choice, concentration and presentation of episode, descriptions of atmosphere, use of dialogue and interior monologue and a varied prose style, Clostermann's diary, "reportage" becomes, in many respects, indistinguishable from a novel. Certainly, he captures the drama and colour of aerial combat, the suspense of the hours between missions, the joys of safe returns and the camaraderie of the units after the solitude of the missions and he can sometimes match both Malraux and Saint-Exupéry[27] in the art of creating contemplative moments.

Many similar qualities are evident in the later *Feux du ciel* which the author describes as a collection of "récits" telling the story of a number of fighter pilots' experiences. It had been Clostermann's aim to write a history of the war in the air, but having researched the subject thoroughly, he could not bear to bury the energy, greatness and passion of fighter pilots beneath a mass of historical detail. *Feux du ciel* is not "autobiographical" in the sense that the author recreates campaigns he did not fight, using various documents, but the descriptive and narrative powers of *Le Grand cirque* are very much in evidence once again. Clostermann finds in war a source of emotion and idealism, but his intoxication with the life of the pilot, the whole organisation of missions, his fascination with the technicalities of planes etc. do not make him forget that war is waste of life and suffering. With Clostermann "reportage" achieves the status of an authentic art form.[28]

In his novel about post-Liberation France, *Les Justes causes* (1954), Jean-Louis Curtis describes one of his hero's reactions to the discovery of concentration camps. Thibault Fontanes observes: "Huge posters on the walls of the town revealed to us the existence of certain places of rest and repose called Buchenwald, Dachau, Auschwitz . . . with photographs attached. We collapsed in horror at the sight of them. Here was something so scandalous that no intelligent person could assimilate it. Consequently, we are going to rid our minds of it. You can build a religion on a single crucified prophet, not on several million people burnt to death in slavery. We shall go on dancing and looking for nice beaches on the map for our holidays. Yet the topography of the camps will henceforth add a new dimension to our picture of life: the dimension of fear. And guilt in varying degree will for ever cling to us."

Curtis, through Fontanes, indirectly lays down a challenge to the writers who wish to describe their experiences in concentration camps. The monstrous inhumanity of such experiences will not be assimilated; the camps are a world apart, a universe of their own, unintelligible and incommunicable to those who did not suffer in them. Jean Cayrol had voiced similar ideas in "D'Un Univers concentrationnaire" (*Esprit*, 1949), an article in which the author claims that the camps produced a race of outsiders, a people apart, and he points out the difficulties confronting the writer who attempts description of the camps. In *Lazare parmi nous* (1950) Cayrol uses Lazarus to symbolise this race of resurrected and isolated dead.

In the main, one feels that the literature of the camps does suffer from what Curtis said it would: an inability to communicate such experiences. The principal works in question are: David Rousset, *L'Univers concentrationnaire* (1946), *Les Jours de notre mort* (1947); Robert Antelme, *L'Espèce humaine* (1947); Pierre Daix, *La Dernière forteresse* (1950); Louis Martin-Chauffier, *L'Homme et la bête* (1947); Paul Tillard, *Le Pain des temps des maudits* (1965); Pierre Gascar, *Le Temps des morts* (1953), *Les Femmes* (1965); J. Semprún, *Le Grand voyage* (1973).

In a variety of ways, all the authors concerned express the pressing need which they felt to tell of their experiences and describe the problems they had in finding appropriate techniques of representation and description to capture the atmosphere and reality of the camps without appearing to be culpable of morbidity or sensationalism.

David Rousset's *L'Univers concentrationnaire* is relatively short in comparison to much of the literature of the camps, and perhaps because of this or its very compactness makes a greater impact than many such works. Rousset dwells on the fundamental features of camp life in Buchenwald and Auschwitz. Much attention is paid to aspects of organisation and to its multi-national antagonisms, to its creation of its own particular norms of rationality and social behaviour. Kafka and Jarry are cited as artists who have come close to anticipating the nightmare and unreality of camp life. In both this work and the later *Les Jours de notre mort*, Rousset rejects fiction. In the preface to *Les Jours de notre mort*, he says that although he is using novelistic techniques, invention has no part to play in his work. Details, events, characters are all authentic and no fiction is needed in a world such as the camps where everyday experience is already beyond imagination. Pierre Daix does describe *La Dernière forteresse* as a novel, but the work bears many similarities to that of Rousset; thus the distinction between fact and fiction is once again difficult to grasp. Both works can be compared to Antelme's *L'Espèce humaine* described as

"un récit" about the Gandersheim "Kommando" of Buchenwald, and there is no greater technical difference between this
work and many novels. Martin-Chauffier uses "souvenirs romancés" to tell the story in *L'Homme et la bête* of his arrest in
Collonges for being a suspected Soviet spy, his imprisonment in
Fort-Montluc and Compiègne and eventual transfer to Neuen-
gamme and Belsen, but the whole work reads like a novel. The
literature of the camps throws into sharp focus questions about
fiction and fact. Many of the above-quoted writers "reject" the
label of fiction because they are using lived experience. They seem
to forget, however, that writing about the camps does not require
personal experience as a precondition; nor does personal experience guarantee success in writing about them. Although Robert
Merle's *La Mort est mon métier*, an imaginary autobiography of
Rudolf Höss, the camp commander of Auschwitz, has no great
claims to distinction, it does at least show that biographical base
in the camps is not a necessary element in their recreation.
(William Styron's *Sophie's Choice* [1979] is another example.) It is
also interesting to note that such debates which in the past gave
rise to the term "faction" have been given new life by the award of
the Booker prize to Keneally's *Schindler's Ark* in 1982, a non-
biographical recreation of camp life.

The literature of the camps contains a multitude of themes but
the principal question posed is the nature of man. The reader is
provided with a vast panorama of human beings under great
stress and deprivation caused by other men who subject them to
torture and degradation. But, as Antelme, Martin-Chauffier and
many others point out, in their oppression and in their oppressors,
they did not discover, at the extreme limit of their suffering,
solitude and absurdity or despair but "an ultimate feeling of
belonging to the human race" (Antelme) or "the sense that the
human race is one" (Martin-Chauffier). Certainly, it can be said
that French literature of the concentration camps has given us
new and extensive images of human brutality and of man's
resilience under pressure, and the war has created a new dimension to the literary image of man.

The description of the impact of defeat and occupation on the
people of France, the antagonisms and divisions of loyalty to
which they gave rise in everybody's life, the question of collabora-

tion with Vichy and the Germans, and the role of black-market profiteering offer a wide canvas to the writer wishing to create a picture of French society under threat and oppression. Whether such a picture is created through the perspective of a single individual's reaction either in fiction or "souvenirs romancés", or through a multicolour of perspectives in a village, or town or the capital, the works under consideration possess an identity in their emphasis on social considerations and the disruption of everybody's existence. There is a multitude of relevant texts. Emmanuel d'Astier wrote two volumes of "souvenirs romancés", describing his individual reactions and observations during the war: *De la Chute à la Libération de Paris* and *Sept Fois, Sept Jours* (1947). Certainly not "mémoires" but not quite fiction in the usual sense, d'Astier's work provides us with descriptions of the *exode*, attacks on the too easily defeated military establishment and aspects of Resistance, described as "the most precious manifestation of life." D'Astier travels through Paris, Lyon, Clermont and Marseille evoking "a sedentary France" which is slowly finding itself confronted by "a France which has started to move again".

His comments on the Liberation underline his disappointment at the phoenix-like capacity of the ruling class – "the mountain gave birth to a mouse: we were present at a mediocre rebirth". Jewish député Pierre Bloch in *Mes Jours heureux* (1947) uses a similar hybrid genre to describe his war years, some of which were spent in prison and some with de Gaulle in London. More obviously fictional are Alexandre Arnoux's *Hélène et les guerres* (1945), Michel Bataille's rather puzzling *Patrick* (1947) – about a father reconstructing the history of his son, killed in action during the war – Pierre Daix's *Classe de 42* (1951) and perhaps Boisdeffre's *Les Fins dernières* (1952), a fictional transposition of Pétain's trial of the Liberation period.

Arnoux's work is of particular relevance since its protagonist is an ex-fighter in the great war. When the Second World War is declared, Savrit, the hero, is reminded of the first and longs for the same intensification of existence that he found then. His experiences of the first war were set against his love affair with the beautiful Hélène who died in 1939. Savrit finds the war lacking in the mythical beauty of 1914–18, but in the reign of a resisting France and during the celebrations of the Liberation he finds the resurrection of his ideals, in great contrast to d'Astier's mouse.

Despite the interest of such works and many more besides it is perhaps in Jean-Louis Curtis's *Les Forêts de la nuit* (1947) that we find the best portrait of France under occupation. The author gained the Prix Goncourt for his book and it followed in the wake of another Goncourt prize winner writing on the same subject – Jean-Louis Bory's *Mon Village à l'heure allemande* (1945). Curtis's novel is far superior to Bory's but both have their interest.

*Mon Village à l'heure allemande* begins on 24 April 1941. The village in question is an imaginary one, Jumainville (an amalgam of Germain and Jumelle perhaps?), described as nothing more and nothing less than any other French village, and Bory uses it as a microcosm of France, anticipating Curtis's use of Saint-Clar and Camus's use of Oran. Bory's technique is to avoid external narrative and to present events through a multiplicity of first-person perspectives to present a panorama of personages giving different views of events, a technique used in a more sophisticated form and with many modifications by Sartre in *Les Chemins de la liberté*. This approach enables Bory to capture well the atmosphere of fear and suspicion and the zones of non-communication between the inhabitants of Jumainville. The author extends his use of the relative point of view to allowing the village itself to address the reader and express its alarm at the presence of the Germans and its fear of losing its French identity. In addition the dog of the schoolmaster Tattignie is allowed to express its thoughts (the Germans after the abandonment of Korrektion were referred to as "animals who speak"). The arrival of the Germans transforms a pre-existent network of social relations and antagonisms constituting normal village and French life. The village gossip Mademoiselle Vrin turns to informing; the village flirt Denise Véchard fornicates in collaboration; the mayor Morize is anti-German but fears reprisals against him if he does not co-operate; l'Abbé Varèmes, pro-Inquisition and pro-German, dislikes the early soft approach of the Germans, symbolised by von Scheer and Bachmann. Anticipating Camus' attack on the church in *La Peste* and his character Paneloux, Varèmes denounces resistance and calls for the village to be purified of clandestine activity and for full co-operation with the "defenders of order"; the collaborating village baker Lecheur finds himself and his business under threat from Resistance but the resister in question is a former enemy settling old scores, the poacher Léon; the Boudet family occupies a central place: the father, a farmer,

finds collaboration with Bachmann profitable, and his son Auguste speculates with the black market. The daughter Elisa is
pro-de Gaulle as is her Resistance boyfriend Pierre. The family is
split by violent quarrels. A Resistance network forms in the village
and Tattignie the schoolteacher joins it. He is eventually shot by
Auguste Boudet who begins working for the Germans in a bitter
spirit of revenge against his sister and the resisters who set fire to
his secret store of black-market petrol.

The general atmosphere of suspicion and latent hostility between individuals grows into scenes of violence and open struggle
as the war develops, and the novel degenerates as a result of this:
events become over-dramatised and actions exaggerated particularly in the section during which Juine lives out an assignment in
terms of a Buffalo Bill adventure romance. Bory's work rarely
goes beyond social description of the village to probe more
searching questions, but it is interesting both for its techniques of
representation and portraiture of the French under occupation.

Curtis's *Les Forêts de la nuit*[29] explores the occupation through
the imaginary town of Saint-Clar, situated at the extreme end of
the occupied zone. Passive collaboration is widespread and dominant but the English-hating Madame Costellot is quick to
fraternise, as are many of the women in the town. Saint-Clar
receives a Vichy merit award eventually for its good behaviour
and cooperation.

Into this imaginary structure, Curtis, using conventional third-
person narrative, projects his experiences of France under Occupation. The author is at pains to point out in his preface that the
work is a novel, not a document or piece of sociology, that he has
deliberately kept Resistance activity and heroism in soft focus to
allow for a certain unity of tone in the presentation of the tableau
of Occupation. Curtis's characters present, like Bory's, a panorama of perspectives on events, but social description tends constantly to give rise to more general preoccupations in a story
which is much more exciting to read than many war books. A
variety of themes is explored by Curtis: Francis Balansum is the
young idealistic resister. We see him at work helping people to
cross the line (the work begins in November 1942 just before the
zoning system is abolished), wanting to be more active and finally
being tortured without giving in, shot and mutilated by the group
under Merkel, a viciously sadistic collaborator working in the
French Gestapo. Francis is the son of a relatively poor aristocrat,

Count Balansum, who is pro-Pétain and anti-Stalin but he is presented sympathetically and is so proud of his son's work that he switches allegiance to de Gaulle. In contrast to Francis is his former schoolfriend Philippe Arregui, an ambiguously presented character, ruthless but likeable for his quick wits and energy. Arregui operates the black market but eventually joins with Merkel. Arregui is a rather Nietzschean individual; he has no time for Francis's social conscience. Francis has a sister Hélène who shares initially her brother's idealism. She is in Paris, separated from her fiancé Jean de Lavencourt who has fought for Spanish Republicanism and is now believed to be in the RAF. Francis uses Arregui to deliver a message about Lavencourt to his sister. Arregui is quick to sense beneath the idealistic postures of Hélène a lonely and frustrated virgin: he speedily seduces and abandons her but not before she breaks off her engagement. Lavencourt's death is soon reported: the young idealist was killed on a mission but his plane was not shot down, he crashed it deliberately. Arregui, working under Merkel, soon finds himself instructed to clean up the resisters of Saint-Clar whose operations under Francis have been uncovered to the Germans by Madame Costellot. Arregui does try to a limited extent to protect Francis but he fails, and in a rather weak section of the text Francis is shot.

With the death of the idealists, Francis and Lavencourt, and with Hélène's posture of idealism punctured, Curtis begins to turn his attention to a central concern of the novel – the way in which the Resistance movement became infiltrated after Stalingrad by political opportunists, thus leading to a prostitution of the rare and elevated ideals which originally inspired it. The slippery character Darricade who has played a two-way game slowly emerges as the hero of Resistance and consolidates his political power. Quite the most bitter outburst against the Darricades of France and the hypocrisy and iniquities of the *Epuration* (the post-Liberation purges) spring from Curtis's pen in the closing pages of the text. For Curtis, the genuine idealists and heroes have been few, and many are dead like Francis and Lavencourt; the self-styled heroes and opportunists of the Liberation represent a return to the self-interest and mediocrity of the past, not a new dawn for France. Through the apolitical but perceptive son of Madame Costellot, Jacques (now the lover of Hélène), Curtis expresses deep contempt for the intrigues and duplicities of political life, a theme pursued in *Les Justes causes* (1954). Even the amoral but attractive Arregui doesn't survive the war: as the German defeat draws near, he joins the army to protect himself but in a gesture of defiant self-affirmation, he skies across enemy lines and is shot.

Curtis's tableau of the Occupation is impressive and informative, but in the final analysis the novel transcends its social descriptions to explore the general themes of youthful idealism, cynicism, opportunism and hypocrisy, thus displacing the Occupation to a secondary dimension of the narrative.

To be read in conjunction with *Les Forêts de la nuit* is Gary's *Les Cerfs-volants* (1980). Written 35 years after *Education européenne*, the work not only testifies to the lasting impact of war on Gary but to the durability of the subject as a fictional base. Dedicated to "Memory", *Les Cerfs-volants* is a largely biographically inspired novel telling of the war-time experiences in occupied France of Ludovic Fleury, the narrator and of his uncle Ambroise, a famous kite-maker of Cléry where the main action of the novel takes place. The image of the kite is used by Gary to symbolise the heroism and idealism of Resistance, and the novel generally traces the development of Ludovic from his inability to believe that Fascism can gain popular support, his sense of unreality at the outbreak of war, to his eventual commitment. The novel also traces his emotional involvement with Lila Bronicki, daughter of an expatriate Polish aristocrat living in France. Lila is a collaborator but Ludovic's love for her survives and he rescues her from the recriminations of the *Epuration*, thus transcending hate and contempt and pointing to a humanism which enhances Germans, collaborators and resisters alike. The novel presents a wide variety of themes, the inadequacy of pacifism, the collapse of France, human duplicity and heroism, barbarism and love, suffering and the possibility of establishing a humanism capable of transcending the double face of human nature. Distanced from events, Gary is able to create in *Les Cerfs-volants* a work of greater power and insight than his earlier *Education européenne*. The time lapse also gives rise to a far more wide-ranging approach as the events of war assume a variety of symbolic dimensions in the mind of the author.

Worthy of mention also under this heading is Louis Guilloux's long work *Le Jeu de patience* (Prix Renaudot 1949).[30] This is a vast fragmented chronicle, written from four principal perspectives, one of which is the Occupation. The town is Saint-Brieuc and the narrator is trying to recreate the history of his birthplace from World War One onwards. Various events disrupt the chronicler, including the arrival of the Germans in the town in 1940. The narrator begins to chronicle the Occupation and piece together events. Slowly *Le Jeu de patience* poses essential questions about historical reconstructions and whether history has any meaning or direction. As in Butor, narrative reconstruction salvages events from oblivion and gives a direction to the human adventure in time. Saint-Brieuc becomes a focus for the contradictions and overlaps of experience. Both in the importance accorded to the war as one of the privileged viewpoints of the chronicle and in terms of the questions posed by the author about narrative, history and meaning, *Le Jeu de patience* is one of the most interesting books about war and Occupation.

For the writer of comic fiction, the subject of war with all its gravity, drama and emotion, offers a particular challenge. It is worth recalling that Malraux, with the gambling mythomaniac Clappique of *La Condition humaine*, and Céline, with Bardamu in *Le Voyage au bout de la nuit*, are both capable of finding, amid the sufferings and torments of war, sources of humour. Nor can it be said that Sartre and to a lesser extent Camus are insensitive to the comic aspects of individuals and situations in war. However it is to Jean Dutourd (*Au Bon Beurre*, 1952; *Les Taxis de la Marne*, 1956), Marcel Aymé (*Le Chemin des écoliers*, 1946; *Uranus*, 1949) and the more "popular" Antoine Blondin (*L'Europe buissonnière*, 1949; *Les Enfants du bon Dieu*, 1952; *L'Humeur vagabonde*, 1955) that we owe the most humorous representations of war, although such humour is admittedly very sardonic and full of satirical intention.

Dutourd's *Au Bon Beurre* is perhaps the funniest and most biting representation of France under the Occupation. The novel starts in 1940 at the time of the *exode* and describes the lives of Charles Hubert and Julie Poissonard and their two children as the family amass a fortune from black-market and collaborationist trading in their "crémerie" business. Strongly pro-Vichy and convinced that all resisters should be shot, the Poissonards betray Léon Lecuyer, a neighbour's son who has escaped from German imprisonment, is active in the Resistance and is trying to assassinate Laval. By 1943 and with a lot of money in the bank, the Poissonards slowly realise that the war might go against the Germans and they switch allegiances. Having helped a young German soldier for money, they strategically betray him to give themselves a respectable Resistance identity and emerge safely from the *Epuration*. By 1948 they are worth 47 million francs and marry off their daughter to a Resistance hero, now a député but at one time a member of the Vichy cabinet. The young Léon is politically educated during the war by a noble CP member, Alphonse, who is later on executed. Léon does not join the Party, becomes a university teacher and has the privilege of instructing Poissonard's son. Poissonard organises Léon's demotion when he discovers that his son's marks are not very good.

In the preface of the book, Dutourd tells us that he felt that he had to write the work, and in the style in which it is written. He appears to mean by this that the bitterness and rancour that he felt at the successful treachery and opportunism of the Poissonards of France ("la canaille" – the rabble – as he calls them) presented a particular challenge to his comic art. An oblique comment on the fragile assumptions which frequently underlie approaches to war literature is provided by Dutourd when he denies that he had been a "crémier" as many critics had assumed...!

*Au Bon Beurre* contains many memorable scenes: Léon's escape from prison and encounter with a Hamburg transvestite soldier, the Poissonards' visit to Pétain bearing ducks' eggs and other gifts; the extremely sarcastic attack on and pastiche of René Benjamin who writes a newspaper article celebrating the visit; the exchanges between the Poissonards, the anti-German Madame Lecuyer and the pro-Nazi collaborator M. Lebugle. As well as its humour, *Au Bon Beurre* is immensely rich in detail about the French under Occupation in the same way that *Les Taxis de la Marne* provides much information about the Liberation and immediate post-war years.

Aymé's *Le Chemin des écoliers* is best read in conjunction with Pierre Daix's *Classe 42* (2 vols, 1951) which traces the impact of war and the lessons derived from it on a group of mainly young people of various persuasions. *Le Chemin des écoliers* shows the younger generation quick to seize the opportunities provided by the black market in war and showing the way forward to their seniors, represented by two personages reminiscent of Flaubert's Homais and Bournisien: M. Michaud and M. Lolivier.

Michaud and Lolivier manage a rented accommodation agency, "la Société de gérance des fortunes immobilières de Paris". The business has become less profitable because of the war, particularly after the *exode*. Michaud is strongly opposed to the black market but his partner feels they are part of it despite themselves. Both men are concerned with their families. Lolivier has a son Tony who gives his father cause for concern when he burns out the eyes of a chicken that he has plucked alive. Michaud has two children, Antoine, active in the black market, and Yvette, unfaithful to her husband away fighting the war. Molinier, a friend of Yvette's husband, provides added humour as a pro-German, anti-Jewish, Communist, Cubist, poet, and freemason collaborator (he has a particular dislike for Jews who own Cubist paintings).

Eventually, Lolivier's growing sense of his own hypocrisy during the war leads to many quarrels with Michaud. He tells his partner that they are merely posturers of Resistance and that their real concerns are not with humanity and values or freedom of others but with their own comfort and feelings. Finally both men abandon their postures of commitment and accept that the war is not their concern and has not changed them: they are still the self-satisfied, self-interested bourgeois of pre-war days. Much of the change is guided by the activities of their children.

Michaud commits adultery with a cabaret girl whom he has met in a bar, a centre of black-market activities, where he has gone in order to protect his son. With Lolivier helping, he quickly amasses a fortune through the black market. Lolivier's son uses the same market to sell off as meat the carved-up body of a girl he has killed with the assistance of an Arab. The work ends happily. Aymé's clear-sighted and sometimes sardonic assessment of his fellow countrymen was already apparent in the work he produced during the Occupation. Here, he completely defeats any image the French may have had of themselves as a nation of resisters. He continues along the same vitriolic lines in *Uranus*, where he denounces the inequities of the *Epuration* and post-Liberation France, as Curtis does in *Les Justes causes*.[31]

When all is said and done it is principally to Sartre, Camus and, to a lesser extent, Simone de Beauvoir that the reader must turn to find the literary masterpieces inspired by the war. The literary qualities of *La Peste* need no underlining, nor the range and depth of Sartre's *Les Chemins de la liberté* (1945–9), and few war works can match the interest of Simone de Beauvoir's complex novel about responsibility and freedom, *Le Sang des autres* (1945), despite its evident limitations as a novel. Such works are too well known to require much comment here; but they do give rise to a number of important questions about the nature of war literature and the significance of war in the lives of these artists.

We can only speculate as to how Camus's and Sartre's thought would have developed if there had been no war but it certainly seems that the impact of war on their ideas is vital. In addition, so apposite and suitable is war as a vehicle for their philosophies and notions of existence that it could be argued they would have had to invent it, if it had not occurred!

Sartre was mobilised in October 1939. Quickly taken prisoner, he spent nine months in a German prison. In *Avec Sartre au Stalag 12D* (1980), Father Marius Perrin records his impressions of Sartre at the time and of his play *Bariona* which, under the pressure of events in Europe, begins the process whereby the rather negative conclusions of *La Nausée* are transformed into the positive concepts of engagement embodied in *Les Mouches* and *Les Mains sales* with their emphasis on action and social change. This evolution is also the principal theme of *Les Chemins de la liberté*. The civil war in Spain, the Munich crisis, the *exode* and the "drôle de guerre" are used by Sartre to articulate his notions of contingency, freedom and responsibility. Mathieu, the disenchanted philosophy teacher of the thirties, and Brunet, the over-confident CP member, are brought under the impact of war to a re-examination of their lives and attitudes.

The war attracted Sartre because it provided extreme circumstances capable of illustrating in stark relief his basic philosophical ideas. He uses it as a vehicle for the articulation of his metaphysic: the war is existence made clear, the lifting of the veil of "mauvaise foi", the discovery of contingency and "historicité" (cf. *Situations III*). In a sense it is questionable whether the work can be described as a "war novel" since the subject matter of war is simply a contingent "historical" event used as a pretext for exploring issues which far transcend the war. It is really, in the hands of Sartre, an extremely apt metaphor of our condition.

In the course of *Le Sursis*, Mathieu reflects on the war. He would like to know what it is and where it is. Sartre used the occasion to echo ideas developed in *Situations I* and *La Nausée* about history as a structure of consciousness, the impossibility of objective description, the philosophical relevance of the notion of relativity to the novel. In a sense, his remarks anticipate the Robbe-Grillet of *Dans le labyrinthe* and lead us to Guilloux's *Le Jeu de patience*. The upshot of Sartre's analysis is to make our very notion of an event a structure of consciousness and thus to make a literary structure a secondary symbolic organisation. There is no pre-existent reality, event or experience to which the literary artefact gives "order"; thus the history of the war is in itself a "fictional" creation of consciousness. Ideas such as this converge in a variety of ways in *Les Chemins de la liberté* and give the work great complexity and interest, but with the result that the war as subject matter seems slightly dwarfed.

Such observations are perhaps even more applicable to *La Peste*. The experience of war had possibly a greater impact on Camus than on Sartre. The already fragile individualism and hedonism of his early work is transformed by deeper reflections promoted by the war into the (perhaps equally fragile) humanism of *La Peste*. However, the war, Occupation and Resistance are but one dimension of *La Peste* and all such matters are transposed through the basic choice of the plague symbol. The war may well have been for Camus a metaphor of existence but he chooses a different metaphor to express its many possible dimensions. Camus was probably more conscious than most artists of the possibility of getting bogged down in particulars and history, and of the dangers of using immediate events as a subject matter for art. Like Sartre, Camus is also conscious of the extreme complexity of the nature of the relationship between fiction and history. Calling his work a "chronique" he uses a retrospectively revealed narrator and the edited diaries of Tarrou to pose the problem of reconstruction and transposition of events into narrative. *La Peste* poses in an acute form the question of what a war book actually is: it can certainly be read without necessarily thinking of the war, or even war, and as time goes by the historical context will fade away more and more. For this reason it is perhaps best to describe *La Peste* as a work inspired by war rather than a war book.

Simone de Beauvoir's *Le Sang des autres* (1945), completed before the end of the war and originally destined for Les Editions de Minuit,[32] eventually appeared with Gallimard. Here Beauvoir uses the Resistance movement as a set of general perspectives through which to explore in detail the question of freedom and responsibility. The problem of action in the Resistance is analysed but there is no description of action as such, rather the work abstracts from Resistance action a multitude of conflicts and paradoxes which confront the protagonist, Blomwart. There is also only the briefest evocation of the Occupation when Hélène realises that collaboration is impossible because it implies acceptance of anti-Semitism.

As with Sartre and Camus, Beauvoir's preoccupations in *Le Sang des autres* far transcend the question of war. It does end on a spirited defence of freedom by Blomart and is thus a "Resistance work", but the freedom envisaged goes beyond the question of occupation and national sovereignty. Much the same could be said of Vailland's *Drôle de jeu* (1945) where the Resistance movement is used as a base for the writer's exploration of private notions unrelated to war, although largely rooted in the author's personal experience of Resistance.[33]

The works of greater depth and interest, like the best war books of the past, pay more attention to art than to fact, and subordinate recreation of the war to exploration of the human condition. This is ultimately true even of those works of Resistance primarily intended as a call to action: *Le Silence de la mer* and other Editions de Minuit texts possess the power to transcend their historical moment. War in itself is a contingent event, a neutral backcloth and vehicle, capable of articulation in a wide variety of ways. Although much information on the war can be gleaned from them, the war is not so much the text of the best works as their pretext.

## English Translations of Works Mentioned

Aymé, Marcel, *Le Chemin des écoliers/The Transient Hour*, trans. by Eric Sutton (London, 1948).

——, *La Vouivre/The Fable and the Flesh*, trans. by Eric Sutton (London, 1949).

——, *Uranus/Fanfare in Blémont*, trans. by Norman Denny (London, 1950).

Beauvoir, Simone de, *Le Sang des autres/The Blood of Others*, trans. by Yvonne Moyse and Roger Senhouse (London, 1948).

Bory, Jean Louis, *Mon Village à l'heure allemande/French Village*, trans. by D.P. and P.J. Waley (London, 1948).

Camus, Albert, *La Peste/The Plague*, trans. by Stuart Gilbert (London, 1948).

Clostermann, Pierre Henri, *Le Grand Cirque/The Big Show*, trans. by Oliver Berthoud (London, 1951).

——, *Feux du ciel/Flames in the Sky*, trans. by Oliver Berthoud (London, 1954).

Curtis, Jean Louis, *Les Forêts de la nuit/The Forests of the Night*, trans. by Nora Wydenbruck (London, 1951).

——, *Les Justes Causes/The Side of the Angels*, trans. by Humphrey Hare (New York, 1954).

Dutourd, Jean, *Au Bon Beurre/The Milky Way*, trans. by Robin Chancellor (London, 1955).

Gary, Romain, *Éducation européenne/Forest of Anger*, trans. by Viola Gerard Garvin (London, 1944).

Kessel, Joseph Elie, *L'Armée des ombres/Army of Shadows*, trans. by Haakon Chevalier (London, 1944).

Merle, Robert, *Weekend à Zuydcoote/Weekend at Zuydcoote*, trans. by K. Rebillon-Lambley (London, 1950).

——, *La Mort est mon métier/Death is my Trade*, trans. by Alan Ross (London, 1954).

Modiano, Patrick, *La Ronde de nuit/Night Rounds*, trans. by Patricia Wolf (New York, 1972).

——, *Les Boulevards de ceinture/Ring Roads*, trans. by Caroline Hillier (London, 1974).

Nimier, Roger, *Le Hussard bleu/The Blue Hussar*, trans. by John Russell and Anthony Rhodes (London, 1952).

Pozner, Vladimir, *Deuil en 24 heures/The Edge of the Sword*, trans. by Haakon Chevalier (London, 1943).

Rousset, David, *L'Univers concentrationnaire/A World Apart*, trans. by Yvonne Moyse and Roger Senhouse (London, 1951).

Roy, Jules, *La Vallée heureuse/The Happy Valley*, trans. by Edward Owen Marsh (London, 1952).

——, *Retour de l'enfer/Return from Hell*, trans. by Mervyn Savill (London, 1954).

Saint-Exupéry, Antoine de, *Pilote de guerre/Flight to Arras*, trans. by Stuart Gilbert (New York, 1942).

Sartre, Jean-Paul, *Les Chemins de la liberté/The Roads to Freedom*. I: *L'Age de la raison/The Age of Reason*, trans. by Eric Sutton (London, 1947); II *Le Sursis/The Reprieve*, trans. by Eric Sutton (London, 1947); III *La Mort dans l'Ame/Iron in the Soul*, trans. by Gerard Hopkins (London, 1950).

Vailland, Roger. *Drôle de jeu/Playing with Fire*, trans. by Gerard Hopkins (London, 1948).

Vercors (Jean Bruller), *Le Silence de la mer/Put out the Light*, trans. by Cyril Connolly (London, 1944).

——, *Marche à l'étoile/Guiding Star*, trans. by Eric Sutton (London, 1946).

# 3 Germany

## Alan Bance

Germany was responsible for the outbreak of the Second World War in a sense that is not paralleled by her part in the events which led to the Great War, a European conflagration fuelled by national suspicions and ambitions on all sides. Even if one accepts that it was primarily German militarism and aggression which launched the First World War, that role in no way compares with Germany's agency in creating the Second, the inevitable fulfilment of Hitler's ideology. This fact colours German fiction dealing with the war, and the response of readers, native or foreign, to the German war books. While the fiction of other nations describes a reaction, embodied most clearly perhaps in the French Resistance literature, German writing has the task of coming to terms with the results of an action initiated by Germans and, while almost universally reviled abroad, at least in its early stages undoubtedly accepted if not welcomed by most of their fellow-countrymen. It is true that, in "Sorcerer's Apprentice" style, operations almost immediately escaped from the control of the war's instigators, and gradually they, too, took on the role of victims of a catastrophe so vast as to be almost beyond human imagining. But, while these later developments may cloud the issue, especially in a German popular view of the war, they do not permit German writers to disown their nation's responsibility.

The shape of "their" war, as seen from a German vantage point, can be outlined as follows: after it became clear that this time, in contrast to the settling of the Czech and Austrian "questions", Hitler was not going to get his way by negotiation, i.e. intimidation, he decided to give his new *Wehrmacht* some useful active-service experience by invading Poland. Following the declaration of war on Germany by the European democracies and the fall of Poland, a period of "phoney war" in the West was succeeded by the rapid collapse of France in 1940. The end of hostilities was blocked only by the minor obstacle of Britain, which the *Luftwaffe* and the U-boats could be trusted to deal with. As the air war over the Channel petered out in a stalemate, however, Hitler postponed an invasion of England, a hopeless prospect without German air and sea supremacy, and turned towards the East in the summer of 1941. Now at last Germany faced the real enemy, Bolshevism, which was to be ruthlessly destroyed in order to clear Russian land for German colonisation. The "war of annihilation" began as a campaign of lightning victories achieved by inflicting total tactical surprise upon a cumbersome Soviet command. With the onset of autumn and winter, however, it was clear that the Russians were as yet by no means defeated (despite official announcements to that effect from Berlin), and the German campaign ground to a halt just outside Moscow. In the Russian winter counter-offensive that followed, German losses were appalling (88 977 dead, 23 319 missing). The German summer offensive of 1942 brought only the certainty that the costly and brutal Russian campaign could hope for no quick end, and the suspicion that, with an immense hinterland to fall back upon, the Soviet forces simply could not be defeated. Any lingering German hopes were dashed by the most significant single event of the war, the siege and fall of Stalingrad and the total destruction of Paulus's 6th Army early in 1943. From then on, the end was rarely in doubt. While the population at home endured the inconceivable horrors of day and night Allied blanket bombing, the German forces were driven on to the defensive both on the Eastern and the Western Front, pushed back towards the homeland by the Russians, and unable to beat off a nervously awaited Anglo-American invasion in Normandy in 1944. After the failure of the much-vaunted "wonder weapons", the V–1s and V–2s, one last desperate attempt to turn the tide of events in the West, the Battle of the Bulge in the Ardennes just before Christmas 1944, simply precipitated the end in May 1945; the total capitulation of Germany and its division into zones of occupation.

The history of German Second World War fiction begins for our purposes after the Nazi period itself. With the exception of trivial war stories written to a formula and intended to prepare adolescents for their military call-up (sample titles are *Mit Stukas und Panzern nach Frankreich* and *Achtung – ich werfe!*) the years from 1939 to 1945 produced very little fiction dealing with the war. Any demand for combat literature seems to have been amply supplied by novels produced at the end of the Weimar Republic, dealing with the First World War and incorporating militaristic attitudes welcome to the National Socialist régime: Werner Beumelburg, *Die Gruppe Bosemüller* (1930), Edwin Erich Dwinger, *Die Armee hinter Stacheldraht* (1929), Josef Magnus Wehner, *Sieben vor Verdun* (1930), and Hans Zöberlein, *Der Glaube an Deutschland* (1931). With very few exceptions, such as Hans Wörner with his war novel *Flugschüler Ungenat* (1941), novelists writing during the war years remained faithful to the favourite pre-war themes of National Socialist literature, such as peasant life and historical personalities. The possible explanations for the dearth of war fiction are various. Those with first-hand experience of Second World War combat were otherwise engaged between 1939 and 1943, when the tide of war turned; and thereafter few Germans would presumably have had the stomach for novels glorifying a war they were not winning. Realism, the hallmark of the novel form, was not only dangerous politically, but officially discouraged. The preference for the lyric and dramatic genres in the Third Reich has to do with traditional German esteem for these "higher" forms, deemed suitable vehicles, therefore, for the aspirations of the new Germany. In 1942 a leading Nazi *Literat*, Gerhard Schumann, typically rejects the novel as too analytical a genre for war writing. While prose fiction "casts its flickering light on events", the lyric is "the fire itself", the flame of myth, irrationalism and purification of the race through war. The novel could not compete.

Any outline of the phases of war book production after 1945 can only be a rough one. The desire of Germans to learn about the war from fiction was not quickly satisfied: it was only by the end of the forties that war novels began to appear in any numbers. Not surprisingly, in view of the ruthless suppression of opposition under the National Socialists, the earliest novels were expressions of pent-up wrath and condemnation of the régime and the war, books like Theodor Plievier's *Stalingrad* (1945), written in exile in Moscow, and Walter Kolbenhoff's *Von unserem Fleisch und Blut* (1947), a novel about a fanatical young "Werwolf" whose Nazi indoctrination leads him to continue the war long after defeat has become inevitable: this, too, written not on German soil but in the American re-education camps, Forts Ruston and Kearney. The indictment of war and inhumanity continued with, for example,

Hans Erich Nossack's powerful collection of stories *Interview mit dem Tode* (1948), including the famous description of the destruction of Hamburg by Allied bombing in 1943, "Der Untergang"; Heinrich Böll's *Der Zug war pünktlich* (1949), concerning a soldier travelling towards the Eastern Front and the certainty of death, or his *Wo warst du, Adam?* (1951), a series of loosely related scenes epitomising the pathos and irony of war for Böll's largely passive subjects; and Alfred Andersch's *Die Kirschen der Freiheit* (1952), an account of the author's decision to desert to the Allies in Italy towards the end of the war.

The political circumstances of Germany in the Cold War era account for the short life-span of this phase, the period of freedom to explore and experiment with the new democratic concepts proudly bestowed upon Germany by the Western Allies, and to attempt a brutally honest confrontation with the immediate past. Quite early on, with the freezing of relations between eastern and western power blocs, any literature taking up a critical (i.e. independent and thoughtful) stance towards the Allies was suspected of pro-Communist leanings; so, for instance, the American military government in April 1947 banned the liberal-progressive journal *Der Ruf* for its "nihilistic" standpoint (the response was the formation by Hans Werner Richter in the autumn of 1947 of the Gruppe 47, which was to become the biggest single influence in post-war literature). There were many factors at work in West Germany to encourage a suppression of recent memories; the formation of a stabilised Federal Republic constructed out of the Western Zones of Occupation; the need to assimilate enormous numbers of refugees from the East; the Berlin blockade; the emerging "economic miracle"; the debate about, and eventual (1955) adoption of re-armament as a result of the outbreak of the Korean War in 1950 – all required the assumption of a prematurely achieved "normality" and conspired to muffle the voices of the small group of writers genuinely concerned to come to terms with the past. The 1950s were a period when politics was pushed into the background and ideologies were suspect. The self-evident virtues of the free-market economy were equated with the right to withdraw into the private sphere, be it the nuclear family or one's own self-sufficient conscience, now free of discomfort as the past became sanitised through the operation of "the whole catalogue of [German] incorrigibility", as Ralph Giordano's hero calls it in the brilliant new novel *Die Bertinis* (1982): "Hitler was solely responsible", "there were good sides to the regime (the Autobahn) as well as bad", "it was the British in the Boer War who invented concentration camps", and the neatly self-contradictory assertions that (a) "we didn't know what was going on" and (b) "there was nothing we could do about it if we did know".[1]

The reflection of all this in war literature was not so much books attempting to justify militarism (such attitudes being confined, so far as serious literature was concerned, to extreme right-wingers like Erich Edwin Dwinger in *Wenn Die Dämme brechen* [1950], an account of the onslaught of the invading Russian forces on East Prussia), but a trend towards, on the one hand, the "tough", value-free novel limiting itself to depicting the horrors of war *à la* Remarque (*All Quiet on the Western Front*), without explicit political or ideological comment or content (Gert Ledig's *Die Stalinorgel* [1955], or Reinhart Stalmann's *Staub* [1951], are examples); and, on the other hand, a more private, even existentialist view of war, as a-political and a-historical as the philosophy of the free play of market forces itself.[2] Examples of the latter type of novel (reminiscent of the writings of Saint-Exupéry) are Gerd Gaiser's *Die sterbende Jagd* (1953), about a "dying squadron" of fighter pilots whose independent pride in their élitist branch of the profession of arms is overshadowed elegiacally by knowledge that they are hopelessly outnumbered and the war is being lost; or Herbert Zand's *Letzte Ausfahrt* (1953), presenting the situation of a cut-off and surrounded fictional city in the east of Germany as symbolic of the human condition in general; or the much-acclaimed *Nichts in Sicht* by Jens Rehn (1954), the story of a German submariner and an American pilot *in extremis*, drifting and dying in a rubber dinghy in mid-Atlantic.

The number of significant war novels gradually declined after 1955, although the popular, adventure-story kind of war book still thrived.[3] The Gruppe 47, whose members had been young men during the war and had for the most part served in the German forces, lost coherence and influence in the sixties. Important war novels continued sporadically to appear, such as Siegfried Lenz's *Stadtgespräch* (1963), set in occupied Norway, or Böll's *Entfernung von der Truppe* (1964: it contains a "recherche du temps perdu" by an ex-soldier, now a grandfather, of the wartime period and especially an episode where he went absent without leave), or Alexander Kluge's Stalingrad-book, *Schlachtbeschreibung* (first published 1964, but in a revised version as *Der Untergang der 6. Armee* in 1969). The theme of war also loomed large in the epoch-making novels, Günter Grass's *Die Blechtrommel* (1959; see especially the chapters "The Polish Post Office", "The Ant Trail" and "Inspection of concrete") and Siegfried Lenz's *Deutschstunde* (1968; a vastly inflated "punishment essay" on the very German theme of "the joys of duty", written purportedly by a young man in a reform institution, attempting almost total recall of his wartime years as the son of an over-conscientious country policeman in northernmost Schleswig-Holstein). But it was precisely these great achievements in the field of *Vergangenheitsbewältigung*, or coming to terms with the past, which demonstrated a need to break out from the limitations of preoccupation with the war itself and to conceive startling new ways to do justice to the totality of the years from 1933 to 1945.

In the 1960s, in any case, prompted by the Eichmann trial of 1961, new forms of the documentary theatre were emerging which shifted the emphasis of *Vergangenheitsbewältigung* from the novel to the stage. Investigating the war and war guilt in a wider context, a world-wide perspective in some cases, were plays like Rolf Hochhuth's *Der Stellvertreter* (1963), on the failure of Pope Pius XII to intervene on behalf of the Jews in the Third Reich, or his *Soldaten* (1967), accusing Churchill of responsibility, firstly for the inhuman reprisals against German cities like Hamburg and Dresden carried out by saturation bombing, and secondly for the murder of the Polish General Sikorski. Peter Weiss's *Die Ermittlung* (1965) was based on the records of the Frankfurt Auschwitz trial of 1963–64. These playwrights, along with others such as Heinar Kipphardt (*In der Sache J. Robert Oppenheimer*, 1964) began to break down what they saw as the myth of the unique war guilt of Germany – still quarantined in her moral isolation ward – by scrutinising the record of the supposed representatives of democracy or of humane values (the Western democracies, the Papacy, Churchill).

With the extreme political events of 1967 and after – student riots and the radicalisation of the German political scene – the spell of the past might seem to have been broken at last; and indeed the new generation of German writers (Peter Handke, Wolf Wondratschek) intended to "wipe the slate clean" and cleanse the language itself of the old preoccupations. Present-day political issues now dominated almost exclusively. Even so, the early seventies unexpectedly saw the publication of two important war books, Lothar-Günther Buchheim's submarine-novel *Das Boot* (1973), and Alfred Andersch's *Winterspelt* (1974), both curiously belated products. Andersch takes up on a larger scale the themes of his earlier *Die Kirschen der Freiheit* (a German officer just before the Battle of the Bulge makes a half-hearted attempt to capitulate to the Americans with all his troops intact), while Buchheim, who had put to sea thirty years earlier with U-boats as an official war correspondent, now writes up his experiences in the form of a gripping work of fiction which launched a new, hardly novel but very interesting West German controversy over the suspected glamourising of the Second World War, and in particular the creation of a hero-figure in the shape of the attractive young submarine captain. The 1970s also saw the republication of a number of earlier war books, and a gradual increase in West German receptivity to the subject of the war years, as evidenced by the massive viewing figures and positive audience response when the American TV series *Holocaust* (on the deportation and extermination of the Jews) was screened at the end of the decade.

This was also a time of intensified research by historians into such topics as the complicity of the *Wehrmacht* in the atrocities of the Eastern Front, reported in Christian Streit's *Keine Kameraden*, dealing with the Army's involvement in and responsibility for the maltreatment and death of millions of Russian POWs; Klaus-Jürgen Müller's *Das Heer und Hitler*, on the relationship between the upper echelons of the military and the National Socialist régime; Manfred Messerschmidt's study of political indoctrination in the Army, *Die Wehrmacht im NS-Staat*; and above all *Die Truppe der Weltanschauungskrise*, by Helmut Krausnick and Hans-Heinrich Wilhelm, which in 1981 caused a new sensation (duly recorded in *Der Spiegel* in April 1981) by breaking down the convenient distinction between the *Wehrmacht* and the activities of SS or SD units in Russia, a distinction which had maintained intact the myth of the Army's "purity".[4]

On the fictional front, the latest phase of interest in the war has been reflected particularly in chronicles of family life, like Walter Kempowski's *Tadellöser & Wolff* (1971), Horst Bienek's *Zeit ohne Glocken* (1979), and Ralph Giordano's *Die Bertinis* (1982). Running parallel to this recent fiction is a never-ending stream of reminiscences and eye-witness accounts, such as, in 1982, the new volumes *Meine Schulzeit im Dritten Reich*, memoirs of their school-days under Hitler and in the war by German writers, edited by Marcel Reich-Ranicki; and *Das andere Gesicht des Krieges: Deutsche Feldpostbriefe 1939–1945*, a collection of letters to and from the front line, edited by Ortwin Buchbender and Reinhold Sterz. The recent literary activity generated by the Second World War, however critical, bears witness to something of a "nostalgia wave" about the period in Germany (compare Fassbinder's films, *The Marriage of Maria Braun* and *Lili Marleen*), and is crowned in a strangely appropriate way by the publication in 1982 of a museum-piece war novel, Heinrich Böll's *Das Vermächtnis*, set on the Atlantic coast of France and on the Eastern Front in 1943. It was written in 1948, but mislaid and re-discovered upon the transfer of certain Böll papers back to Cologne from across the Atlantic.

This outline of the history of German Second World War literature is necessarily schematic where books do not lend them-selves to unambiguous classification, where authors who pro-duced early war books hardly change their attitudes to the war in later ones, and where themes and problems persist through three decades. Another way of looking at the phases of war literature is in terms of generations of writers,[5] rather than of the dates at which their novels happened to appear. By this reckoning, of authors writing in the first twenty years after the war, the three main groups are, firstly, the so-called "Lost Generation", those who grew up under Fascism and were called up to fight in a senseless war for which they felt no responsibility, but which robbed them of their best years: secondly, the generation before them, those born between 1900 and 1914, who had more oppor-tunity to form a mature political outlook in the pre-Nazi years and, in contrast to the "deadbeat" and sceptical attitudes of the "Lost Generation", fought, however desperate their situation, to maintain some kind of moral toehold: and finally, those born around the turn of the century or earlier, the generation of the First World War (e.g. Remarque, Jünger, Plievier, Dwinger, Hartung). The latter tend to respond to the Second World War in broader, less personal terms, and on the whole are in possession of an intact world-view. Most did not see active service in 1939–45, though there are notable exceptions such as Ernst Jünger.

While such divisions into phases or generations are interesting, I do not propose to make them the basis of the observations that follow, although it will be useful to refer back to them from time to time. There is enough consistency in the questions raised by German war literature between 1945 and the present to justify an approach along thematic rather than purely chronological lines. This approach also permits the occasional glance at works which are not primarily "war books" (e.g. Siegfried Lenz's *Deutsch-stunde*) but concern themselves centrally with the issues of the war. Moreover, the exploration of themes is a way of side-stepping the question raised in the preceding sentence: what *is* a war book? The first chapter of this book has examined the considerable problems of definition. I shall take a broad view of the question and look beyond the front-line or combat novel, on the one hand, and beyond purely fictional forms, on the other, to include diaries and memoirs where these possess literary qualities and seem to throw light on central themes. To limit the scope of interest to books dealing only with combat would not do justice to the German experience of the war, which found its victims and its heroes both on and off the battlefield. But a line must be drawn somewhere, and this means the exclusion from the category of war books works (in some cases the most outstanding that were produced in the period) into which the war-theme enters, some-times even centrally, but which in the final analysis are not books "about" the war. In this category must be placed Grass's *Die Blechtrommel* (1959); Thomas Mann's *Doktor Faustus* (1947) – possibly the most penetrating analysis of the connection between the German psyche and the origins of the Second World War; Hermann Kasack's surrealistic novel *Die Stadt hinter dem Strom* (1947), which begins very much in the reality of a civilian population living an underground existence after the destruction of their city (eventually, however, the hero, Lindhoff, discovers that he is the only living soul in a city of the dead); Walter Jens' *Nein, die Welt der Angeklagten* (1950), a Kafka-esque, anti-utopian projection forward into the post-war years of the paranoia of the Nazis as it rose to new heights during the war; Ernst von Salomon's *Der Fragebogen* (1951), containing enormously ex-tended answers and excursus in response to one of those naive Allied de-nazification questionnaires post-war Germans were obliged to complete when applying for key posts; Alfred An-dersch's *Die Rote* (1960), the attempted flight from life in the

*Bundesrepublik* to Venice by a young German woman who is then
embroiled in events which lay some of the ghosts of the Second
World War; Heinrich Böll's *Billard um halbzehn* (1959), in which
the war period forms a climax to a survey of the life of three
generations of a family in this century; and many more.

The majority of German war books can be seen to offer responses to questions which are not generally openly stated. (Böll
is different from most other war writers in his willingness to ask
the *simple* questions: "My God, how many times have I asked
myself how colossal the power must be that makes millions of
people, completely without volition, despite cowardice and fear,
trundle towards death as we are doing tonight", says the narrator
of *Das Vermächtnis*.) There is a quest for innocence; a tendency to
look for ways to express the concept of heroism despite all the
difficulties the notions holds in our age and in such a war; and a
desire to find alternative identities, to evade the wholesale condemnation – of the German soldier along with his odious political
masters, in whom, it must be said, he had not been so loath to
place his trust when the war started – which poured in upon
Germany from all sides after the war. The war novel seeks
redemptive means of meeting the problem of war guilt without,
on the one hand, giving way to total despair or nihilism, or, on the
other, offering an outright exoneration of Germany in action in
the Second World War. Simplified assumptions of collective guilt,
such as those entertained by some representatives of the Allies in
the early days of the occupation, were not found particularly
useful by a nation which had to go on living with itself, and
intended to do so with as much dignity as it could muster
(especially since dignity had been an early and long-term victim
of the bullying régime of which the Allies had just relieved it).
The war novel had a part to play in rehabilitating some vestiges of
German self-respect. It is a perfectly understandable function
which, perhaps rightly, has been held in some suspicion by
Germans themselves, as falling in all to easily with precocious
Cold War "normalisation" and offering a politically dangerous
exoneration (*Entlastung*) of genuine war guilt, Fascism, or militarism. The outsider looking in can perhaps afford to be more
detached and tolerant.

I propose to group my remarks under a few broad headings
which, while not entirely discrete or free of overlap, offer a
convenient way of accommodating some of the complexities of the

subject: the social, political and literary aspects of the Second
World War in German fiction.

The state of mind of the average soldier or, for that matter, civilian
living through the war is commonly reflected in war literature as a
sense of unreality. Again and again there are expressions of
incredulity at the grotesque forms that "normality" has taken on,
and a corresponding mistrust of surface appearances. Günther
Weisenborn in his prison diary *Memorial* (1948) offers the least
confused statement of this dichotomy. (Typically, Second World
War prison literature, by its very nature, does make issues more
clear-cut than they appeared to the average citizen or *Landser*
[ordinary soldier] not classed as official opponents of the régime.)
It was in the subterranean prisons of the Gestapo, among the
"captive army of freedom", and not in the "sunlit, rabid everyday
world" of the Nazi Reich, that "the beauty of human greatness"
was to be found. It is a commonplace experience of the time that
everything sane and decent has gone underground, making way
for a perversion of normality brazenly parading as the real thing.
The title of Hugo Hartung's novel on the fall of Breslau, *Der
Himmel war unten* (1951), concisely expresses the central idea of a
"Himmelfahrt nach unten", an "ascension into the depths",
summarised at the end of Book I of the novel as "the Hell above
has been traversed. Heaven is beneath the earth". The same novel
provides an example, duplicated time and again in war literature,
of the violence done by this war to familiar reality, in this case the
description of well-known city streets which have now, amazing-
ly, become a battlefield: "Rönnig is wide awake and yet he thinks
he's dreaming. This was the route he took every day in peacetime;
there was his tram-stop. Peter sometimes used to hide behind that
big tree. On that bench on the left Lisa would wait for him
countless times with the children." In his "Der Untergang",
Hans Erich Nossack asks in the course of the description of the
survivors of the terrible bombing of Hamburg in July 1943:

> What did those affected expect [from their hosts in the country
> villages where they sought refuge]? ... We expected that
> somebody would call out to us: 'Wake up! It's only a bad
> dream!.'

At "the still heart of the cyclone", in the Führer-bunker in Berlin, Felix Hartlaub (*Im Sperrkreis*, 1955, originally published as *Von unten gesehen*, 1950, a war diary by a writer who disappeared in the final battle for Berlin) was noting the discrepancy between the demonically efficient military machine, and the reality "out there": "As long as the papers are in order – but the reality they relate to is taking place on another planet." In Hermann Lenz's autobiographical novel *Neue Zeit* (1975), the narrator, Eugen, is provided with a "dream-time", turn-of-the-century Vienna, to which to escape from the realities of war. Such a fantasy world is only a positive counterpart, however, to the "dream-time" the Germans as a nation have allowed themselves to live through under Hitler as they sleepwalk towards disaster, for the most part firmly convinced that they are fully awake, hard-headed and practical. To quote from the same novel (*Neue Zeit*): "Your daughter Margarethe, though, she knows how you've got to be in this life: solid and down-to-earth. Not living in some dream hiding-place, even if this hiding-place is something like Old Vienna with the Emperor Franz Joseph." She knows that "the quality of the sun and the Spring had stayed the same even under Hitler" – a common delusion of unchanged normality which leads to the German difficulty, recorded in so many war books, in accepting as the reality, and not a bad dream, the rude awakening brought by the war. A traditional German propensity to separate inner from outer life is apparent here, and it is remarked upon in much war fiction, as it is for example in Franz Fühmann's story "Das Gottesgericht", "The Divine Judgment" (essentially a modern story of *hubris* by an East German writer, set in occupied Greece, and published in the collection *Die Elite*) where the comment is supplied by the thoughts of the Greek cook, Agamemnon, about his masters:

> ...how strange all these German soldiers were, so tough and yet so dreamy at the same time: tough in the day-time, when they shouted 'Hey, you, Greek, come here!' and dreamy when they were sitting around at night, when the moon was shining, listening to the sounds of the sea, and singing.

It is in Heinrich Böll's war books that the delusion of normality is most fully realised and exploited. When one of his wartime characters shows a sense of the unreality of the "real" events

happening around him, he does so as a demonstration of faith by
Böll in a higher reality, or of his character's need for such a faith.
In *Wo warst du, Adam?*, the doomed Jewish girl, Ilona, "seemed to
know that it was better not to live very long and not to build one's
life upon a love which was only real for a few moments at a time,
whereas there existed another, eternal love". The nihilistic vacuum experienced by Böll's soldier in *Das Vermächtnis* can only
properly be filled by a similar belief (though Böll is far from
condemning his narrator for not developing such a faith). One of
the most complete accounts of the sense of unreality in wartime in
Böll's works is "Aufenthalt in X", from the collection of stories
*Wanderer, kommst du nach Spa*. A soldier finds himself in a strange
town, alienated from his own inauthentic role, spending the night
with a strange girl:

> This life, I thought, is not my life. I have to play this life and I'm
> playing it badly. . . . Somewhere in this perfect silence was the
> war. . . . I was completely alone in this town, these people did
> not belong to me.

The narrator claims to have often "walked along the edge of
reality"; and in another story in the same collection, "Die Es-
senholer", surrealism takes us completely beyond the limits of a
normality which is unworthy of the name: "so-called reality was
inflated by the dark and shadowy laws of another reality which
made mock of it". Later fiction consistently maintains the theme,
so that in Andersch's *Winterspelt* (1974) Major Dincklage is
reassured by an army psychiatrist(!) that the powerful sense of
unreality which not infrequently comes over him as the war
progresses is a "nice little neurosis" which is a sign of health in
these times, when the dangerous people are those who find
everything quite normal. Siegfried Lenz still fights to gain ground
for a different sense of reality in post-war Germany in *Deutschstunde* (1968). Both the hero-narrator Siggi and his father, the
dour policeman Jepsen, can be diagnosed as "abnormal" at the
end of the novel; but whereas the father's warped sense of "duty"
is easily concealed behind a policeman's uniform and survives
unscathed from the Nazi period (where it did untold harm) into
the present, Siggi's exaggerated version of a humane sense of
duty, which finds its expression in a compulsion to oppose
destruction (even where "normal" people would see no threat of

it) is the one which is officially labelled by the psychologist
Mackenroth as an illness.[6] And in a recent novel by Horst Bienek,
*Zeit ohne Glocken* (1979), an average law-abiding citizen, Valeska,
is shaken and confused when she realises the full implications of
the race laws the Nazis have introduced (the possibility of a
death-sentence for a female associating with an *"Ost-Arbeiter"*, a
foreign worker from Eastern Europe employed as forced labour):
"She had always thought she knew what reality was. . . . Perhaps
the only reliable reality was death." (And yet the Nuremberg race
laws had been in operation for some years before the war.)[7] So
bizarre was the period 1933 – 45 that German authors trust very
largely to their basic senses, of smell, sight, touch, hearing, taste,
as touchstones of reality and the most reliable means of gaining
access to a past which no amount of documentation seems to make
credible. The recurrence of these sense-impressions in *Deutschstunde*, in Böll's *Billard um halbzehn*, in *Zeit ohne Glocken* or Walter
Kempowski's *Tadellöser & Wolff* may be welcome to the nostalgia-
industry, but is not merely a product of it. It is in relation to the
theme of unreality that the various prison diaries of the Second
World War (Weisenborn's *Memorial*, Luise Rinser's *Gefängnis-
tagebuch*, 1946) establish their credentials as war books, for their
authors were fighting in isolation, "in the front line", to uphold
their own sense of normality against the worst effects of a totalitarian government in wartime to subvert reality, with the aid
of all the plausible rhetoric about "betraying the nation in its hour
of need". One is reminded of the use made by the psychopathic
Roland Freisler, President of the "People's Court" which tried the
conspirators of the 20 July 1944 plot to kill Hitler, of the full
power, panoply and spurious legitimacy of the Nazi State to
destroy the resistance and the dignity of its isolated show-trial
victims.

A problem with which the Germans were faced, as their opponents were not, was a sense of the futility of the war. It is probable
that in the initial successful phase the bulk of the German
population did not feel that Hitler's war was pointless. But very
few of the war books choose to reflect this early near-euphoria.
Two diaries of the Eastern Front form notable exceptions: Jochen
Klepper's *Überwindung*, 1952 (Klepper was married to a con-

verted Jewish lady, was eventually forced to leave the army on those grounds, and later in the war committed suicide with his wife and daughter); and Curt Hohoff's *Woina Woina* (1952). Hohoff's unusual honesty about what he saw – and to an extent he enthusiastically participated in them – as the expansive "Alexandrian" dreams of the Germans, by which they were sustained through the early trials of the Russian adventure, only serves to heighten the effects of the disaster at Stalingrad: "the reversal from the highest expectations to the degradation of a merciless abandonment even to death broke the back of German army morale". Strictly speaking, of course, the war was literally a pointless exercise from the very beginning, irrespective of the outcome, for German war aims in the traditional sense were barely defined and by nature indefinable, apart from glorification of war itself as an expression of the national will and vigour. In so far as war aims received a definition at all, it was one which included asssumptions either criminal beyond the point of most ordinary Germans' tolerance (wholesale genocide against Jews and Slav "subhumans") or incredible in scale (world domination on behalf of the "Aryan" race). But the futility of war was, all too humanly, not as easy to perceive in victory as in defeat, when the disastrous results of Hitler's increasingly megalomaniac leadership began to manifest themselves. In Plievier's trilogy *Moskau, Stalingrad, Berlin*, written in a highly critical spirit, the sense of futility present from the beginning comes to the fore, especially in his *Berlin* volume (1954) as the message of enormous, tragically wasted effort is now literally brought home to the Germans and delivered in high explosives on their doorstep in the capital. Plievier thereby exploits the perhaps largely unthinking assumption, among the bulk of the population, of German intentionality as having lent some sort of point – however criminal – to the war in Eastern Europe. It puts a cruel edge to his satire in a passage in *Berlin* (insistently repeating a cliché defensive phrase often heard in post-war Germany, "Das haben wir nicht gewollt!"[8] – "That isn't what we wanted!"):

That was not what the Berliners wanted, to see their houses turned into blazing heaps of charcoal, the slates from the roofs shooting through the streets like flocks of birds.

By implication, the Berliners *did* want (or did not object to) a similar work of destruction in Eastern Europe and elsewhere.

Most war books are not as ideologically or politically clear-cut in their response to the war's futility as Plievier's, but tend to look for some meaning within or despite the senselessness. Hugo Hartung falls back upon a native Silesian mysticism to suggest that German bombs dropped upon a German city (Breslau)[9] in April 1945 represent a kind of retribution: "as in the Bible, fire falls from Heaven". Hartung is not alone among German writers in seeing the outcome of the war as a Divine Judgment, which at least makes a kind of sense out of some part of the destruction. Another attitude is that of Heinrich Gerlach, one of the tough and cynical school of war-book authors which is especially well represented in the 1950s. He is drawn to the most sickening aspects of battle, but he also exemplifies a not uncommon way out of the futility-trap. In *Die verratene Armee* (1957)[10], Stalingrad is a "miracle without a meaning", a miracle of sheer endurance. However senseless strategically and morally, the unbelievably tenacious defence fought in bitter conditions by sick and starving German troops was impressive enough to lend an intrinsic meaning to events on the individual level – one which is underlined by the grudging respect for his ragged, emaciated, dysentery-ridden foe which the narrator attributes to the ordinary Soviet soldier. Sometimes the senselessness of war brings out by negation the human values it denies, as in Dieter Meichsner's *Weißt Du, warum?* (1952), where the futility of a particularly pointless act of resistance against units of the American occupation in May 1945 by German soldiers holding out in the Bavarian Alps is contrasted with a delicate love idyll and the beauty of the mountains. By contrast, Hans Helmut Kirst's trilogy, *08/15* (1954–5), finds a popular-novel, detective-story way of bringing order into chaos, for while the hero, Gunner Asch, is as cynical about the war, the army and comradeship as any other character of the period ("he had spent five and a half years in the muck with some of the soldiers around him. In the muck. And what did it mean? Just that – muck!"), in volume three he is given his own successful private vendetta to carry out against two war criminals, whose greatest crime, in his view, was to betray their own comrades. For others, like the character Plaas, quoting Ernst Jünger in Salomon's *Der Fragebogen*, there is "an immanent justice" in war, so that the crimes committed against the Jews will also be committed against the Germans ("we shall be dragged off and killed"), thus restoring sense to a senseless universe. Of course, this prophecy was not carried out to the letter, but it is a subtle contribution to the common German mode of thinking that enough Germans *were* "dragged off", i.e. displaced and deported, or killed by enemy action, starvation or disease, for their sufferings to constitute the working of an 'immanent justice' and relieve the Allies of the burden of putting the German nation on trial. This latter, incidentally, was a self-imposed Allied obligation which few, if any, Germans were happy about, and many regarded, together with the re-education programme, as having deprived the nation of a chance to put its own house in order and thereby, at least, do something actively to overcome the sense of futility with which the war had left it, and which the war books reflect.

Gerd Gaiser (*Die sterbende Jagd*, 1953) adds a new twist to the futility theme. For his hero, Vehlgast, the *peace* is senseless and does not justify the enormous effort of the war. But Gaiser is quite content to allow war an intrinsic value, "the fun of the thing for its own sake", incommensurate with any cause for which it might be fought, and grant his fighter pilots the nobility of a warrior caste taking a pride in their prowess; though in doing so, and in his hero's dismissive attitude to peace, he rather shockingly blurs some basic distinctions between good and bad causes. Böll, at the other extreme, has a transcendental religious faith which allows him to derive a sardonic satisfaction from the manifest pointlessness of war, most clearly perceptible to a truly naive eye like that of the peasant woman in *Wo warst du, Adam?*, whose own husband has been dragged off into the army, when there is a mountain of work to be done at home: "Probably war was all about men doing nothing and going off to other countries for the purpose, so that nobody would see them at it . . .". Böll presents the horrors of war (of which combat is the least) and of Nazi terror in sentences which contain a repetitive, insistent rhythm and a minimum of comment: such senseless cruelty as he relates of the concentration camp in *Wo warst du, Adam?* takes him right off the end of his language register. By contrast, he restores meaning to the universe by talking of the simple peacetime values, such as Gaiser's hero despises, in words that are normally almost bereft of meaning, like "schön" (beautiful, nice), but now regain an inexpressible burden of content. Ilona, about to be shot by the Camp Commandant, recalls her days as a school music teacher, when her pupils "sang words which they didn't understand but which were beautiful. Life appeared beautiful to her . . .".

The distrust of language characterises particularly the "Lost

Generation" writers like Böll and Wolfgang Borchert, and it is out of a similar suspicion of too easy a way of injecting meaning into the futility of war that most war writers reject the traditional German *Bildungsroman* (novel of education) option of personal development converting experience, however negative, into the positive value of spiritual growth. Apart from East German literature, where the growth of political awareness through war is an almost invariable theme,[11] there are few parallels to the formulation by Rönnig, the hero of Hartung's *Der Himmel war unten*, of the learning advantage he has gained from his war experiences ("something like an inner usefulness"). The formulation may be rare, but the content of the lesson he has learned ("Since I shot my grand piano to pieces along with a few other things I thought necessary to sustain life, I've been looking for new ways to 'realize my existence'"), turns out however not to be very different from the conclusions drawn by Borchert, who died in 1947 at the age of 26 from the ravages of imprisonment, war service and the post-war famine. He had only two years to finish his slim oeuvre of short stories and the famous *Heimkehrer* (returning soldier) play *Draußen vor der Tür*; and he above all was the impatient prophet of the "Zero Hour" (*Nullpunkt*), of the fresh start without encumbrances from the past: "We don't need poets with good grammar. We haven't got the patience for grammar. We need the ones ... who call a tree a tree and a woman a woman, and say yes and say no: loud and clear and three times over and without subjunctives" ("Das ist unser 'Manifest"). There has been a controversy over the last decade or so as to the legitimacy of the term *Nullpunkt*, denoting what for many years after the war was popularly regarded as a complete break with the past in 1945. No doubt the notion was essentially a fiction: it is hardly possible for a nation, part of whose self-definition lies in the memory of a collective past, to discard the past completely. But the illusion of a *Stunde Null* (Zero Hour) was one that was beneficial to the mental health of the "Lost Generation" after the war; a subjective conviction conveyed, with full consciousness of its subjectivity, by Hans Erich Nossack in his story "Klonz", whose opening paragraphs urge the necessity of piecing the world together again from all its constituent elements. Merciful amnesia is not actually obtainable, but many post-war authors of war fiction like to assume it: "We no longer have a past" (Nossack in "Der Untergang"). On the negative side, this means that writers refused to contaminate *their* war experiences by any reference to a now tainted cultural heritage: "Can you still hear Hölderlin? Do you recognise him, drunk with blood, in fancy dress and arm in arm with Baldur von Schirach?" (Borchert). On the positive side, rejection of the past was the premise on which to build the future. Borchert's "we live in huts of wood and hope" is the typical zeugma of the German *Heimkehrer*. The closer the war writer can get to a value-free representation of his experiences, the greater his contribution to a fresh start.

In the light of what has already been said about the sense of the war's unreality and futility, and many writers' reservations about earlier cultural canons, it is interesting to see what becomes of the concept of heroism in German war literature. Plievier puts the problem in a nutshell in the last pages of *Stalingrad*:

> And this was accepted: all moral and ethical qualities are inevitably vitiated, and must inevitably achieve the opposite of what is intended, when their possessor carries out orders and obeys a law which is not the law, but an article from the charter of a conspiracy.

Heroism is a clear case of the good quality turning to the bad when employed or exploited in an evil cause. The climate of intellectual opinion in Germany since the Second World War has made the heroic ideal highly suspect, and for the reasons that Plievier neatly formulates. A glance at a recent British contribution to the debate about the heroic in realist fiction shows up a difference in attitudes. Andrew Rutherford argues against the fashionable view that realism and the heroic are incompatible, and that to show war as it really is, with all its chaos and brutality, is to rule out the possibility of heroism.[12] Rutherford, on the contrary, believes that, since history records many well-attested cases of heroism, realism has the option, if not actually the obligation, to include the heroic in its repertoire. In Germany, this reasonable statement would be controversial and would call down upon its author's head some dark political suspicions. Witness the discussion surrounding the "heroism" of Buchheim's submarine novel, *Das Boot* (1973), which was heated enough to produce a volume of commentary and collected controversial opinions put together by Michael Salewski, an academic and a reserve officer in the Federal Republic's navy (*Von der Wirklichkeit des Krieges*, dtv, Munich 1976). What the Buchheim controversy shows is the continuing sensitivity of the issue of (particularly) Second World War heroism in West Germany today, and that any German war novel (like any Russian one) is inevitably received as a political statement. Non-Germans can achieve some feel for the atmosphere in Germany by comparing the impact of the Vietnam War in the USA. Like the Second World War from a German point of view, for most liberal Americans Vietnam was a conflict mistakenly undertaken, ineptly fought, futile, wasteful and (to some minds worst of all) lost. There may be American voices dissenting from part of this view, but certainly Vietnam has made thinking about heroism a little more complicated than it was for Americans after the Second World War. The heroic ethos has been forced on to the defensive, as it is in James Webb's Vietnam novel, *Fields of Fire*. In West Germany after the 1939–45 conflict the same effect emerged, but greatly magnified, in proportion to the scale of the reversal of values that took place abruptly in 1945. Before the war, Karl von Ossietzky concisely summed up the German ethos (not confined to Nazi ideologists): "Nowhere is love of peace so thoughtlessly equated with cowardice."[13] After the war, by the same token and by the operation of the kind of polarization for which German intellectual history is famous, any sympathy towards the heroic ethos was automatically assumed to be militaristic. (It is interesting that the leader writer of *Die Zeit*, in the issue of 21 May 1982, reacted to the Falklands crisis with the fear that the atmosphere of "heroism" prevailing in Britain at the time might infect his fellow *Bundesbürger* and promote a new militarism.) After 1945, as Salewski says, only two Second World War images of the heroic were acceptable in West German public life: that of the "small man" who could be assumed to possess no overview of events or ability to analyse them, and was therefore exonerated from political guilt (the majority of war novels do indeed present the so-called *Obergefreitenperspektive*, or "corporal's point of view", thus avoiding political reflections); and the "big man" in the higher ranks of the General Staff who could see what was happening, and had the courage to resist (Beck, Stauffenberg, Rommel): the latter type, however, is rarely a subject for serious literature (apart from some works appearing very soon after the

end of the war: see p. 123), though Hans Hellmut Kirst's *Die Nacht
der Generale* (1962) comes to mind as a popular novel featuring the
20 July as a focus.

The vigilance which has been thought necessary in West
Germany since the war is epitomised by an article by Günter
Grass in 1970,[14] "What are our soldiers reading?", against the
exposure of the *Bundeswehr* to extreme right-wing and neo-Nazi
propaganda, which he claimed had been infiltrating the army
libraries. (In 1965, Grass himself founded five libraries for the
*Bundeswehr* and one for the "Alternative Work-Camp for Conscientious Objectors" in Heidelberg, and Uwe Johnson compiled
a model list of titles suitable for *Bundeswehr* bookshelves.) Grass
quotes a riposte, to liberal criticism like his own, from a spokesman for right-wing factions: "Do you say I am preaching war?
Not war, but courage, which eradicates rot."

The heroic is, however, inseparable from the subject of war, so
that the problem of German writers, sometimes perhaps an
unconscious one, has been to find ways of presenting heroism by
which they do not expose themselves to suspicion. Sometimes
heroic themes creep into books whose political credentials are
impeccable, like Plievier's. In *Moskau* (1952), written back in
Germany *after Stalingrad*, though preceding the latter in the
chronology of the trilogy, he describes a group of ex-Lufthansa
pilots who, very much like the submarine captain in Buchheim's
*Das Boot*, represent one acceptable face of heroism in Second
World War books; the non-conformist, totally unmilitary in
bearing, who keeps his own council but, once pressed (however
reluctantly) into service, does his "job" extremely well. Plievier
ironises his presentation of these veterans, who are twice the age of
the average *Luftwaffe* pilot, but he encourages the average reader
to admiration by the tone adopted: "The fantastic thing is – they
can fly, they possess unique flying skills, and for that they can be
excused everything else." In the same volume, there is an un-
spoken but telling contrast between the position of the German
soldier left with no choice but to fight on in Russia ("here we stand
and must go on and cannot ... lower our arms; we have fallen in,
and we must march ...";  note the Lutheran echo in "here we
stand") and the ignominious panic in Moscow which leads to an
undignified scramble of the pampered Soviet intellectuals (like
Ilya Ehrenburg) to escape from the threatened city. Later in the
novel, the attractive figure of the tank commander, Vilshofen,

stands for German heroism in misery and defeat when he is described as "ein sterbender Elch" (a dying elk), with a suggestion of Victorian heroic images of "the stag at bay". What above all creates something like a heroic atmosphere in Plievier's trilogy is the monumental, epic scale of events, and of the novels (some 1200 closely printed pages altogether). This very monumentality appears to show Plievier in thrall to the spirit of his times, in direct contrast to Böll's conscious opposition to them through the brevity, understatement and indirectness of his evocation of war. To quote an attitude represented by the time-serving intellectual Dr. Wittstock, in Plievier's *Berlin*, "evil is no longer evil when it is committed on the grand scale". In the trilogy as a whole, a similar conversion of quantity into quality takes place in the transformation of the vast scale of intrinsically senseless events into a meaningful, even – by suggestion – heroic phenomenon simply *because* of the grandness of scale, almost that of a latter-day Nibelungen tragedy.

In other works on a less pretentious scale, devices permitting an heroic aura without militarism include the presentation of combatants as men who "play hard and fight hard", a clean, manly image: see for example the wild Christmas celebrations in Hartung's *Der Himmel war unten*, the heroic drinking orgy in the notorious brothel scene at the beginning of *Das Boot*, and many other war time excesses which serve the dual purpose of expressing a proper, although perhaps subconscious, desperation at the prospect of entering battle burdened with a guilty conscience, and at the same time the larger-than-life, Valhalla behaviour of the warrior-hero consuming his life with an intensity that dwarfs the pale virtues of peacetime. Many a "cynical" novel overtly rejects heroics, as Wolfgang Ott does through his mouthpiece Heyne in a long monologue in *Haie und kleine Fische* (1956), only to claim, through the same mouthpiece, that there is a contemporary heroism consisting in facing, alone and without solace, the prospect of death in a senseless cause – "What is courage without loneliness?"[15] Asch in Kirst's *08/15* is the typical tough anti-hero hero. His primary fictional role is to fight the army and defeat its hierarchy. At the beginning of volume two, for example, he establishes his status as a wily front-line veteran by scoring a moral victory over the arrogant new commanding officer and his peacetime, rear-echelon notion of discipline. But Asch always knows what to do in a tight spot, always puts the safety of his men before his own, and is a father-figure to his troops. The fact that he occasionally reveals his humanity by giving way to a little fear only enhances Asch's true heroism. As far as the fair sex are concerned, he is more solicitously gallant than any officer and gentleman. Curiously, such heroes seem to spring up fully armed; for what Kirst does not show us is the stage when Asch is first bloodied in battle, any more than we are shown the related figure of the submarine commander in *Das Boot* acquiring his heroic presence. Would that in some way diminish the mythical status of these hero-figures? The apotheosis of the heroic anti-hero is seen in the episode which concludes volume two of *08/15*. In his address at the funeral of his friend Vierbein and others, Asch demonstrates how heroes – who are very sparing with words, as against deeds – ought to talk when they break their silence. There is, first of all, the stress on the *voluntary* attendance of many comrades at Vierbein's funeral, a striking contrast in this command-ridden military system. The funeral address is the true climax of the whole trilogy; claiming total simplicity and rejecting histrionics, it proposes a rhetoric of *anti*-rhetoric:

"It can well be said that these men died bravely. But none of us knows exactly what courage is. It can be the silence before death, the acceptance of what is called fate. I never heard any of these men cry out, I never saw them cry – the war was too loud ..." Asch was silent and so were the soldiers around him. Their faces were expressionless. Nobody wept. And the sky stared down grey and indifferent upon them all.

In its way the scene is as dramatic a set-piece as any to be found in traditional heroic literature. Heinrich Böll presumably well knows the seductive power of such unofficial heroism, and for that reason he scrupulously avoids the direct, orthodox presentation of combat and manly comradeship, and concentrates on the isolated individual trying to shake off the grip of war. (If he uses the word "hero", it is only with profound irony, as in *Der Zug war pünktlich*: "... then the [troop] train starts moving, lighter by a few heroes, and a few heroes the richer"). Only in the East German novels can heroism still wear its *official* face, and then only with a special meaning: "to live for the poor, mortally wounded Germany of tomorrow, that is heroic, that takes courage" (Dieter Noll, *Die Abenteuer des Werner Holt*, vol. 1, 1960).

In a latter-day war novel like Andersch's *Winterspelt*, conventional heroism is broken down into an account of courage as a physiological reaction of the peripheral nervous system, or countered with a moral alternative, the courage to declare oneself lacking in physical valour. Such a cool and detached attitude belongs, however, very much to a later decade. Fiction closer in time to the war felt constrained to make allowance for isolated acts of heroism. One of the most striking examples is to be found in Hans Werner Richter's *Sie fielen aus Gottes Hand* (1951), and it serves at the same time to remind us that in this war the distinction between front-line and civilian life is often blurred. The Polish patriot Hanka has to suffer in isolation the pain and ignominy of being thought a collaborator by her fellow-countrymen, while actually working for the Resistance by eliciting intelligence information from her German "lover", for the sake of which she is, at the same time, deceiving her Polish fiancé, Stanislaus; and, to make matters morally more confusing, she is attracted to her German informant, despite herself. Her situation requires a kind of courage for which there is no recognition; and there is no chance to share the burden with comrades. It is also a type of heroism which lies safely beyond the suspicion surrounding the heroic in post-war Germany.

Although, in a tight spot, membership of a group, or merely sharing danger with one other fellow-sufferer, is often comforting at a basic animal level in Second World War fiction, comradeship is not the straightforward boon that it was in, say, Erich Maria Remarque's *All Quiet on the Western Front*. Many of the "tough" war novels reject the notion (like Ledig's *Die Stalinorgel*) as outmoded cant to delude the soldier about his situation in this war, where in the last cynical analysis the survival of the individual is all that counts. Besides, *Kameradschaft* is one of those words the Nazis have exploited and polluted, as Max Walter Schulz, another East German war novelist, makes brilliantly (but almost untranslateably) clear in his "novel of development", *Wir sind nicht Staub im Wind* (1962: the novel is significantly subtitled, as a rebuff to the West German "Lost Generation" concept, "novel of a generation that was not lost"):

The old lure of brothers under the same cap, the invitation to go
through hell and high water together, the proposition to join an
alliance of boozing and brawling, of living and dying with a
whoopee and a wotcher and a get stuffed, the credo of all
troopers under the Swastika.

For Alfred Andersch, in *Die Kirschen der Freiheit*, the much-
vaunted comradeship simply meant never being able to achieve
privacy, and Böll in *Der Zug war pünktlich* makes his hero Andreas
say that "when you're alone you're not so lonely any more". At
best, comradeship in Second World War fiction has to do, not
with facing the enemy, but with solidarity against the military
machine, "the prison-house of the military collective" (as Andersch points out in an excursus on the subject in *Winterspelt*).
One of the few war books in which comradeship is present as a
pure and undiluted value is Peter Bamm's *Die unsichtbare Flagge*
(1952) and that, significantly, does not concern a combat unit but
a team of army medics totally free of ideological pressures and
serving not under the Swastika but under the banner of humanity
(the "invisible flag" of the title). Otherwise, there is usually an
ambivalence about comradely membership of a combat group, as
there is about the concept of heroism, and for not dissimilar
ideological reasons (exceptions are to be found, especially in the
more popular kind of war novel, like Willi Heinrich's *Das geduldige
Fleisch* [1955] where comradeship is the chief redeeming feature of
his soldiers' deperate war).

A certain kind of German fiction about this war often takes a
grim delight in breaking down such conventional "values", by
way of revenge upon Nazi distortions of them. Stalingrad, as an
appropriate symbolic climax to the war, provided a ready-made
vehicle for this nihilistic tendency. In the *Kessel*, the doomed
pocket from which no breakout is possible, the war ethos collapses in upon itself. As if on a macabre version of the Admirable
Crichton's desert island, distinctions of class and rank are gradually broken down. After the better-connected high-ranking officers have had themselves flown out, all ranks are in the same dire
straits, and the promotions, decorations and commendations
regularly telegrammed through with due pomposity from the
Führer-headquarters become a grimly ironic part of this "desert-
island syndrome" in most of the Stalingrad-novels (very explicitly
in Chapter 15 of Gerlach's *Die verratene Armee*) along with the *King*

*Solomon's Mines* theme of loot acquired by German soldiers which becomes worthless as the prospect of escape rapidly fades and the only goods worth having are food and fuel, not to be purchased at any price. Stalingrad (or Russia) is one of the two symbolic poles of German recall of the Second World War, the diametrical opposite being Paris (or France). It is striking how often this juxtaposition is made, and how much of the German fate it encompasses. The occupation of Paris is the rightful prize that had been withheld in the First World War, despite the millions of German casualties. The easy fall of France in 1940 offers the most dangerous kind of realised wish-fulfilment, the making good of all the injustices Germany has suffered since 1918, especially the Versailles settlement, and a temporarily almost unchallengeable vindication of the policies of the Third Reich. Paris is the First World War re-run as it ought to have been, and within a relatively civilised framework far short of the total war which Goebbels was to declare in his famous Sportpalast speech of 1943, and which was to some extent the product of Stalingrad as well as of Allied bombing. Paris and Stalingrad are images of success and failure, belief in Hitler's construct and the revelation of its total artificiality. Paris is within the compass of the old European conflicts: Stalingrad is the culmination of something new, peculiarly Hitlerian and insane; the first modern attempt to carry out in practice Germany's ancient mission to colonise the East, and the first avowed campaign of genocide. Its outcome is not only the end of the old Prussian officer caste (where Paris by contrast was the last of their finest hours), but even of a whole line of development in European philosophies of vitalism and the "life-force" associated with Bergson, Klages, Lawrence (D.H. *and* T.E.), Nietzsche, Georges Sorel, the Futurists. Gerlach puts it well: "Stalingrad... has become more than a geographical concept ..." ... "This drink [French cognac] in this place [Stalingrad] and at this time symbolized, quite consciously for everybody, an almost 4000 kilometre long path right across Europe, a dubious path, dubious because of the end to which it had led."

One is tempted to ask: was it dubious *only* because of that? However, the insight Gerlach is reporting is not necessarily his own, but attributed to a group of Prussian-style officers, for whom it is a shattering one. It ought not to have required a military débâcle of Stalingrad proportions to produce such an insight, but Gerlach's implication that it does is compatible with the historical facts. (The events of 20 July 1944 would never have happened if Hitler had not been losing the war.) The ruthless abandonment of Paulus's 6th Army at Stalingrad – necessitated largely by Goering's crazy undertaking to supply the Army from the air – was the beginning of the end of another, very important established value, a German military tradition based not only on solid achievements but on absolute trust in the loyalty of the German military to its oath of allegiance. This is too large a subject, with too long a history, to expand upon here, but the Prussian concept of duty had already given rise to two classical dramatic works some century and a half before Stalingrad, Lessing's *Minna von Barnhelm* and Heinrich von Kleist's *Prinz Friedrich von Homburg*. Without some awareness of the power of this tradition, hallowed by such names as Kant and Schiller (Siegfried Lenz's *Deutschstunde* explores the theme) it is hard to grasp an aspect of the Second World War with no clear parallel in other Western nations' awareness, but central to that of the Germans. A spokesman in Plievier's *Berlin* formulates the essence of the problem:

> But he knew only too well what a terrible, binding power this solemnly-given word could have, and that even in the best it was capable of repressing deeper insight, all sense of responsibility, even one's own nagging conscience.

Even since the war, feelings have been known to run high over this issue, the classical statement being Hans Egon Holthusen's attack in *Ja und Nein* (Munich 1954) on Alfred Andersch's *Die Kirschen der Freiheit* (especially on the chapter entitled "Eid", the oath) under the heading "Reflections of a deserter".[16] Few foreigners will understand the heat of this debate about whether Andersch's action in deserting to the Allies in Italy was the right course, or the right course pursued for the wrong reasons (which is Holthusen's argument). Andersch was still worrying away at the question, but with much more detachment, in *Winterspelt*, where he makes the Americans reject as treason Major Dincklage's offer to surrender to them intact with all the troops under his command ("We don't want anything to do with a traitor") – so that even the Western democratic enemy reinforces German preconditioning to acceptance of the almost sacrosanct concept of loyalty. It is not an inconceivable outcome (to a very unlikely situation), although perhaps an implausible one; but the whole *Problematik* Andersch is grappling with illustrates the sensitivity of the loyalty issue in Germany, demonstrated in the (to outsiders) surprisingly hostile response by their fellow-countrymen to certain returning German exiles after the war. Although, even one day after the capitulation, there were very few Germans prepared to declare themselves Nazis, Thomas Mann's reception in many quarters was less that of a representative of the better Germany than that of a traitor, because of his anti-Nazi publicistic activities in exile. Willy Brandt, returning from hiding in Norway, bore the stigma of treason against his fellow Germans, and the epithet "the émigré", for the greater part of his subsequent political career.

It must be said that most of the war books seem reluctant to destroy the positive image of the *Wehrmacht* as the repository of uprightness and loyalty. Certainly, some of the war novels place the Prussian officer caste under attack, as Plievier does in *Moskau*, or more virulently in *Stalingrad* (written during his war-time Moscow exile), particularly in a set-piece tirade by the hero Vilshofen against Prussian attitudes. Alexander Kluge's *Schlachtbeschreibung*, too, maintains a consistent campaign against the officer class, but Gerlach (*Die verratene Armee*), while sporadically critical, does not offer a thoroughgoing analysis of the Prussian military code. Occasionally, as for example when he devotes a page or so to one General's struggle with the oath-question in the last days of Stalingrad, he reveals considerable understanding for this mentality. In another case, a captain begs for food from the lower ranks on behalf of his General (not himself); tears of gratitude well up in his eyes at the response, and the other ranks bite their lips (Chapter 15). Such a scene suggests a reluctance to relinquish lingering attitudes of respect for the *Wehrmacht*. The war books generally do not show the army involved to any great extent in the atrocities committed by the Germans in Eastern Europe, from which, as historical research is beginning to show, it appears that the *Wehrmacht* itself cannot be exonerated. Gerlach suggests, for example, that the army scarcely heeded the infamous *Kommissarbefehl* of 1941 (the order to shoot captured political Commissars on the spot). Hohoff in *Woina Woina* makes the customary distinction between the actions of *Wehrmacht* and SS or SD forces, but is honest about the shooting of Russian prisoners of war by the *Wehrmacht*: Jochen Klepper in *Überwindung* maintains that "the army acts correctly wherever it preserves its freedom [from the State]". To concentrate on what is left of the reassuringly independent tradition of the *Wehrmacht* is obviously therapeutic, and identification with the tradition can, in extreme cases, offer almost complete detachment from implication in the black side of the war, which is safely left to Hitler and his SS minions. Ernst Jünger, in the first part of his war diary, *Strahlungen I* (published already in 1942 as *Gärten und Straßen*, but revised for later editions), takes refuge from the pain the Nazi régime obviously caused him (see e.g. the entry for 1 July 1942) in his pride of lineage as a member of the Prussian officer caste whose achievements run in an unbroken sequence from 1814 through to 1870, 1914 and 1940! Gottfried Benn joined the *Wehrmacht* as a medical officer as early as 1935 to escape from the Nazi vice without having to emigrate, for, as he says, 'the army is the aristocratic form of emigration' (*Doppelleben*, 1961).[17] He claims that until the spring of 1938, when Keitel became supreme commander, four out of five officers were openly anti-Hitler.

Benn and Jünger were particularly "aristocratic" representatives of the older generation of writers: but with that generation in general is associated a kind of cultural rearguard offering a conservative sanctuary "inside the whale" (the Nazi edifice). It leads at times to a schizophrenic separating out – reminiscent of the 'vulgar idealism' of the Wilhelmine period – of a 'good' native cultural tradition, and "bad" imported influences. So in *Strahlungen II*, for example, Jünger links the progressive de-culturation of inter-war Berlin, and the de-humanizing of the Nazis, with creeping materialism and modernity in general, derived of course from America: "America is conquering the sites of the ancient culture – I mean that America which became more evident from year to year in modern Berlin." Gottfried Benn in his wartime letters expresses his disgust at the opportunity created by the war for America to be the final arbiter in settling a European peace – "But the USA! Jews and jobbers, what a deal that will produce!."[18] (In the same volume of letters, Benn reports that there is a new wartime enthusiasm for Rilke). Germans of the older generation (Benn, Hartung, Hohoff, Weisenborn, Jünger) create for themselves a reassuring sense of continuity through cultural references in the midst of war. What is disturb-

ing in this, for the younger generation, is the assumption of
European, and indeed especially *German* cultural superiority;[19]
and that in itself, although grotesque at such a historical juncture,
would not be so dangerous were it not that, in the Cold War
climate that sets in so rapidly in the post-war years, the German
claim to be a bastion of culture, particularly against Bolshevism
(note, for example, Benn's reference to the Russians in 1941 as
"this scum of humanity"),[20] which had enjoyed a great deal of
popular credence as a justification for Hitler's Russian invasion,
gains a renewed respectability and diverts attention from the ugly
truth of the recent campaign in the East. Peter Weiss's narrator in
*Die Ästhetik des Widerstands* (vol. II, 1978) reminds us of the
pre-war European bourgeois fear of red Russia, greater than their
fear of Fascism, which lends even the Nazis' struggle with the
Soviets some kind of spurious crusader value (at the end of
Plievier's *Moskau*, Vilshofen comes to the conclusion that the
Germans *do* have a mission in Russia, but one which has been
ruined, "in practice", by the SS and SD). A whole complex of
thinking – the cultural citadel, a German heritage preserved
intact within Nazi Germany, the cultured Prussian officer contrasted with the vulgar US invaders, the bulwark against Bolshevism, Meinecke's notorious counsel to the Germans in 1946, after
their disastrous failure, to read Goethe to each other[21] – was
deeply suspect to younger writers. As Herbert Zand puts it in
*Letzte Ausfahrt*, in wartime "the Magic Flute was silent, Mozart
had received the Iron Cross Class I and died of it, Tamino was a
fighter pilot gone missing". A character in one of Nossack's
stories, a writer, declares that music in wartime is just "whoring"
(i.e. selling cheap distraction). Cultural pretensions after 1945
tended to be regarded as deeply undemocratic: intellectuals like
Jünger were suspect for having contributed to the false "normality" of the Third Reich (in Chapter 15 of Bienek's *Zeit ohne Glocken*
an interesting intertextuality is set up when Jünger's *Gärten und
Straßen* is mentioned, and appears to play a role of this kind). In
Adorno's famous dictum, "to write poetry after Auschwitz is
barbaric";[22] and any attempt to draw sustenance from earlier
literary tradition was open to misconstruction in the Cold War
and political restoration periods of the 1940s and 1950s. Hence a
good deal of the deliberately un-literary, undemonstrative, de-
clarative style of the younger generation of war writers.

Almost the only neutral territory left for a German writer hoping to salvage something positive out of the national catastrophe lay in the themes of wartime love relationships – productive in war literature at any level, from the most popular to the most belletristic – and the medical profession. Both themes embody a humanity that transcends politics or the moral problems of war. However, 'love and war' are discussed in Chapter 1, and I do not intend to dwell on the subject of separation, fidelity and alienation between the sexes in wartime, because its treatment is little different in the German war books than in those of other countries. (A particularly saccharine exploitation of the "love in wartime" theme is to be found in Remarque's exile war novel, *Zeit zu leben und Zeit zu sterben*, 1954.) The role of medics is worth a brief comment, however, since it does fulfil a requirement that is particularly evident in the German books; a positive, humanistic diversion from the moral disorder and the inhumanity of the fighting war. Peter Bamm's *Die unsichtbare Flagge* has already been mentioned, but the function of medics is no different, even if there is a difference in the quality of the presentation of the theme, in Heinz Konsalik's *Der Arzt von Stalingrad* (1956), which deals with the efforts of a heroic doctor attempting to minister to the needs of the captured troops at Stalingrad. In Bamm's book, German medical personnel and captive Russian doctors work together to tend the wounded of both sides at Sebastopol. Many other authors focus on the medical profession: Kluge, Plievier, Hartung, Nossack, and Zand all make more or less extensive use of the theme. The central redemptive metaphor of hospitals in wartime is that, although largely futile (like the war itself) in their effects in comparison to the amount of destruction of human life that is going on around them, they are unreflectively and unquestioningly humane. It is a cruel paradox that they often heal soldiers only in order that they may be sent back into the fighting. But at least the medics are not identified with the system in which they operate: they simply make the best of a very bad job, and hence they can serve as a centre for respect within the general madness, like the voice of the war book's narrator himself, and so reinforce his own humane and anti-war message without any need of rhetoric. In a world where values have been reversed – so that heroism can be a negative when it serves an unworthy cause, and "what was right was wrong and what was wrong was right" (Herbert Zand)[23] – they are restored by the straightforward categorical imperative, an unproblematical version of the soldier's unquestioning devotion to duty; a part of the war experience, but insulated within it.

Various other means that are essayed by writers to redeem something from the moral wreckage of war are more problematical and likely to backfire. One such means is present, at least by suggestion, even in some of the most thoroughgoing dissenters from war and militarism. It lies in a search for the origins of the present disaster in the mists of time, thereby suggesting a general diffusion of guilt or responsibility. As usual the popular writer puts it most unashamedly. In Johannes Mario Simmel's *Mich wundert, daß ich so fröhlich bin* (1949) – the novel concerns a group of people trapped in a cellar after an air raid in Vienna, and the attempt of the token fanatical Nazi type to find a drastic and dangerous way out – the Nazi is described as "the stupid victim of a chain of events going back so far that one loses sight of them". Jünger in *Strahlungen III* traces the present troubles back as far as the French Revolution and even the Renaissance; Alexander Kluge suggests a similar panoramic view in his chapter "Rekapitulation" in *Schlachtbeschreibung*, or the historical information provided in the chapter quaintly entitled "Wishes ... are something very simple around the year 1200." Plievier's *Moskau* begins with an historical document from the year 1537, and offers reminders of earlier invasions of Russia (sometimes by even worse barbarians than Hitler), as does *Stalingrad*, along with a reference to seventeenth-century hostilities between Russians and Germans on German territory. A soldier in Gerlach's novel declares that "we have the ballast of centuries to shake off". Plievier makes the unilluminating vulgar-Marxist equation of capitalism and Fascism, or sees the Second World War as a crisis of Europe ("Quo vadis, Europa": *Berlin*, Part 5). Others make the war an outcome of base human nature in general: Simmel, again, in *Alle Menschen werden Brüder* (1967): "I was no hero, never wanted to be one, this war wasn't my war.... And like the millions ... who [were] ... too young, too stupid, too gullible, too lazy or too cowardly to prevent this Adolf Hitler from coming to power – like these millions, I didn't have much luck": or, in *Mich wundert, daß ich so fröhlich bin*, the wife whose husband has been called up to fight refuses to think about the rights and wrongs of the war, for she knows "that the workers of all countries, the poor and underprivileged had been condemned since the beginning of time to fight for others and die

for others" (a very seductive argument, this; and one has to
remember that Simmel's novels run to enormous editions, since
he enjoys by far the biggest sales – 55 million to date – of any living
German author). In particular, the tough kind of novel that is
attracted towards describing the horrors of war in detail also
attributes the lowest motives to mankind ("everyone kills if they
get the chance")[24] and thus makes any search for ultimate responsibility almost otiose. There are many insidious suggestions, too,
that the war represents the workings of fate, or that it is a natural
disaster, an Act of God like a landslide, essentially beyond the
control of human agency. Demonizations of Hitler carry a related
implication: for example, the hypnotic effect of the Führer, even at
the end of the war, on the *Wehrmacht* officers Krebs, Boldt and
Loringhoven in Plievier's *Berlin*, Part II.


Not many novels offer a clear analysis of the German political
situation during the war, and this lack of direction stands in
contrast, particularly, to the Communist books, such as Anna
Seghers' *Die Toten bleiben jung*, or Schulz's *Wir sind nicht Staub im
Wind.* It seems that one must know clearly what one is for, in order
to be able to analyse what one is against. The political vagueness
of most war books is realistic, since war is not conducive to clear
thinking, but it also reflects the vulnerability of Western liberal
society with its pluralism and drift[25] (the symptomatic title is that
of Rudolf Krämer-Badoni's satirical novel *In der großen Drift*, 1949,
which is a picaresque account of an anti-hero buffeted about by all
the winds that blow in Germany from the 1930s to the 1940s) and
its ideological vacuum which invited Hitler to step in in the first
place. The perspective of many narrators is a-political and limited. Peter Bamm, who pre-empts serious discussion of the
Hitler phenomenon by referring to the dictator invariably as "der
primitive Mann", projects an a-political image of the army as
being, for the most part, equally remote from the resistance
movement of 20 July as from allegiance to Nazism. According to
him, "whole armies" evaded the Hitler salute, which was imposed on the *Wehrmacht* after 20 July 1944, by making sure that a
mug or mess tin was carried in the right hand at all times. For an
analysis of the appeal of Nazism one does not look to the war
books, which deal mainly with effect rather than cause, but to
books that consider the war within a broad political context and

time-span. (Anna Seghers in the first volume of *Die Toten bleiben jung* offers a good analysis of the German nationalist mentality; Peter Weiss in the second volume of *Die Ästhetik des Widerstands* deals with the reasons for the German working-class underreaction to Hitlerism.) The treatment of Nazi figures in the war novels is usually stereotyped and sketchy, and there are in fact surprisingly few committed Nazis – except in the East German books, of course, where they tend to be caricatured (one thinks of Herbert Ott's *Die Lüge* [1956] and its stereotype Nazi torturer having his way with the beautiful blonde Russian partisan girl). The caricature Nazi is not absent from West German books, either: there is the deadly concentration camp commandant Filskeit, fanatical, neurotic, fastidious and a lover of music, in Böll's *Wo warst du, Adam?*. Other-rank Nazis are often brutal and stupid: Nazi officers are rare and distinct types, usually bad soldiers; but there is also a class of decent idealistic officers deluded and misled by Nazism, like Wedelmann in *08/15*, or (a much worse case) Hinrichsen in the third volume of the trilogy, who is described as "not bad but stupid", "not a Nazi but a National Socialist". (The scarcity of Nazi attitudes among the officer class hardly squares with the historical facts. A recent study of representative first-line, "first-wave" conscription formations deployed on the Eastern Front shows that one third of the officers in the sample belonged to the Nazi Party, and that Party ideology had very heavily infiltrated army thinking, especially influencing attitudes to the Russians.)[26] One has to look to later books about the war period, like Bienek's *Zeit ohne Glocken*, for a more subtle analysis of the effects of Nazism among the ordinary wartime population, and to Andersch's *Winterspelt* for a moderation of the now stereotype interpretation of Nazism as perverted *Kleinbürgertum* (the petty bourgeois outlook). It is only in the more recent books, too, that one finds more than a passing reference to the fate of the Jews, with the obvious exception of the concentration camp literature, such as Ernst Wiechert's *Der Totenwald* (1946), Bruno Apitz' *Nackt unter Wölfen* (1958) and E.M. Remarque's *Der Funke Leben* (1952). The majority of war novels imply at most only a hazy half-knowledge on the part of the fighting troops of the atrocities being carried out in the name of Germany. The emphasis tends to shift from "why we're fighting" to "how well we fight". (Heyne, the hero of Ott's novel of the war at sea, *Haie und kleine Fische*, is convinced that the German High Command is ignorant of the concentration camps. Little is done to disabuse the reader of this mistaken notion.) In Kirst's novel, written primarily in the picaresque mode, the detailed description, in volume two, of the execution of two Russians by German military police breaks into the light-hearted narrative as a shock for the reader. The trivial tone is resumed immediately afterwards. The basic historical fact of German aggression (the Second World War as a German responsibility) is often masked by presenting a situation, like the last stages of the U-boat war or the fate of Gaiser's hopelessly outnumbered fighter pilots, which can be called "the adventure against unfair odds", creates the possibility of an appealing gallantry within defeat, and allows a certain amount of self-pity.[27] This scenario is played out anew in Buchheim's *Das Boot*, but it is to his credit that in one respect he does not shrink from political reality, but in a central episode shows how in a position of authority even the most humane character, the young submarine commander known as "the Old Man", is led by the a-moral ground-rules of Nazi warfare into committing a war crime (parallel to a historical case for which the Allies executed a submarine captain after the war), the attempted destruction of a neutral passenger ship. He fails only by a fortunate accident.

Attitudes towards the enemy are also fairly stereotype. In accordance with the implicit "bulwark-against-Bolshevism" assumption about the war on the Eastern Front, the Russians *en masse* are often seen as a menacing, almost animal, primitive Asiatic horde, and the individual soldier as an ignorant, confused peasant, though also a tough and worthy opponent. The British do not make a very prominent appearance, though there is some attempt in Gaiser's *Die sterbende Jagd* and especially in Wolfgang Ott to break down the irritating British assumption of moral superiority by describing acts of war by the British which fall below the chivalrous standards observed by their German counterparts. The Americans emerge generally as facile and juvenile, cautious fighters who "became victors without being heroes" simply by virtue of their crushing material superiority. Stefan Heym is in a special position to criticize the hollowness at the centre of the Americans' "crusade" in Europe. *The Crusaders* was written in America and appeared only later (1950) in the author's own translation as *Der bittere Lorbeer*, unique as a sustained representation of the war by a German author as seen through American eyes.[28] (Andersch, however, also assumes an American point of view on occasion in *Winterspelt*.) Elsewhere, there is some criticism of the Allies for demanding the unconditional surrender of Germany, which undermined any attempt at resistance within the country itself.

Not that resistance occurs very frequently as a theme in the war novels: where it does it is of a minimal, passive kind. The hero of Hermann Lenz's *Neue Zeit* is deliberately unmilitary and never fires his rifle once in his five years of combat (in fact, almost all the deaths of Germans in the novel occur through action by their own side, and one has the impression of the Second World War – quite rightly – as an "own goal" of massive proportions). The events of July 20 are mentioned in passing in a number of books, but not shown to have many reverberations. (There are however, some works based on the officers' plot, such as Hans Bernd Gisevius, *Bis zum bitteren Ende* and Fabian von Schlabrendorff, *Offiziere gegen Hitler*, both 1946.) Jünger records the severe measures visited upon even the most casual dissenter, and thus disarms outside criticism of the German failure to resist. Plievier (*Berlin*) rather unconvincingly records the "Romantik" of a Berlin woman offering shelter to fugitives. One of the few attempts at a "resistance novel" is Hans Fallada's last book, *Jeder stirbt für sich allein* (1946), whose plot is closely related to the activities of the ill-starred Munich resistance group, the "White Rose". There are a number of ways in which it is an unsatisfactory book, whose moral is that when it comes to resistance, what counts is the state of mind together with the translation of the thought into the deed – but not the effectiveness of the action. There is a distinction to be made here between brave defiance and purposeful resistance. The best resistance-writing, not unexpectedly, stems from Communist authors. In both Anna Seghers' *Das siebte Kreuz* (1942), probably her best-known novel, and in the most famous GDR war novel, Dieter Noll's *Werner Holt*, the young hero is educated to the point of resistance. In the latter novel another soldier, Wiese ("the real hero among us") is shot for attacking an SS guard who has "finished off" an exhausted concentration camp inmate. This positive act of resistance is an outbreak of spontaneous humanity which promises – something very important as the foundation of the Socialist utopia – that there is good material present among the German victims of Fascism (compare the inspiring subject matter of the famous and very powerful East German concentration-camp novel, Apitz' *Nackt unter Wölfen*). But of course, politically speaking, common sense and decency are not enough in the GDR literature. There is a contrast here to Ernst von Salomon's attempted rehabilitation of his fellow-Germans in *Der Fragebogen* through the medium of a stalwart Berlin charlady, Frau Imming, a one-woman resistance group who simply ignores the Nazis' nonsense and goes her own way regardless. Salomon tells us, somewhat unconvincingly, that "some eighty percent of the German population belonged to the 'Obergruppe Imming'". (If many did – whatever the percentage – it was certainly only after 1943.) The ultimate proof of a fully-developed resistance mentality, some of the novels suggest, would be an ability to identify one's own interests with those of the "enemy", so that the use of the pronoun "wir" (we) would acquire a different meaning. Various degrees of this kind of identification are in fact achieved in some novels.[29]

What more than anything else in the war literature comes between the average German and a full understanding of the past is the insidious and self-pitying suggestion of the *betrayal* of the ordinary German soldier by a system in which he has naively placed his faith. The paradigmatic title of Gerlach's novel, "The Betrayed Army" (cf. Michael Horbach, *Die verratenen Söhne*, "The Betrayed Sons", 1957), refers to Stalingrad; but Stalingrad was only the finale of the Germans' betrayal *all along*. The most brazen instance of the argument is in Gaiser's *Die sterbende Jagd*, where the German warrior is compared to "a man, some Walthari or Parzival, who sets out to defy death itself if necessary in order to defend his adored one, but discovers she is a whore who has taken up with a black whoremonger, with whom she sleeps. Now the man is in a bad way. What shall we do with him?". Kirst puts the "betrayal" to rights at the end of his trilogy by employing the wonderfully efficient German military machine, so far misused, to a "good" purpose at last, to bring a Nazi opportunist to justice.

Stylistically and structurally, German war books are not particularly avant-garde or experimental. Unlike the Anglo-Saxon reader, Germans had not been spoilt by successive generations of writers striving constantly to renew "the shock of recognition". There was no need for German writers to deal with war in terms of what Lionel Trilling calls "adversary culture", modernistic writing attempting to make over the techniques of war description and create novel sensations for jaded palates. Every German living through the period between 1939 and 1945 had in some sense been "at the front", and required no more than a suitably straightforward processing of his own experiences in conventional fictional terms. Germany had been relatively cut off from the development of literary culture elsewhere, and the first generation of post-war novels was not, and did not "need" to be, much in advance of Remarque's *All Quiet on the Western Front*. It was only at the beginning of the 1960s that novelists started to become self-conscious about literary techniques.

The earliest foreign influences on the returning prisoners-of-war who were to be the next generation of German writers were American. Names like Steinbeck, Dreiser, Sinclair Lewis and Sherwood Anderson were mentioned,[30] representatives of a realist, not an avant-garde school. Hemingway's name recurs frequently in these early years, and his writing serves as the obvious model for Hans Werner Richter's *Die Geschlagenen* (1949), set in the battlefield of Monte Cassino and the prisoner-of-war camps in America, where Nazi elements continue to terrorise left-wing soldiers. The battle scenes are handled in a manner prescriptive for many a German war novel: a series of independent episodes; no overall interpretation by the narrator to link them meaningfully together; details which are given no particular emphasis and remain discrete entities, like the recurrent paratactic sentences; repetition for emphasis; understatement. Many war novels are similarly episodic, loosely constructed, based on isolated incidents together with character sketches and briefly developed relationships. (Ledig's *Die Stalinorgel* is an example). The structure itself expresses the mood of the time, the desire to maintain a "camera-eye" impartiality and a sense of the opaqueness of the war as a totality. No connection is suggested where there was none in fact. As in Böll's *Wo warst du, Adam?*, the dissolving of the closed form of the novel in favour of a fragmented form corresponds to the fractured reality of war.

Stylistically, war novels offer everything from extremely blunt realism – so determined to indict war by sheer cold-blooded presentation of its horrors (see the opening pages of *Die Stalinorgel*) that the reader has a sense of something having died in the author, to match the brutal death around him – to long-established expressionist and surrealist resources of the German language. Gaiser is one author who works within this tradition to stretch language to its limits, sometimes with very successful results, as in his description of a pilot bailing out and temporarily losing his visual orientation (chapter 23). The same author, though, goes far towards a metaphysic of war, a glorifying of the symbiosis of man and machine, or in other words a kind of *poésie brute*, to be found also (despite his anti-war intentions) in Plievier's various descriptions of the impressive performance of the German war machine, and his conjuring up of the vast scale of operations; as well as quite consciously in Ernst Jünger (in the Allied bombers over occupied Paris he sees an aesthetic combination of "conscious, disciplined order" and "the release of elemental forces": *Strahlungen II*); and in Herbert Zand's vivid account of massed *Flak* firing in unison, as an image of battle becoming an independent organism; or Buchheim's infinite care for the details of the superb underwater machine that is man and technology working together with almost unimaginable precision in *Das Boot*, which also gives us some of the most compelling impressions of the life and moods of the sea itself. Both of these aspects clearly helped to inspire the internationally popular film based on the novel.

At two representative extremes, stylistically, are Wolfgang Borchert, with his wonderfully inventive language, creating the sensation of an attempt to revive feelings brutalised and blunted by the war; and Ernst Wiechert, in *Der Totenwald*, with the language of an "inner émigré", poetic in the most cloying sense, looking down upon the squalor of a concentration camp from the heights of Mozart and Goethe.

War literature does not offer much in the way of clean-cut "fictionality". That is to say, war books do not often work towards an obvious point, open to paraphrase as a discursive statement. In West German war writing, Böll comes closest to creating this kind of literature (*Der Zug war pünktlich*), but otherwise one has to look to East German works like Stephan Hermlin's powerful story *Der Leutnant Yorck von Wartenburg* (written 1945, published 1954), similar in theme to a story by Ambrose Bierce, "An Occurrence at Owl Creek Bridge", and concerning the youngest of the July 20 conspirators, who while awaiting his execution finds refuge in a vision which he takes to be the reality. He dreams he has escaped, fled to Russia, and is returning to Germany upon the news of a popular uprising against the Nazis. Then he is jolted back to reality and his execution. Another GDR writer, Franz Fühmann, in the collection of short stories *Die Elite*, shapes his war tales to a fine political analysis, as in "König Ödipus", for example, a re-enactment of the Oedipus legend in modern (occupied) Greece under the direction of a German classics professor, now an Army officer, who is led, by a progressively-developing analysis of the Oedipus story for the benefit of two eager young students-in-arms, to the insight that not only are the Germans' physical and intellectual crimes not to be distinguished one from another as contributory causes of the German "tragedy", but that he as an intellectual is the guiltiest of all: he shoots himself through the eyes.

In the 1960s there began to emerge works which incorporated the newly-fashionable institution of the unreliable narrator. Günter Grass, with *Die Blechtrommel* and *Katz und Maus*, stands godfather to this development. In the latter *Novelle*, wartime events among a group of teenagers in Danzig remain opaque because of the constitutional unreliability of the narrator, Pilenz. Siegfried Lenz adopts a similar technique in *Stadtgespräch* (1963), reconstructing through another such unreliable participant-narrator the events surrounding the deaths of hostages taken in occupied Norway. Böll is infected with the same uncertainty-principle in *Entfernung von der Truppe* (1964), asking for the reader's co-operation in filling in the narrative outlines he provides, and "changing his narrative levels" [sic] in a display of typical self-conscious 1960s writing conveying the threnodic point, consistently made in other works of Böll, that the past cannot be satisfactorily recaptured or reliably reconstituted. Alfred Andersch in *Winterspelt* writes similar carefully opaque fiction, blending documentary elements with invention, in a book written very much *against* the pattern of the popular war novel: as, in a different way, is Dieter Kühn's compilation with the ironic title *Luftkrieg als Abenteuer* (The Air War as Adventure, 1975), a protest, constructed by juxtaposing cheap fictional accounts with comment and documentary materials, against the popularising and glorifying of the war in the air. Something similar is attempted on a much grander scale by Alexander Kluge in his *Schlachtbeschreibung* (revised version 1969), subtitled "The organisational structure of a disaster". He is interested in exploiting the gap between fiction and history in order to show that in an event like Stalingrad "reality is not realistic",[31] and he creates a basic uncertainty by presenting a mass of partial and fragmented documentary evidence. He supplies both pictures and eye-witness interviews, but in neither case does the evidence serve the purpose of convincing us that we are faced with established truth or sheer undeniable factuality, in the sense that a newspaper uses these aids in order to persuade us that we are confronted with "facts". Instead of offering verification, Kluge's non-fictional material stresses the fictionality of the work and of the "facts". He juxtaposes, for example, diagrams of 1930s futuristic projections of "how a metropolis will look in 50 years time" with far less credible documentary photographs of the weird underground life lived by the *Wehrmacht* in Stalingrad (as it was a kind of Futurism which took them there, this seems a reasonable juxtaposition) and with army manuals describing improvised survival methods in sub-arctic conditions, including some figurative drawings of grenadiers wearing absurd bonnets made of newspaper as protection from the cold. The wheel has come full circle. If the early war books were looking for fictional means to present the facts of war, Kluge is attempting to use facts to expose the fiction, the absurdity, the unbelievability, and therefore the terror, of an event like Stalingrad.

## English Translations of Works Mentioned

Andersch, Alfred, *Die Rote/The Red-Head*, trans. by Michael Bullock (London, 1961).

Apitz, Bruno, *Nackt unter Wölfen/Naked Among the Wolves*, trans. by Edith Anderson (Berlin, 1960).

Bamm, Peter [Kurt Emmrich], *Die unsichtbare Flagge/The Invisible Flag*, trans. by Frank Hermann (London, 1956).

Bauer, Josef Martin, *So weit die Füsse tragen/As Far as my Feet will carry Me*, trans. by Lawrence Wilson (London, 1957).

Böll, Heinrich, *Wo warst du, Adam?/Adam, Where art Thou?*, trans. by Mervyn Savill (London, 1955); reissued as *Pray for the Dawn* (London, 1959).

——, *Der Zug war pünktlich/The Train was on Time*, trans. by Richard Graves (London, 1956).

——, *Wanderer, kommst du nach Spa/Traveller, if you come to Spa*, trans. by Mervyn Savill (London, 1956).

——, *Billard um halbzehn/Billiards at Half-past Nine*, trans. by Patrick Bowles (London, 1961).

Borchert, Wolfgang, *Draussen vor der Tür/The Man Outside: The Prose Works*, trans. by David Porter (London, 1952).

Gaiser, Gerd, *Die sterbende Jagd/The Last Squadron*, trans. by Paul Findlay (London, 1956).

Gerlach, Heinrich, *Die verratene Armee/The Forsaken Army*, trans. by Richard Graves (London, 1958).

Gisevius, Hans Bernd, *Bis zum bitteren Ende/To the Bitter End*, trans. by Richard and Clara Winstone (London, 1948).

Grass, Günter, *Die Blechtrommel/The Tin Drum*, trans. by Ralph Manheim (London, 1962).

——, *Katz und Maus/Cat and Mouse*, trans. by Ralph Manheim (London, 1963).

Gregor, Manfred, *Die Brücke/The Bridge*, trans. by Robert S. Rosen. (London, 1962).

Heinrich, Willi, *Das geduldige Fleisch/The Willing Flesh*, trans. by Richard and Clara Winstone (London, 1956).

Hochhuth, Rolf, *Der Stellvertreter/The Representative*, trans. by Robert David MacDonald (London, 1963).

——, *Soldaten/Soldiers*, trans. by Robert David MacDonald (London, 1968).

Horbach, Michael, *Die verratenen Söhne/The Great Betrayal*, trans. by Robert Kee (London, 1958); also as *The Betrayed* (New York, 1959).

Kipphardt, Heinar, *In der Sache J. Robert Oppenheimer/In the Matter of J. Robert Oppenheimer*, trans. by Ruth Spiers (London, 1967).

Kirst, Hans Hellmut, *08/15/Zero-Eight-Fifteen*, trans. by Robert Kee (London, 1955); also as *The Revolt of Gunner Asch* (London, 1965).

——, *08/15*, vol. 2/*Gunner Asch goes to War*, trans. by Robert Kee (London, 1956).

——, *08/15* vol. 3/*The Return of Gunner Asch*, trans. by Robert Kee (London, 1957).

——, *Die Nacht der Generale/The Night of the Generals*, trans. by J. Maxwell Brownjohn (London, 1963).

Kluge, Alexander, *Schlachtbeschreibung/The Battle*, trans. by Leila Vennewitz (New York, 1967).

Lenz, Siegfried, *Stadtgespräch/The Survivor*, trans. by Michael Bullock (New York, 1965).

——, *Deutschstunde/The German Lesson*, trans. by Ernst Kaiser and Eithne Wilkins (London, 1977).

Mann, Thomas, *Doktor Faustus/Doctor Faustus*, trans. by H.T. Lowe-Porter (London, 1949).

Meichsner, Dieter, *Weisst du, warum?/Vain Glory*, trans. by Charlotte and A.L. Lloyd (London, 1953).

Ott, Wolfgang, *Haie und kleine Fische/Sharks and Little Fish*, trans. by Oliver Coburn (London, 1957).

Plievier, Theodor, *Stalingrad/Stalingrad: The Death of an Army*, trans. by H. Langmead Robinson (London, 1948).

——, *Moskau/Moscow*, trans. by Stuart Hood (London, 1953).

——, *Berlin/Berlin*, trans. by Louis Hagen and Vivian Milroy (London, 1956); also as *Berlin: Rape of a City* (London, 1962).

Remarque, Erich Maria, *Der Funke Leben/The Spark of Life*, trans. by James Stern (London and New York, 1952).

——, *Zeit zu leben und Zeit zu sterben/A Time to Love and a Time to Die*, trans. by Denver Lindley (London, 1954).

Richter, Hans Werner, *Die Geschlagenen/The Odds Against Us*, trans. by Robert Kee (London, 1950); also as *Beyond Defeat* (New York, 1950).

——, *Sie fielen aus Gottes Hand/They Fell from God's Hand*, trans. by Geoffrey Sainsbury (New York, 1956).

Seghers, Anna [Netty Radvány (Reiling)], *Das siebte Kreuz/The Seventh Cross*, trans. James A. Galston (London, 1943).

——, *Die Toten bleiben jung/The Dead stay Young*, (London and Boston, 1950).

Weiss, Peter, *Die Ermittlung/The Investigation*, trans. by Alexander Gross (London, 1966); American edn trans. by John Swan and Ulu Grossbard (New York, 1966).

Wiechert, Ernst, *Der Totenwald/The Forest of the Dead*, trans. by Ursula Stechow (London, 1947).

Zand, Herbert, *Letzte Ausfahrt/Last Sortie: The Story of the Cauldron*, trans. by C.M. Woodhouse (London, 1955).

# 4 Soviet Union

**Don Piper**

The magnitude of the war in Russia and the social and political impact it had upon the country are reflected in a diverse and voluminous literature. More than a thousand members of the Union of Writers, a quarter of whom lost their lives, went to the front in various capacities. Indeed, a bibliography of the prose and poetry written about the war during the decade 1941–51 would probably be longer than this chapter. A second wave of novels and memoirs followed Khrushchev's attack upon Stalin's reputation in 1956. Writers like Bykov, Bondarev and others persistently return to the theme in the seventies.

Consequently, any review of this literature must be both thematic and selective. Only those periods to which hindsight gives a certain thematic homogeneity can be discussed. For this reason I have chosen to concentrate upon the literature of the forties, to touch briefly on the "orthodox" post-war Stalinist novels and close with a review of the writings of the Khrushchev period during which Grossman wrote *Life and Fate* (1960), a work which may well become the "definitive" war novel of the 1960s and 1970s.

The persistence of the war as a major theme in literature over four decades attests the chronic physical and mental trauma which it caused in Russia. On conservative estimates the country lost fifteen million servicemen and five million civilians. Three million *Ostarbeiter* were transported to Germany as slave labour. Three million prisoners-of-war perished in captivity. Russian land was blackened by the scorched-earth policy adopted by both sides and the people suffered the real implications of the Nazis' *Untermensch* theories. Yet, despite these losses, Pasternak remarked that, compared with the thirties, "the war came as a breath of fresh air, an omen of deliverance, a purifying storm".[1]

Superficially, the statement bewilders. Nevertheless, al-

131

though the cost of deliverance was high, the war did constitute a respite from crippling internecine strife. Enforced collectivisation had claimed about three and a half million lives; in the resultant famine of 1932–33 about six million peasants died. During the purges of 1935–38 about twelve million Russians had been dispatched to the camps. The country was bleeding from self-inflicted wounds which were immediately exposed by the outbreak of war. The Soviet Union was disunited and unprepared. Half the officer corps had been shot or imprisoned in 1937–38; in the upper echelons of the services 65 per cent of staff had been removed. The Russian armies, badly led by inexperienced officers, ignorant of mobile warfare and fearful of personal initiative, were routed. In those territories annexed after the Molotov-Ribbentrop Pact of 1939 the Germans were welcomed as liberators. The Ukraine, which had borne the brunt of collectivisation, initially displayed little antipathy towards them. Eighty thousand *Osttruppen* served in the German forces and the number of "Hiwis", the indigenous "odd-job" men of the German army, reached half a million by the spring of 1943. SS detachments included Estonian, Cossack and White-Russian units. Eighty per cent of the very first *Ostarbeiter* were volunteers, while Vlasov's Russian Liberation Army, recruited from ill-treated *Ostarbeiter* and prisoners-of-war, numbered between 800 000 and a million men. Even after Stalin's order of 28 July 1942 which established Military Tribunals empowered to impose the death penalty for cowardice and which, by equating surrender and retreat with treason, effectively disinherited Russian prisoners-of-war, sixty one thousand troops nevertheless deserted in the second half of the year.

In brief, the divisiveness of Stalin's internal policies and the collapse of his foreign policy, his disregard of numerous warnings of the invasion and the inane orders which forbad strategic withdrawals and ensured encirclement of entire armies exposed the limitations of his arbitrary regime. Had Germany been less committed to dogmatic racism, it would have recognised in Vlasov's trenchant anti-Stalinism the voice of widespread discontent.

Yet Pasternak's comment is substantially correct. A combination of Russian nous and German stupidity eventually effected a rare unity in the country. Political dog-fighting largely ceased and the atmosphere of suspicion lifted. Always inherent in Stalin's doctrine of "socialism in one country", patriotism, boosted by his speech of 6 November 1941 in praise of such national heroes as Alexander Nevsky and Kutuzov, now became Russia's staple diet. The work of historians like Wipper and Snegirev and numerous historical plays and novels emphasised historical continuity rather than ideological disjuncture and suggested a common identity between the old and new Russia. Guards regiments were introduced into the army, the prestige of the officer was enhanced, parity between the political commissar and the military commander was abolished in favour of the latter and professional soldiers like Zhukov and Rokossovsky replaced such political figureheads as Voroshilov and Budenny. Indeed, Stalin's restoration of the Synod and his reception of the Metropolitan in September 1943 typified the wartime ascendancy which practical patriotism enjoyed over ideology.

German policy also fostered national unity. Convinced of victory by the winter of 1941, naively identifying the Russian people with Bolshevism, their political planning restricted to the dismemberment of the Soviet Union, the colonisation of its people and the extermination of Jews and Party members, the Germans were grotesquely ill-equipped to exploit the fissures in Soviet society. The appointment of such fanatical Nazis as Koch in the Ukraine and Lohse in "Ostland", the abominable treatment of Russian prisoners-of-war, the castration of the education system, de-industrialisation and the perpetuation, until too late, of the collective-farm system exhibited such crass fanaticism that they alienated the very strata of society upon which successful colonisation depended. Hitler's boast that Leningrad would be starved into submission, statements that German requisitioning of food would necessitate the death of millions and reports of the brutal recruitment and treatment of the *Ostarbeiter* provided the Soviet authorities with fertile propaganda and swelled the ranks of the partisans. The belief that Russia's land existed for German exploitation and that its people constituted a German work-force was a profound political weakness which propagandists like Ehrenburg eagerly exploited and the Russian people bitterly felt. The situation precluded a "third choice" and people opted for patriotism.

Pre-war soviet literature had reflected the nation's insularity. The Party's paramount influence in every sphere of Russian life enabled it to suppress all means of international comparison. Thus, as reflected in Soviet culture, the 1930s constituted an unparalleled economic, social and military achievement. The "excesses" of the decade were explained as the consequences of such progress. "One can't make an omelette without breaking eggs" and "Fell a forest and the chips fly" were the stock apologetics of the period. Socialist realism, the official doctrine in the arts since 1934, was an equally closed system. Its principal feature was *partiinost'*, its Party spirit, an ideological component which neutered the element of realism. The latter was equated with the clear presentation of a message, namely the illustration of Soviet industrial and agricultural success. Following the proclamation in 1936 of the victory of socialism and the inception of a classless society, the "no-conflict" novel emerged. Such drama as literature could muster was provided by earnest disagreements between well-meaning technologists about industrial innovations or by survivors of dying species like *kulaks* and misguided intellectuals. Described as "reality varnished" after Stalin's death, socialist realism plotted the historically inevitable progress of a society wisely led by the Party. Gentile in its treatment of sexual matters, lacking depth in characterisation, muting human grief, it spawned a multitude of flat novels barely distinguishable from each other.

The war exposed the invalidity of the myths. The Party's mistaken foreign policy and the defeat of its "invincible" Red Army destroyed all claims to infallibility. It now became impossible to conceal unpalatable truths from millions of bemused Red Army men and a population bombed and blasted throughout European Russia. Soviet society had ceased to be hermetically closed.

Consequently the distinguishing feature of war literature is its realism, understood now as a unvarnished representation of the pain and courage of the Russian people and as a willingness to question matters hitherto considered taboo. The poet Aleksey Surkov, declared in 1942 that the troops were quick to detect "the jingle of hypocrisy in metallic words" and that "only the language of truth, honest and simple" was acceptable.[2] Ideological generalities now give way to a preoccupation with facts, with the immediate and present. There is a revival of poetry, whose graphic vividness, be it that of Inber and Berggol'ts in Leningrad, or of Surkov, Gudzenko and Mezhirov at the front, also characterises the best prose. Scarcely describable as "fiction", the work of Nekrasov, Bek and Simonov is rooted in their experience of war. Thus there is little to distinguish *People with a Clean Conscience* (1946), the autobiography of the partisan leader Vershigora, from Nekrasov's "novel" *In the Trenches of Stalingrad* (1946), save that it is the latter which is less discursive and more factual. Even after the war when "fictional" accounts of events reappeared, it is the enormity and grandeur of the non-fictional elements which impress. In Ketlinskaya's *Under Siege* (1947), Chakovsky's *It Happened in Leningrad* (1948) and Chukovsky's *Baltic Skies* (1954) the description of life in besieged Leningrad transcends the doings of characters reverting to the stereotypes of socialist realism. Similarly in more romantic works like Grossman's *The People are Immortal* (1942) and Gorbatov's *The Warrior Aleksey Kulikov* (1942) and *The Undefeated* (1943) the authentic emotional response which the author makes to the course of the war rivets the attention far more than the larger-than-life characters.

Russian war literature emerges as a chronicle of people's spontaneous and varied responses to a cruel period of history. The poet Boris Slutsky compared *War and Peace*, the most popular book of the times, to a mirror in which the country again recognised itself. Wartime literature possesses the physical, three-dimensional quality of Tolstoy's art, the same sturdy patriotism and variety of human emotion. It remains, however, a kaleidoscope of responses, in which preoccupation with present events precluded broader, more philosophical perspectives. Only in the 1960s in *Life and Fate* does Grossman set the social vigour and camaraderie which this literature embodies in an historical context.

Greater freedom from Party controls and a less rigorous censorship created a confidence and assertiveness which sharply differentiate wartime from pre-war literature. Oblique criticism of the effects of Party policy upon national unity reflected deeply felt reservations. In *The Old Teacher* (1942) Grossman identifies collectivisation as a cardinal factor in the animosities arising in a Ukrainian town under German occupation. Gorbatov's *The Undefeated* stresses the difficulties of organising resistance in a listless, demoralised Ukraine. The narrator of Aleksey Tolstoy's *Tales of*

*Ivan Sudarev* (1942) is the son of a *kulak* who, refusing to join a collective farm, "sold his cow, boarded up his hut and went off to the Far East".[3] This ironic presentation of a *kulak*'s deportation is followed by Ivan's remark that he, a *kulak*'s son, must now defend his country. In Grossman's *For a Righteous Cause* (1952) Commissar Krymov shelters in a peasant's house during the retreat to Moscow. The peasant gloats over the Red Army's defeat. He has memories of 1930 when peasants drank all their vodka, slaughtered their animals and died. In 1943 Dovzhenko voiced the disapprobation latent in many such passages. His scenario for a film entitled *The Ukraine Ablaze*, first published only in 1966, is a lament for a divided country. Its climax is a fight to the death between the loyalist Zaporozhets and Zabroda, once deported to Siberia by Zaporozhets as a *kulak* and now in charge of the *Polizei*: "They talked of the *kulaks*, of deportations, of sufferings on alien soil, of famine, deaths and acts of treachery. They abused and taunted each other with Siberia and the nation's misery, . . . and with Hitler and German pogroms and the burnings and hangings and slavery."[4] The hatred is venomous and tears the Ukraine apart.

Writers also touched upon the politically dangerous theme of the purges. From 1939 onwards batches of men were released from the camps. Amongst them were the future Marshals Rokossovsky and Meretskov, General Gorbatov and S.V. Rudnev, later to become Commissar in Kovpak's White-Russian partisan forces and Vershigora's immediate superior. In his remarkably outspoken autobiography Vershigora recalls the following incident. A certain partisan sergeant called Karpenko, who had received a ten-year sentence and been released, took such exception to Rudnev's political pep-talks that he threatened his life, justifying his indiscipline on the grounds that his experiences as a prisoner had shattered his nerves. A reconciliation took place only after Karpenko had learned of Rudnev's own arrest in 1937. Twenty months later, his Party card was returned to him with the words: "There's been a mistake."[5] Piqued and angry, Rudnev left the army. When war broke out, he volunteered, but was rejected! Hence his appearance amongst the partisans. Simonov's *Days and Nights* (1944) lacked a chapter when it first appeared. Published in 1966, the chapter contains criticism of the social debilitation caused by wave after wave of arrests. One of the most appealing characters in Nekrasov's *In the Trenches of Stalingrad* is the eigh-

teen-year-old orderly, Valega, whose biography is curtly summarised: "All I know is that his father and mother are dead. He
has a married sister somewhere whom he scarcely knows at all. He
was put on trial. He won't say for what. Did time. Did not
complete his sentence. Released and volunteered for the army."[6]
The passage implies the death of Valega's parents during collectivisation, the dispersal of the surviving members of the family
and his own arrest as a result of Stalin's decree of April 1935
extending all penalties to children of twelve and over.

Comments of this kind underline the insularity of a society
which literally and figuratively disarmed itself. In Ehrenburg's
*The Storm* (1947) pre-war society is presented as a closed, fearful
world unaware of the threat posed by the German occupation of
Western Europe. Informed opinion between 1939 and June 1941
was generally pro-German. Remarks like "They smashed the
French beautifully" and "They knocked them out like artists" are
not untypical. Ehrenburg deplores "the crude manners, the
arrests, the soullessness of the bureaucrats".[7] His strictures are
echoed by many another writer. The meaningless jargon of the
politicians, the social stratification created by the Party hierarchy, the primitive level of Soviet culture are subjected to widespread criticism. The insidious effects of enervating propaganda
and political callousness resulted in a diminished sense of social
identity and national purpose. Vershigora mentions the disaffec-
tion of a partisan who feels that his life has been planned "on the
abacuses of the State Planning Department". Dovzhenko attributes these bitterly critical words to a German officer: "Do you
know, they don't study history? Amazing! Their diet for twenty-
five years has consisted of negative slogans. They reject God,
property, the family, friendship. All that remains of nationality is
a derogatory adjective. They have no eternal truths. That's why
they breed so many traitors." Reproached with lack of patriotism,
deserting soldiers reply that they do not understand the
concept. At school they were taught class warfare. Dovzhenko's
thesis is that the suppression of nationalism and the social antagonisms created in the thirties had led to the country's destabil-
ization.

The feeling that the Party was out of step with the national
mood intensified after the outbreak of war. Fadeyev's novel *The
Young Guard* (1945), based upon the organisation of an urban
guerrilla movement by the young people of Krasnodon, sharply

censured the Party's unreadiness for war. The chiefs of police and the Party bosses are the first to flee the German advance. So many vehicles are requisitioned for their flight that the town is left without transport. Dovzhenko describes this common theme in angrier terms. As "nonentities who understand nothing of the national tragedy" depart in half-empty lorries whose load of secret documents precludes their picking up refugees or wounded, a trooper remarks: "What's going on? Tell me, why are we so vile?" In Fadeyev's novel those Party members detailed to organise resistance are out of touch with the young, are ignorant of urban warfare and misguided in their judgment of people. The Party's alienation from the people is always attributed to its bureaucratic attitudes. Party-boss Stepan Yatsenko, in *The Unde-feated* concludes that his heart is "stained with ink"[8] when he finds that his appointees have collaborated with the Germans. Dovzhenko describes a typical chairman of a typical provincial town. He is so lost in a maze of "secret papers, secret doings and secret instructions", so locked into a bureaucracy where such sinister nonsense is important that it allows him "to keep his own provincial obtuseness and his profoundly callous attitude to human beings equally secret".

The Party's conduct of the war itself was criticised. Doubts were expressed about three broad and often overlapping areas of policy – the status of Russian prisoners-of-war, Russian military strategy during 1941–42 and excessive political coercion and surveillance in the armed forces.

Like the Japanese, Russian prisoners-of-war were regarded as traitors. Even troops who broke out of encirclement were disarmed and interrogated by Special Department or *Smersh* agents. With desertion so common, all escaped prisoners were similarly questioned and, at best, sent to the penal battalions. Dmitry Medvedev, an NKVD officer who commanded a partisan unit in the Bryansk area, reflects this orthodox attitude. In his novel *Stout Hearts* (1948) escaped prisoners-of-war are undisciplined and drunken. One has to be shot. In the novels of Gorbatov the standpoint is only slightly less stringent.

Most writers were more lenient. A peasant woman in Was-silewska's *The Rainbow* (1942), after seeing the condition of Russian prisoners-of-war marched through her village, advises her son to choose death before captivity, while Aleksey Tolstoy transforms seven shamed and dispirited ex-prisoners into an efficient partisan unit in his story, *Seven Dirty Faces* (1942). Sholokhov's *School of Hatred* (1942) is a harrowing account of the conditions in which half a million prisoners died during the first six months of the war. Sleeping in piles under the open sky to keep warm, many frozen to the ground, they would fight over the occasional horse-meat thrown to them deliberately to provoke disorders and necessitate shootings. The hero of the story, Gerasimov, escapes and, despite initial suspicions on their part, joins the partisans. Sholokhov's more famous work *Fate of a Man* (1957) is much less honest. Andrey Sokolov's escape in the company of a captured Nazi and his rapturous reception have been rightly condemned by Solzhenitsyn as cheap and shameful.[9] Indeed, the safest sanctuary for escaped prisoners-of-war appears to have been the partisan army of Kovpak and Rudnev. Here the Party line was flouted. Vershigora reports that ex-prisoners were welcomed because their experience of captivity ensured that they would "never surrender a second time". He is also scathing about the *Smersh* interrogators. Sometimes when these "exceptionally demanding people" were themselves captured they proved to be "cowards and traitors". Conduct in captivity rather than the fact of captivity, he concludes, "should determine our attitude to people". It was generally felt that the Party's undiscriminating attitude was impractical and unjust. People should not be "categorized" as traitors.

Nor could the war be won by edict. Von Manstein identified the main defect in Russian strategy in 1941–42 as the policy of fighting for "every inch of ground, with the result that the Germans were able to achieve large-scale encirclement".[10] This tactic of defending established lines is criticised by Saburov, the hero of Simonov's *Days and Nights*. Surveying the miles of useless trenches between the Don and Volga in 1942 he realises that "our ideas are out of date: we retreat and take up position, whereas the Germans are round us in a trice and are there before we are".[11] This inflexibility becomes the theme of Bek's novel, *The Volokolamsk Highway*, which describes the activities of a battalion commanded by the Cossack Baurdzhan in the fighting along a key road to Moscow in 1941. The battalion belongs to the 8th Guards Division under the command of the celebrated Major-General Panfilov. The first two volumes, published in 1944, illustrate the difficulties Russian officers had in welding their demoralised forces together. Even when discipline is re-established, officers must be taught to conserve manpower, to "read" a tactical situation and use initiative. Panfilov emerges as an astute tactician, determined to introduce some mental and physical mobility into the rigidity of Russian military practice, a man ready to ignore orders and countenance tactical retreats if the situation demands such. The 1944 publication ends when Baurdzhan has successfully accomplished such a withdrawal. The continuation of the novel in 1960 presents the repurcussions of Panfilov's unorthodoxy. At one point Baurdzhan is relieved of his command and Panfilov is reprimanded and humiliated.

Indeed, a few writers, weighing the death-toll exacted by the mistaken strategy of 1941–42 and Russia's overall military unpreparedness, raised basic questions about the Party's competence. Two superb stories by Kazakevich verge upon dissidence.

*Star* (1946) is set in the forests of the Western Ukraine, a terrain whose timelessness intimates the transient nature of human existence and whose people are indifferent to the blessings of a Russian liberation. A platoon of scouts, code-named Star, is sent on a mission from which it does not return. The sub-plot concerns an investigation by a Captain Es'kin of a complaint by a surly peasant woman that the scouts have failed to return her horse. Travkin, the platoon commander, unaware that one of his men has traded the horse, denies the charges. Eventually Es'kin arrives to confront Travkin:

> 'Comrade Captain, mightn't it be better if you just went to them and interrogated them there?'
> 'Where are they?'
> 'Behind enemy lines.'
> The investigator scrutinized Katya with cold, humourless eyes.

The story is untendentious, yet creates an overwhelming atmosphere of menace. The men are threatened by the terrain, the local population, the enemy and their own side.

*Two Men on the Steppe* (1948) is more explicit. An officer, Ogarkov, is court-martialled and sentenced to death for failing to deliver a message. The Russians, however, are forced to withdraw and he is left in the charge of Dzhurabaev, his ultra-conscientious guard who insists on marching him back through occupied territory to Russian lines. Dzhurabaev is killed, but Ogarkov returns and is pardoned. The story's impact lay in descriptions like this:

> Towards evening, when the sun was at their backs, Ogarkov would see Dzhurabaev's shadow beside him. He soon began to feel a deep antipathy, almost hatred for that shadow. Not for Dzhurabaev, but for his shadow. He felt no hostility towards Dzhurabaev himself – the man was doing his duty. But his shadow ... which never failed to keep pace, which seemed to be fixed, attached to him, reduced Ogarkov to a state of impotent exasperation and he tried to ignore it completely.[12]

The passage conveys the sense of being constantly stalked, the realization that the menace is of inhuman, not human, dimensions, the despairing recognition that this impersonal force will never falter and a consequent awareness of a permanent impotence and injustice.

Nekrasov's *In the Trenches of Stalingrad* appears to be an unsensational, diaristic account of a soldier's experience at Stalingrad. It is, however, a mine-field of innuendo. Terse references to disasters like Kharkov and laconic calculations of losses belie a cold anger. Artless conversations disguise their irony:

> 'But, nevertheless, he's got will-power ...'
> 'Who has? ...'
> 'Stalin, of course. Managing to contain two retreats on this scale.'

Or they raise vital questions:

> 'You knew there would be a war?'
> 'Maybe.'
> 'No "maybes", you knew.'

The leading character, the semi-autobiographical Kerzhentsev, shows a bitterness and scepticism uncharacteristic of wartime literature. The work itself ends in anti-climax, even bathos. On 19 November the Russian counter-attack begins, and Kerzhentsev's battalion is ordered at gun-point to capture some water-towers heavily defended by German machine-guns. Twenty-six men, half the "battalion", are killed. One of the dead,

Karnaukhov, had two portraits in his dug-out – one of Stalin, the other of Jack London. Kerzhentsev takes the picture of London as a keepsake. Stalin's picture is not reclaimed. Finally, after a stay in hospital, Kerzhentsev returns to find his men still trying to take the same objective and talks to Chumak, a former criminal: "Just think of it – some two hundred lousy metres – We've been through the whole of White Russia, the Ukraine, the Donbass, the Kalmuck steppes, and now we can't take two hundred metres. And Chumak asks me – why not?" The novel ends not with a celebration of victory, but with a squalid episode in which men are killed so that absurd orders from above may be fulfilled.

Chumak asks whose is the responsibility for the Russian débâcle. Dovzhenko provides an answer in his scenario. It too involves a picture of Stalin. Zaporozhets takes it down: "Good-bye, comrade. You and I did not expect that such things would happen in our country, but they have. And the cost in life has been immense. . . . What will become of our people? Will they survive or vanish without trace? . . . We are all gall. . . . Comrade, you said that the people were immortal. Our immortality weighs heavily upon us."

Someone was responsible for the social disharmony, the military improvidence and the inept strategy that caused such slaughter. Later, in 1958 Mezhirov, an ex-soldier, summarized the theme in three lines of verse: "Under-shoot. Over-shoot. Under-shoot. / The artillery shells its own men . . . / They are felling no forest, but still the chips fly".[13]


Such dissidence was not widespread. In general, criticism of the Party was intended to be constructive, not destructive. Almost all writers regarded the relationship between Party and people as a partnership towards which Stalin had made the first gesture in his broadcast of 3 July 1941 which began: "Comrades! Citizens! Brothers and sisters! Warriors of our army and fleet! My friends, I turn to you." Simonov's description of Saburov's reaction typifies the response of the majority of Russians. The warmth of the address, the gurgle of water being poured into a glass, the long pauses, the controlled anguish persuaded Saburov that "whatever might happen, he, Saburov, was with him to the end".[14]

The austere figure suddenly became human and was largely

exonerated from blame for Russia's woes. He became a symbol of national unity and the frequent, apparently sycophantic invocations of his name were then sincere. His voice prompted Vera Inber to remark that "he knows everything and will never be a hypocrite".[15] The poet Isakovsky "prostrated himself" before him in honour of "the purity and truth which your life embodies".[16] The poet Antokol'sky deified him, inviting him to rise in Marshal's uniform "So that seas again be blue / And fields again be green."[17] The authenticity of many such sentiments is attested by Aliger. Zoya Kosmodem'yanskaya, the partisan-heroine of her poem "Zoya" (1942), died with the words "Stalin is on guard" on her lips. Republishing her poem after Stalin's death she wrote that, although Zoya's attitude now seems dated, then "there were no such differences between us".[18]

The general view was that the thirties had passed into history and that the people in alliance with a *cleansed* Party would jointly face the common enemy. Berggol'ts believed that "the bitter years of persecutions and evil" were over.[19] The poet Kurosheva shared the current optimism: "There can be no return to old deeds and thoughts:/ All has been cremated in a monstrous conflagration."[20] Vershigora described his life as a partisan as "a time of truth and beauty" which would straighten the back of many a "bureaucrat, red-tape merchant, informer and pusillanimous editor". A new spirit was in the air and attitudes to the Party changed. When membership meant instant death if one fell into enemy hands, joining the Party became an act of patriotism. It was, as Ketlinskaya remarked in *Under Siege*, equivalent to "going to the front, into the line of fire".[21] The idealism of 1918 revived. Sel'vinsky composed his "Ballad of Leninism" (1942), Inber invoked the popular name of Kirov in "He is Ours" (1942) and Tikhonov wrote one of the war's finest martial poems, "Kirov is with Us" (1941). In response, the ideological criteria determining Party membership became so relaxed that two of Vershigora's wayward partisans – Karpenko, who had been sentenced to penal labour in the thirties, and Mudry, an escaped prisoner-of-war and former speculator, were enrolled in the Party's ranks by partisan commissars. Inber, Vershigora and Slutsky became members in 1942. Other criteria now prevailed. In *The Young Guard*, for instance, young Radek Yurkin's request to join the *Komsomol* is speedily granted. He is asked to outline the obligations of membership:

'The task of a member is to kill the German-Fascist invaders until none of them is left . . .'

'Well then,' said Turkenich, 'in my opinion the lad's grasp of politics is perfect.'[22]

The tacit agreement between Party and people resulted in the efflorescence of a literature which Aleksey Tolstoy described in 1942 as being "genuinely national".[23] The desire for truth, however, which now distinguishes this literature cannot be wholly explained by the relaxation of Party censorship and discipline which attended the concordat. It was also dictated by the quality of experience which writers derived from the war and which Semyon Gudzenko, himself a soldier, elucidates in his poem, "My Generation" (1945).[24] The brutality of the poem's refrain – "There is no need to pity us, for we would pity none" – is deceptive. Despite its horror, war intensifies the commonplace experiences of joy and suffering: the intensity of feeling is such that one lives on an ultimate level of three-dimensional reality. A truer insight into life and people emerges. Pity demeans the dead who had that knowledge. Surkov writes in similar vein. The demeanour of the troops has become "more captious and abrupt", for the true worth of "deeds, people and things, caught in the shimmering light of battle, shines out visibly". The measure of literature became its approximation to the realities of the front and its distance from the cant of the past decade.

Hence there was no attempt to disguise German superiority and Russian weakness during the humiliating pre-Stalingrad months. Officers in Grossman's *The People are Immortal* talk freely of the Germans' élan, discipline and brilliant deployment of tanks and airborne troops. German military prowess was held in awe. Gershenzon, an interpreter killed in 1942, relates that during the battles around Vyazma two figures came out of the darkness towards him. He bellowed: "Hände hoch!" and approached. They were Russians: "I bawled them out: do Red-Army men really raise their hands when they hear a word of German?"[25] Baurdzhan in Bek's novel describes the arrogance of the German advance "without reconnaissance, without patrols . . . , all their amenities with them, in lorries, confident of routing the Russkies as soon as they met them". He needed a victory, be it only in a skirmish, to prove to his men that German were not "scaly, long-tailed monsters or fire-breathing dragons, but men".[26] Simonov's Saburov recovers from panic in battle on the Moscow front, rallies a few men and makes a stand. His men wonder at the dead Germans, "men they had killed . . . and whom it was in fact possible to kill". Similar consternation characterised the retreat to Stalingrad. Grossman's *For a Righteous Cause* (1952) describes the excitement which the prospect of withdrawal from the battlefield generates. It is reflected in "the animated eyes" of the lightly wounded troops escaping "the hell of the trenches" and in "the busy bustle of people preparing to leave along the road to the East".[27] A character in Nekrasov's novel remarked: "Only a miracle can save us. Otherwise they will crush us. With their organisation and tanks." In terms of matériel the miracle was performed in the Urals: in terms of morale the crucial factors were German atrocities, Russian patriotism and the immense shame felt by the retreating armies.

Grossman captures the magnitude of the catastrophe on the Bryansk front in October 1941:

> I have never seen or imagined a flight of this scale. A Biblical Exodus! Vehicles moving in eight lanes abreast. The hysterical wail of dozens of lorries simultaneously extricating themselves from the mud. Enormous flocks of sheep and herds of cattle are driven across the fields; further back, columns of horse-drawn transport wagons and thousands of carts covered with brightly-coloured canvas, plywood and tin, all carrying refugees from the Ukraine, squeak and creak their way along the roads; and still further in the distance are crowds of pedestrians with sacks, bundles and cases. It is not a river or a flood, but the slow movement of an ocean current, hundreds of metres wide to right and left. From under the canopies raised over the carts gaze children, dark-haired and fair, Jewish elders with Biblical beards, peasant women in shawls, Ukrainian old-timers in their caps, black-haired Jewish girls and women. . . . And what peace there is in their eyes, their grief is philosophical, what a sense of fate, of a universal catastrophe!
>
> In the evening the sun appears from behind tiers of blue, black and grey clouds. The shafts of light are broad, enormous, stretching from heaven to earth as they do in Doré's paintings of

dread Biblical scenes of the descent of austere heavenly hosts. Amidst these yellow beams of light the movement of the old men, of the women with babes in their arms, of the flocks of sheep and soldiers seems so majestic and tragic that at times I really feel that we have been transported back to the era of Biblical catastrophes.[28]

The transmigrations which followed the retreating troops and the reception they had from those who remained in the villages were humiliating. Slutsky recalls that in 1941 he could not eat because neither he nor the army "had earned our rations".[29] The prose of Nekrasov and Sholokhov and the poetry of Simonov and Surkov detail countless scenes of gaunt, silent women standing outside their houses and sullenly watching the bitter, shamed and equally silent soldiers march past. The anger of the troops was exacerbated by their realisation of the fate to which they were abandoning the civilians. German conduct had initially provoked horrified astonishment. In August 1941 Sholokhov was bewildered by the "senseless, aimless" destruction.[30] Blank incredulity characterises Svetlov's poem, "The Italian" (1943). A Russian soldier who had so often dreamt of warm Italy's gondolas looks, uncomprehending, at the body of an Italian he has killed. What on earth made him come to die in a Russian winter? "The blue skies of Italy" are glazed in the open eyes of a corpse freezing on the plains.[31] Interrogations of German prisoners-of-war increased amazement. Prisoners had no knowledge of Hitler's works and little of German classical literature and music. The reasons they gave for the invasion – booty and living space – seemed fatuous in the context of such carnage.

This sense of bewilderment, however, soon gave way to hatred. The plight of Russian territories liberated in December 1941 decisively altered attitudes. Apart from hangings, rape and requisitions, the Germans had desecrated Tolstoy's home at Yasnaya Polyana, destroyed churches in Novgorod, looted Tchaikovsky's house at Klin. The first evidence was discovered of the extermination of the Jews and of the starvation of Russian prisoners. The cumulative impact of such scenes throughout the war is difficult to over-exaggerate. The Red Army marched through its own razed villages and towns, unearthed pits containing the bodies of its own countrymen, witnessed the devastation of its fields and the malnutrition and famine of its own people and

eventually stood aghast at Mauthausen, Maidanek and Auschwitz. The Germans appeared to be unthinking instruments of
a cruel machine bent only on destruction. Indeed Grossman is the
only Russian writer who tentatively explores the philosophy of
Fascism. In *For a Righteous Cause* Peter Bach's disgust with
Nazism is slowly eroded by public opinion, the omnipresence and
omnipotence of the Party and the prodigious achievement of the
German army. Having reached the Volga, he questions the
self-pride which his spiritual opposition to the regime has given
him and senses the ecstasy of power: "Suddenly out of the dirt and
the smoke, this foreign sky and immense alien land which lay
vanquished became physically palpable to him and in that instant
his entire being felt the grim power wielded by that cause of which
he was a part." The exercise of brute force has its delights: "All
that power which slumbered in *Beyond Good and Evil* . . . , in Fichte,
was today physically marching across the plains."

Most writers, however, were more concerned with the effects
than with the psychological nuances of Nazism. The realisation
that they were being treated as "sub-humans" led to an ironic
reversal of the popular images associated with East and West.
The Germans were compared to the hordes of Genghis Khan and
Russia became the bastion of civilisation. In 1941 Lebedev-
Kumach, launching the concept of a Holy War in a poem of that
name, called upon Russia to destroy "the accursed horde" and
"the dark power" of Fascism.[32] The conflict was less ideological
than Biblical, a clash between Darkness and Light. Pasternak
adapted Biblical imagery to the battle of Stalingrad in his poem
"Revivified Fresco" (1944). For Berggol'ts the war was a "hallowed, righteous battle".[33] The poet Prokof'ev saw it as a fight
against "evil and darkness"[34] waged on Russian soil which Tvardovsky described as "hallowed and pure".[35] In his story, *The
Meeting* (1942/3), Tikhonov compared besieged Leningrad to
Troy, while the siege itself was associated with Hell: "It is as if
ancient things had crawled forth – / Foes, blockade and
darkness."[36]

Written in July 1941, Surkov's *A Soldier's Oath* expressed a
loathing of the Germans which soon became endemic: "The blood
of defiled and murdered mothers, wives and sisters, the blood of
slain children has coagulated and become in my heart a clot of
immeasurable hatred." The incantatory quality of Surkov's prose
reflected the quasi-religious terms in which the war was popularly

viewed. Whereas little animosity was displayed against Italians and Rumanians, Russian detestation of the Germans was unabating. Quoting from captured documents, diaries and letters and also from SS publications, Ehrenburg conducted a masterly campaign of mockery and vituperation against the master-race in the press. The spleen of his article, *Kill!* (24 July 1942), retains its power today.[37] Literature itself became saturated with hatred. Aliger defined it as "unerring gun-fire".[38] A character in *Under Siege* is possessed by it: hatred is "a living creature which stirred in her breast and made her body shake from head to toe". Wassilewska's *The Rainbow*, an unrelieved catalogue of German atrocities, nevertheless conveys the popular spirit of brooding malevolence. The Germans patrol a village at night:

> It was as bright as day. The moon's light gushed and blinded, spilling the lustre of silver glance over the entire area. The columns of light blazed: they had never seen such light before. In the moonlight the snow, azure snow, scintillated and its blueness was alien to them. And the snow ground beneath their feet: the frost was of an intensity they had never known and never suspected. Not a soul anywhere: only peasant shacks watching the road and the pupils of their frozen windows resembled human eyes.[39]

The demand for vengeance was equally unrelenting. The Old Testament code of an eye for an eye, wrote Inber, offered inadequate compensation for the horror of Leningrad's blockade. Germany would pay "in hundreds" for each Russian death.[40] Revenge, declared Antokol'sky, is "sweeter than a lovers' meeting", it is "incorruptible and inflexible". Tvardovsky sought "death for death! Blood for blood! Grief for grief!" Surkov describes a mundane scene of 1941 and draws the inevitable conclusion: "In the wind the poplar shivers, chilled and dying. / The windows are opened wide. The dark peasant home is empty. / A mother weeps over the body of her dead son. / An orphan wanders off aimlessly, at random. / Our burier, the raven, grey from hot ashes, / Drops into the black night from the charred gates . . . / Our people will pay this bloody account / With fire, steel and inordinate revenge."

These attitudes were a defence-mechanism against unwarranted aggression and barbarous inhumanity. The Germans, wrote Sobolev in *One Wish* (1942), "possess neither human heart nor human mind. A steel axe feels nothing when it shatters living tissue and cuts short human life".[41] The story is about an orphaned boy who has seen his father, the president of a collective farm, tied to two German tanks and torn apart. In *The Science of Hatred* Russian prisoners-of-war are crushed for sport by German tanks. In *The Rainbow* a pregnant partisan is stripped and made to run naked in the snow. She gives birth in a barn under the eyes of jeering troops and is then bayoneted and thrown into an ice-hole with her dead child. The theme of Antokol'sky's "The Undispatched Letter" (1944) is a German slave-market where five hundred Ukrainian girls and five hundred Russian youths are sold like goods and chattels in a circus. Sel'vinsky's "I Saw It" (1942) records his impressions when seven thousand bodies were unearthed at Bagerovo: "They lie, they sit, they crawl up towards the parapet. / Each has his own gesture, / wondrously personal! / Winter has frozen in the corpse / the man's feeling at his death. / And so the bodies rave, threaten, hate ... / This deathly silence wrangles like a meeting."[42] By the time Grossman described with clinical fury the obscenity of Treblinka the "fictional" horrors of *The Rainbow* had long been a feature of Russian life. The threat people felt was the physical extinction of Russia. When Dovzhenko's native village was razed, he felt "that it was not my village which was perishing, but the entire nation". His own sufferings epitomised the nation's agony throughout the long war:

> I too burned in that fire then, I too perished together with the people, the animals and the plants. I blazed like a tree, like a church, I swayed on the gallows and dispersed into the dust and smoke of catastrophic explosions. ... from my muscle and shattered bones they made soap in mid-twentieth-century Western Europe. My skin was used for book-bindings and lamp-shades: my skin also lay along the paths of war, filthy, trampled and flattened by the heavy tanks of humanity's last war.[43]

The ferocity of the struggle in Russia necessitated total commitment. There were no vacillations or qualms of conscience about killing. In *The Divisional Commander* (1944) Berezko compares the aesthetic pleasure which his hero has in observing the execution of his battle-plan to that of a composer hearing a performance of his symphony. The odd reference to the German proletariat emphasises by its rarity the absence of a sense of international brotherhood. Writers identified with their country's struggle for life and discovered their birthright not in the First World War but in the Napoleonic War. Vershigora found the works of Remarque and Hemingway irrelevant, while Yury Krymov in his *Letters from the Front* (1944) noted that "Remarque's *All Quiet on the Western Front* is totally at variance with my impressions. *War and Peace* is much closer."[44]

For Russian writers the Great Patriotic War was a just war which demanded not only an excoriation of the invader, but also a homage to the suffering and endurance of the people, a commemoration of the dead and a celebration of victory.

As the army marched through burned villages in 1943, Kazakevich, numbed by the condition of peasants living in dug-outs like "troglodytes", observed that their grief was matched by "an endurance to which there really is no limit".[45] Simple fortitude becomes a major literary theme. In her poem "To a German Woman" (1942) Aliger embodies in her own sorrow the plight of many Russian women. She has lost both husband and child, but is still eager to struggle on. Kataev's novel, *Son of the Regiment* (1944), provided the customary biography of the many children who figure in the literature of the times. The boy's father was killed at the front. His mother was shot. Others in the family die of hunger. He fends for himself until he attaches himself to a military or partisan unit. Writers spontaneously attempt to generalise personal grief. When Taras in *The Undefeated* goes to find food, he joins a phalanx of peasants with wheelbarrows which "squeaking and clattering rolled over the stones and dragged the exhausted, sweaty, dust-blackened people behind them". Antokol'sky's *Son* (1943), written on the death of his own boy, is informed with the humanity of Russian family life, while his son's delight in woodwork and stamps, the excitements of his first drink and first love, the "manly" letters he writes home from basic training do not differentiate his brief life from that of millions. In poems like "The Mother" (1942) Surkov "freezes" a commonplace event and gives it the universality of a Dutch painting: "A camp-fire's smoke. A heap of damp greatcoats. / The comfortless life of a soldier. / A woman, come from 'over there', / Mourns her dead daughter. / Her voice is more muffled than the forest's murmer. / It rustles like withered grass. / Her still, sad words / Scorch our souls with pain." Grief's anodyne is the consciousness of its universality and of the general will to endure and overcome.

The stoicism of front-line literature is most strikingly expressed in attitudes to death. Vershigora jovially relates that in 1941 he rose within ten days from platoon to battalion commander. Nekrasov strikes a sour note as Kerzhentsev prepares for another costly attack in Stalingrad. If there are eighty men in his "battalion", then the regiment has about 240 in all. Add about one hundred signals, scouts etc. "But how many are fit? Not more than a third'." Elsewhere the mood is almost always fatalistic. Fear becomes so habitual that Sel'vinsky in his poem, "Fear" (1942), likens it to a minor physical ailment. It is "the chronic catarrh of the front-line trooper". Surkov explains the syndrome. Asleep, the soldiers dream of "mutilated bodies on the black mutilated earth". They awaken with but one thought – to remain alive until nightfall. They fall asleep with a prayer to survive until morning. They dream ... We scamper "over the phases of the day / Like hamsters over a wheel", Surkov wrote in an untitled poem of 1943. "We swilled down the icy vodka / and with my knife I picked the foreign blood out from my finger-nails", declared Gudzenko in "Before the Attack" (1942). Indifference to spilling German blood was matched by the cool fatalism with which they shed their own. Sometimes this coolness verges upon indifference as it does in a scene described by Surkov in 1943. The snow is spattered with a "bloody dew", sleek dogs, gorged on human flesh, roam the battle-field beneath a black cloud of carrion-crows, while the troops nonchalantly march past chatting about personal matters. Often the fatalism is moving. Surkov's "To Outsiders" (1942) announced: "We bloody soldiers are candidates for death, / We stand in fate's queue for our turn." *For a Righteous Cause* portrays the stand made by Rodimtsev's 13th Guards Division at Stalingrad. A battalion advances into the German lines and the men, awaiting the inevitable counter-attack and certain of their own death, talk to each other in the past tense: "'I was a widower and never had kids,' said Rezchikov ... 'Oh, mate, I used to love vodka, I supped it like a bitch does milk and, as for women, they never did me any wrong'."

The epitome of Russian nerve, however, was Leningrad. During the siege, at its worst in the savage winter of 1941–42, between eight hundred thousand and a million Russians died from bombing, shelling and starvation. Without electricity, fuel and water, daily rations down to one hundred and fifty grammes per person, Leningrad became a ghost city. Chukovsky likened it to a submerged town in which the gait of its starving citizens was so slow "that they seemed to be moving through dense water".[46] Chakovsky's description is similar: "It was if I was reading some fantastic novel about the earth's last days, about life's extinction as a result of some cosmic cooling process and cities standing devoid of life and covered in snow."[47] Berggol'ts saw it as a necropolis whose inanimate features had also become unreal: "Everything in the city was dead or, better, seemed transported to 'another world' where everything . . . is different: the same, but soulless."[48] Lost in "eternal night and frozen stars, / eternal moonlit snow and ice",[49] paralysed by bitter frosts, Leningrad resembled a vast sarcophagus.

According to Ketlinskaya, people, exhausted by hunger and cold, died "quietly, soundlessly like candles burning out". In such conditions death had its attractions even for Berggol'ts, her mood of still submissiveness being followed by a desire "to melt into those huge drifts, into the purple-bricked, hoar-frosted warehouses, into the lowering slate sky". At first women took their dead to cemeteries, but, as famine became chronic, the dead were left lying in the snow or in their apartments. Economy of effort and of emotion became the law of survival. In "The Blockade" (1943) the poet Shishova explained: "We shall not even nod in greeting, / saying good-bye we shall not wave a hand."[50] Crossing to unoccupied territory Inber was struck by the rapid speech and deep breathing of people there. In Leningrad, where the trite expression "gnawed by hunger" became a reality as muscular distrophy crippled thousands, speech was so soft that the breath released was barely visible even in winter. Only the most pressing need dictated activity. Gazing fixedly ahead, their faces swathed in bands against the wind, people would go for water to the ice-holes in the Neva or pull a sledge with a body to the cemetery, no longer stopping when others fell exhausted or dead. Few were strong enough to make coffins and the coffin-maker would demand payment in bread. In her "Leningrad Poem" (1942) Berggol'ts relates a harrowing incident when, having collected her bread-ration, she met a neighbour whose daughter had died. More concerned with the needs of the living, Berggol'ts refused her friend's request for bread for a coffin: "As if on the world's edge / alone, in the fog, savagely quarrelling, / two women walked side by side, / two mothers, two women of Leningrad. / And, like a mad woman, / she long entreated me, bitterly, timidly."

A scene from *Under Siege* incapsulates the city's plight. A soldier, Kocharyan, has lost his wife in the bombing and returns in search of his son, Stasik, who is in a children's home. The streets are deserted: a solitary lorry passes by carrying corpses. At his ruined home he helps two weak girls extricate a beam for firewood. He learns from a neighbour of Stasik's whereabouts and of the cemetery where his wife was taken. Against his neighbour's advice he sets out for the cemetery and begins to overtake people harnessed to sledges on which appear to be the swaddled bodies of children. They are in fact adults whom emaciation has shrunk. Bodies line the road to the cemetery and inside they lie in huge piles. He abandons his search for his wife and goes to the children's home, bursting into tears when he is asked if he is the child's father. A nurse puts him up for the night and only in the morning does he find the bodies of her father and mother carefully laid out on the kitchen table: "I thought you wouldn't have stayed if ...". He is accustomed to death, but its casualness in a civilian context seems sacrilegious and arouses in him an anger and hatred deeper and more bitter than he had known at the front.

However, the most impressive feature of Leningrad life was the will to endure. An awareness of the imminence of death seemed to purify the spirit and rebaptize the five senses. Platitudes, wrote Shishova, like "Thank you", "My dear" and "Have a good journey" were spoken with a "special intonation" which restored "the lost but original meaning of words". The heroine of Chakovsky's novel remarks upon this lucidity: "One sees through to the depths of language. Everything has become as clear as crystal, like the ice on Ladoga." In a city which consumed everything – dogs, cats, birds, glue and belts – the rye bread brought across Ladoga became an object of reverence. Inber described it as "sacred" bread, "whiter than snow".[51]

The city rallied. The young succoured the sick and cleaned the flats. Some factories still functioned. Tikhonov's *A Winter's Night* (1942) is set in one such factory which resembles "a cave of stalactites. ... The dark sky showed through the shell-holes: a satin surface of ice covered the vaults and walls." A worker collapses and dies with the words, "My soul's ablaze."[52] Berggol'ts' "Leningrad Poem" illustrates just how "the spirit, holding fast, overcame the body's treacherous impotence." Ketlinskaya referred to the prevalent "feeling of freedom and independence from the body" resulting in an almost religious love of the city: "This is our city. It cannot be taken by storm, nor by intimidation. Nor by famine. We shall stand firm. We shall endure." Chakovsky defines its eerie spiritual power: "The city seems empty. After dusk one doesn't see any people and one never sees troops. But the city cannot be taken. It is as if its defenders were invisible. Touch it and it will kill."

Broadcasting on 20 September 1942 Berggol'ts claimed that an umbilical cord united Leningrad and Stalingrad. The resistance and self-sacrifice of each were spontaneous. Each exhibited a spirit which inspired and unified the nation.

In Nekrasov's novel two soldiers at Stalingrad disguss the land's fertility. There is a warmth in their voices: "Tolstoy called it the latent heat of patriotism. It could well be that this was the miracle ... which would prove more powerful than German organisation and tanks with black crosses." Patriotism was the decisive factor in this battle described by Grossman as an elemental conflict between two states "locked in a life-and-death struggle waged with a mathematical, pedantic exactitude for a storey of a house, for a cross-roads". On New Year's day 1943 he listened to a record of one of Beethoven's Irish Drinking Songs:

> Milady Death, we beg you,
> Tarry outside the door.

The words and the naive genius of Beethoven's music rang out with indescribable power. This was perhaps for me one of the greatest experiences of the war, for at war a man knows many passionate, joyful or bitter feelings, he knows hatred and anguish, grief and fear, love and pity and vengeance. But sadness is a rare visitor. Yet in those words, in that music of a heart's lament, in that condescending, ironic request:

> Milady Death, we beg you,
> Tarry outside the door,

there was an inexpressible strength, a sadness that was noble. ... The soldiers listened to it as solemnly as they would a church service, men who had spent three months face to face with death in that ruined, maimed building which had not yielded to Fascists.[53]

Likened by Simonov to an unbroken series of "cairns haphazardly raised over houses which had gone underground",[54] Stalingrad was to engender the same legend of indomitable courage as Leningrad did. Like the people of Leningrad, the troops felt isolated and left to their own devices. Isolation fostered independence and cameraderie. Life was reduced to basics and the formalities of military custom were largely abandoned. Rank became less important. According to Grossman, who was present throughout the battle, there existed "a brotherhood and equality amongst all the men at Stalingrad – from trooper to general".[55] Russian morale is nowhere better illustrated than in the closing pages of *For a Righteous Cause* which describe the destruction of one of Rodimtsev's battalions. All differences between regular, conscript and penal troops suspended, communications with divisional headquarters severed, conversing in the past tense, the men die doggedly unyielding and serene. His comrades dead, the peasant Vavilov climbs out of his shell-hole with a grenade: "Submachine-guns ... avidly rattled their fire at him... , and when he disappeared from view, it was as if he had not collapsed like a clod of dead, bloody flesh, but had melted into the dusty, milky-yellow mist which eddied and gleamed in the rays of the morning sun."

The tension created by the ordeal of the two cities was immense. There was a palpable excitement in the air and an awareness of the nation's historical destiny. Berggol'ts felt that she was living on a different plane of experience: "And time shall be no more.... I know exactly how this happens.... Time stopped, it contracted and became a single point of radiating light within me. Time and being were one. And the barriers between art and life, between past, present and future joyfully collapsed." She talks of a new psychic dimension which enabled her to enjoy "all of life simultaneously, all its poetry and all its tragedy". In "The Third Zone", a poem of 1942, she heard a stringed instrument at the front and wrote: "Life will simply incandesce and cease abruptly, like a string full of song." "Your Journey" (1945) describes a happiness which was "untender, stern and sleepless". Although it may at times "have ruin in attendance," it nevertheless transports one to "peaks so solitary, tender and bare/ that the gods would envy them". Tikhonov's *The Apple Tree* (1942) is about a dejected Leningrad artist who, returning home after an air-raid, sees an apple tree covered in frost and caught in moon-light: "The tree burned with a cold, wondrous light: like a white fire it cast snow-white flames which never for an instant ceased to blaze and gambol." Comforted by this symbol of Leningrad, he dismisses thoughts of leaving his "astounding world of beauty, heroism, toil and majesty".

Many factors contributed to this ecstatic, quasi-mystical mood. Aliger's "Your Victory" (1944–69) recalls the gentleness and fellowship of people at war. Everything was shared and "we became more expansive, simpler, younger", for "our love was more tender and our comrades more dear". Vershigora compared the moral integrity of his partisans to that of Leningrad. As Gudzenko declared in his "Ballad on Friendship" (1942–3) that "we nursed our friendship as jealously as infantrymen guard a metre of blood-stained earth", so Chakovsky observed that everyone in Leningrad possessed an emergency supply of cour-age, rarely used *in extremis* to save self, but ready to expend itself for others' sake.

However, the principal element in the euphoria was a deep pride in a common achievement. In "A Second Conversion with my Neighbour" (1944) Berggol'ts reminds her friend that "we whom life's humdrum cares intoxicated/took nameless heights/which are not mapped". Bek's Baurdzhan opined that Russians had never spoken of themselves so eloquently as on the battlefield. Sel'vinsky's "Letter" (1943) elevates this national pride into a sense of historical mission. Time lengthens in war: an hour in battle becomes eternity. Under such constant pressure a soldier adapts to timelessness. Self dissolves: a philosophical, eternal perspective obtains. Consciousness becomes selfless and one's being is "warmed by a secret flame". One is absorbed into history whose "battle-pitted, yet intimate face" one goes out to meet "as if it were the sole point of life". The troops, wrote Surkov in "Keys to the Heart" (1942), knew that they were "standing in the draught of great events,/Believing to the end in their star". Vishnevsky provided a more prosaic interpretation of the same patriotism. Neither Hoover nor Lady Astor could now deny that Russia had set the world an example and had emerged as one of the world's spiritual leaders.

After Stalingrad the patriotism inherent in all Soviet wartime literature becomes more buoyant and confident. Tvardovsky's "Vasily Tyorkin" (1941–45) is a nice blend of that realism and improbability characteristic of folklore. Tyorkin's pithy aphorisms and his musical talents, the aplomb with which he pees on the battle-field and bags an enemy plane with a rifle, his fondness for drink and physical strength, the modesty of his demeanour and derring-do in battle secured instant popularity and spawned many lesser Tyorkins.

Kozhevnikov's *Stories of the War Years* (1941–5) celebrate the versatility of the ordinary soldier. These cock-sure tales reflect the author's conviction, even in the darkest days, that the phlegm, inventiveness and courage of the Russian character would ultimately triumph. Kozhevnikov delights in eccentric characters and colourful situations. Russian troops advance under a drained lake's cracking ice; a sniper diets on vitamin pills and carrots; a fanatical mechanic is genuinely hurt to discover that a tank commander, whose tank he has lovingly repaired, has died in hospital.

This vein of unpretentious patriotism continues in such post-war works as Polevoy's novel, *A Real Man* (1946), his stories, *We are Soviet Citizens* (1948), and Panova's *Travelling Companions* (1946). Polevoy's stories are based on actual events and his novel is the biography of the Russian counterpart of Douglas Bader – Aleksey Mares'ev who, despite the loss of both legs below the knee, resumed his career as a fighter-pilot. The matter-of-fact manner in which the pilot's crawl to the safety of a Russian village is described precludes any romanticism and relates exceptional heroism to a common fund of Russian valour. Panova's novel is set in a hospital-train. The personnel ranges from a representative of the Leningrad intelligentsia to the social flotsam and jetsam who service the train. Few have common interests, but the exacting daily routine of nursing, amputations and operations welds this motley assemblage into an efficient, proud unit.

Startlingly different is Leonov's *The Capture of Velikoshumsk* (1944), a Gogolian, romantic commemoration of Russian prowess, loosely based on the fighting at Zhitomir in the winter of 1943. Written with all Leonov's verbal virtuosity and rhetoric, its characters in the heroic mould, the novel pays homage to a veteran tank, No. 203, whose exploits are so awesome that mechanics doff their caps when it arrives for repairs. The tank becomes a personality in its own right, wreaks havoc behind enemy lines and finally dies a martyr's death in a literal blaze of glory.

The poetic counterpart of Leonov's patriotic celebration of victory is Prokof'ev's famous "Russia" (1944) in which the country's diversity – its trees, plains, its wheat and industrial produce, its heterogeneous people and monolithic Party – is synthesised and given a timeless pedigree by the evocative use of the imagery, vocabulary and metres of Russian folklore, song and epic. Indeed, a deep love of the land and countryside is common to all writers. The landscape constitutes a permanence and a continuity of life of which the troops crave to become a part again. The flora and fauna of the countryside awaken a longing for peace and a nostalgia for home and family. The men identify with the eternal urge of plant and animal to survive and live. In Surkov's "A Battle in the Forests near Polotsk" (1944) morning breaks, the battle quietens and the soldiers realise "that the woodpecker is at work like a sprightly carpenter...; / that a canvas of blue shows through the branches; / that the road to the next battle is shorter; / that life is immortal and in its name / we shall still serve our country".

Tyorkin also claimed that he fought "not for fame, but for life on this earth".[56] As the war drew to its close, it was viewed less as a struggle for national survival than as a victory of humanity and civilisation over barbarism, a victory to which Russia had made the greatest contribution. Although no open animosity is displayed towards the allies in the literature of 1941–6, their failure to open a second front until 1944 indubitably rankled. Vishnevsky's belief that the allies would fight to "the last drop of the Russian soldier's blood" and that their intention was "to put Germany in its coffin and Russia in hospital"[57] was confined to his diaries and expressed a rancour which Stalin was to exploit after the war. Published literature, however, limited its exasperation to occasional references to the comparatively minuscule scale of the fighting in North Africa and to Stalin's remark that the partisans would have to serve as a second front. Nevertheless, there was a proud consciousness that Russia had borne the brunt of the war and had been mankind's principal standard-bearer. In January 1942 Inber noted: "The USSR is being called the Saviour of Mankind and indeed it is so." Sel'vinsky's poem, "To Russia" (1942), argued that the defeat of Russia would rob the world of hope, for Russia had become "Humanity". Indeed, Leonov's claim in his novel of 1944 that the Russian victory "had opened our eyes wide in astonishment at ourselves and at the world" indentifies the two main trends in Russian literature at the end of the war.[58] The first is a strong sense of national identity and unity based upon a rediscovery and love of the ordinary people of Russia. The second is a heightened awareness of Russia's international prestige and standing, a feeling that the country did uphold common human values against barbarism and that, after its own pre-war dark age, it was again ready to make a contribution to the comity of nations.

These ambitions were to be frustrated. During the Cold War the Party resumed its ascendancy. The awesome power of the state ended the wartime partnership between Party and people and stifled democratic aspirations "akin to those entertained by young officers returning to Russia after the campaign abroad in 1815".[59] The transformation of patriotism into rabid nationalism and a propaganda campaign to "reconstruct" the country obviated discussion of the Party's pre-war and wartime miscalculations and silenced demobilised soldiers who had sampled higher standards of life in Eastern Europe and an intelligentsia dangerously preoccupied with "truth". The claustrophobic normalcy of the 1930s returned. Chauvinistic obscurantists like Aleksandrov and Lysenko dominated the arts and sciences. The Leningrad Case of 1949–50 and the "Doctors' Plot" of 1952–53 reflected renewed political in-fighting and initiated fresh waves of arrests. An "anti-cosmopolitan" campaign of a distinctly anti-Semitic character was launched to eradicate western cultural influences and neuter the culture of the minority peoples of the Soviet Union. In his novel *Quiet* (1964) Bondarev describes the reactions of a demobilised soldier as follows: "There had been four years of lull ... the defence had been stubborn. ... Now forces which Sergei could not resist were surrounding him ...".[60]

By 1949 a series of Party decrees inspired by Zhdanov in 1946 had uprooted "cosmopolitanism" in Soviet theatre, literature and cinema with devastating effects upon war literature. The post-war works of Nekrasov, Kazakevich and Vershigora were part of the "stubborn defence" which nursed the spirit of front-line literature. Grossman's *For a Righteous Cause* was a remarkable anomaly in 1952.

Such works, however, became unpalatable. To appease Stalin's wrath at the political implications of his *Two Men on the Steppe* Kazakevich wrote the dishonest *Spring on the Oder* (1949). Kataev's *For the Power of the Soviets!* (1949), an inventive story of underground resistance in Odessa, was deemed to lack a proper assessment of the Party's role. A second version appeared in 1951 involving both Stalin and Khrushchev in the action. Fadeyev's *Young Guard* was also considered unworthy of such a pillar of the literary establishment. Consequently in the re-written version of 1951 the ineffective Party of 1945 appears as the mentor of the Young Guard. After a savage attack by Bubennov, Grossman undertook to re-write his novel.

Orthodox post-war literature therefore is indeed "fiction" in the pejorative sense of "deceit, dissimulation, pretence" (*OED*). In works like Il'enkov's *The Main Road* (1949), Kazakevich's *Spring on the Oder*, Bubennov's *The Silver Birch* (Part 1, 1947; Part 2, 1950), Biryukov's *The Seagull* (1950) and Popovkin's *The Rubanyuk Family* (1951) the Party's military omniscience eliminates all dramatic tension, and history is accommodated to the current Party "image". In Kazakevich's novel Nazi provocateurs rather than Russians commit atrocities on German soil, Berlin falls with minimal losses and the officer who repatriates Russian prisoners-of-war is "proud and happy" in his "historic role".[61] Bubennov's immense work illustrates the degeneration of the war novel. It opens with an excellent account of the ferocity of the German attack at Rzhev in 1941. At the end of Part I, however, the hero's regiment, having broken out of encirclement in the most unlikely fashion and untroubled by *Smersh* investigators, is inspired by Stalin's November speech to stand firm against the foe. Part II demonstrates the Party's preparedness for war, reflected in its far-sighted organisation of a superb partisan movement, and the strategic genius of Stalin who master-minds the Russian counter-offensive.

This distortion of history also necessitated the deflation of the war hero. Writers were encouraged to enhance the role of the civilian population. The result was a spate of long, tedious novels like Panfyorov's *Battle for Peace* (1947), Pavlenko's *Happiness* (1947), Azhaev's *Far from Moscow* (1948), Babayevsky's *Cavalier of the Golden Star* (1948) and Medynsky's *Mar'ya* (1950). Often contrasting the fickle instability, albeit temporary, of the demobil-ised soldier with the enduring ideological rectitude of the civilian, these effete and tendentious novels totally fail to convey the magnitude of the civilian war effort.

In short, "orthodox" war literature became an instrument of Party propaganda and the war itself a retrospective extension of the Cold War. Writers lambasted the West, interpreted Fascism as the creature of American capitalism, wallowed in a self-glorifying nationalism akin to Nazism and deified Stalin. Like their pre-war equivalents, the novels are based on the "no-conflict'" concept of a society so sagely organised that disagreements may arise only between the good and the excellent, and are populated by smug, self-righteous people of astonishing sexlessness. Resembling literary dinosaurs in their massive, uncoordinated bulk and minuscule intellectual content, works like those of Panfyorov and Babayevsky were soon to become by-words of sycophancy and pretentiousness.

Once the principle of Stalin's infallibility was challenged, the artificial life of the "orthodox" novel ended. Khrushchev's "secret speech" of 1956 demolished Stalin's military and political authority and generated numerous articles and memoirs critical of his military competence.

Literature inevitably followed suit. Even such apparently uncontentious works as Bondarev's *Last Salvoes* (1959), Sokolov's *The Invasion* (1963) and Anan'ev's *The Tanks Move in Diamond Formation* (1963) put much more emphasis on the people's contribution to the war than on the Party's. Elsewhere the perspective changes. A new "humanism" appears; experience of war is particularised rather than generalised and the country's political problems come to the fore. Indeed, those objections to Party policy earlier raised by Nekrasov, Dovzhenko and Kazakevich were bound to revive. Once that fear of national extinction which had produced the thematic homogeneity of wartime literature had disappeared, political issues, formerly considered of secondary importance, but very much alive two decades later, had to re-emerge. The resultant concentration on "secondary" issues, often criticised as "unhistorical", was the inescapable outcome of the anaesthetisation of wartime tensions.

Hatred of the Germans, however, remains a constant theme. If Kuznetsov's *Babi Yar* (1966), a documentary novel about life in occupied Kiev, is the most detailed account of the effects of German atrocities, then perhaps Bogomolov's classic story, *Ivan* (1958), is the most incisive. Ivan is an eleven-year-old boy employed as a scout. His father and young sister have been killed and his mother is missing. He has fought with the partisans and been in a death-camp. This "pre-history" is never described. His conduct attests its effect. He is inordinately proud and peremptory. Icy self-control follows childish misbehaviour. He collects knives and takes vodka with his meals. His spiritual sustenance is hatred and his exploits have given him the authority of a senior officer. The soldiers' attitude to him is a mixture of awe, tenderness and guilt. Eventually he is sent to a military school but absconds. After the war it is revealed that, caught watching a railway line in the winter of 1943, his fingers and toes gangrened, insolent under questioning, he was shot.

Other writers introduce motifs new to war literature. Okudzhava's *Good Health, Scholar* (1961) and Nekrasov's *Second Night* (1962) were censured for "anachronistic" pacifism. In each the presentation of war is restricted to the view-point of a raw recruit. The schoolboy still longs for his home, falls adolescently in love and is preoccupied with the state of his boots and his loss of a spoon. Okudzhava's disregard of broader national and military perspectives and his more explicit attitude towards sex were clearly designed to shock, while the personalisation of war accentuates the impact and consequences of an excessive death-toll: "Schoolboys crawling along the trenches, dying of wounds, returning home without arms and legs.... A young girl as a sergeant-major.... What has happened?"[62] In Nekrasov's story Len'ka Bogorad is taken by Captain Orlik on his second day at the front to locate the position of enemy mine-fields and to capture a German for interrogation. The plan goes wrong and Len'ka has to strangle the German. Later Orlik ostentatiously displays the man's belongings and Len'ka feels disgust and shame. The narrowing of perspective magnifies the scale of an isolated event. War appears vile.

Greater attention is also paid to the personal reasons which determined the behaviour of the civilian population under German rule. In Nilin's *Through the Cemetery* (1962) the once clearly defined concept of loyalty blurs as Nilin, like Dovzhenko, explores the social fissures in the countryside. Sazon Ivanych, whose brother was sent to Siberia, is witheringly critical of the regime:

patriotism alone moves him to help the partisans. They in turn rely upon the services of a mechanic who has lost two sons in their ranks. His wife therefore does not welcome their arrival, fearing for her third son who is a Christian and is appalled by the reprisals which the exploits of the partisans provoke against the villages. Eva, the widow of a partisan, was expelled from the Party in the thirties. She aids the partisans, but finds German society congenial and has German lovers.

The change of emphasis, however, is most tangible in the presentation of the relationship between Party and people. Russian policy from 1937 to 1942 is now savaged. If "orthodox" literature interpreted the Russo-German agreement as a gambit whereby Stalin gained time to prepare for the war he foresaw, post-Stalin writings insist that his inane faith in its inviolable legitimacy cost millions of lives. Thus his failure to respond to the imminence of invasion is comprehensively portrayed in such works as Smirnov's *In Search of the Heroes of the Brest Fortress* (1957), Kaverin's *Seven Unclean Couples* (1961), Yarmagaev's *When We Matured* (1962), Vorob'ev's *Killed at Moscow* (1963), Baklanov's *July 1941* (1965) and Rozen's *The Last Two Weeks* (1965). Baklanov's novel incapsulates most of the obloquy. Russia continues its grain supplies to Germany despite the obvious concentration of German forces at the frontier. Reports by commanders are ignored and insistent warnings lead to dismissal and arrest for provocation and panic. The old frontier defences have been dismantled, although fortification of the new frontier is incomplete. Russia's humiliation is reflected in her communiqué of 14 July which dismissed rumours of war as provocation. As the Germans were uninterested in denying the rumours, the Russians act "on their behalf".[63] Rozen's novel explores the pre-war atmosphere of terror which aggravated the effects of Stalin's misjudgments. Gleb Zimin is recalled from his trade delegation in Berlin to investigate Russian complaints of faults in an imported German turbine. Stalin declares the complaint "provocation" and Gleb is involved in an NKVD investigation designed to cast the anti-Nazi manager of the German firm and his Russian counterpart as provocateurs and fellow-conspirators.

There is scarcely a novel which does not touch upon the devastating repercussions of the military purges. A common figure is the officer arrested in 1937 and released between 1939 and 1941. Serpilin, the hero of Simonov's massive trilogy: *The*

*Living and the Dead* (1959), *People are not Born Soldiers* (1964) and *The Last Summer* (1970), was arrested in 1937 because of the suspicion aroused by his study of German military strategy and theory. Objective assessments of Germany's military strength and intentions similarly led to the arrest on charges of treasonable connections with German Intelligence of General Balashov in Zlobin's *Missing* (1964). Indeed the many casual references which the heroine of Rzhevskaya's *From Home to the Front* (1965) makes to the sackings and arrests of her friends' relatives illustrate the virulence of the social cancer.

The loyalty of these "politically suspect elements" during the war highlights the tragedy and waste of the many gifted officers of the Tukhachevsky school who perished in the camps. In *People are not Born Soldiers* Simonov claims that a review of 225 regimental commanders after the Finnish War revealed that none had attended the Frunze Academy and only twenty-five had been to a military college. Baklanov's *July 1941* and Simonov's *Panteleyev* (1961) detail the incompetence and pusillanimity of prematurely promoted and inexperienced officers who "fear reporting failure more than failure itself, fear responsibility for losses more than actual losses".[64]

The psychological consequences of the 1930s were no less debilitating than the loss of qualified personnel. Shalayev of the Special Section in Baklanov's novel explains the Russian débâcle as the result of that treasonable conspiracy whose eradication in 1937 had been too lenient! This might appear to be an author's flight of fancy, were it not for the abundant evidence of endemic suspicion furnished by these novels. In Solzhenitsyn's "Incident at Krechetovka Junction" (1963) circumstantial evidence persuades the good-natured Kotov to surrender an old actor to the Special Department. Simonov's *The Living and the Dead* is a caustic indictment of political lunacy in 1941. 150 men, the remains of Serpilin's division, accompanied by stragglers, break out of encirclement, weapons and standard intact. They are isolated, disarmed and sent to the rear for questioning. A jam at a bridge bisects the column and those stranded are mown down unarmed by encircling German troops. The novel itself hinges on the fate of Sintsov whose Party documents are taken by a friend, when he is left for dead. He recovers consciousness, but, returning to Russian lines, is taken for a spy and then for a coward who has buried his documents. Party officials shun him and requests for re-entry are refused.

The Party's harsh treatment of Russian prisoners-of-war also re-emerges. Two works by Pilyar, *All This Took Place* (1955) and *People Remain People* (1966), and Zlobin's *Missing* are based on their authors' experiences in German camps. Pilyar himself was sentenced to hard labour in the Urals after his release. The books pay tribute to those Russians who did not succumb to the blandishments of the Vlasov forces. As so many of them were victims of the military ineptitude of a Soviet government which disowned them, it is astonishing not that so many joined Vlasov, but that so few did. Treated by the Germans as sub-humans, placed in penal battalions on escape, despised by the troops who freed them, were these millions of loyal Russians, Zlobin asks, "cowards or traitors?"[65] Indeed, a few writers broached the subject of Vlasov's army. In Kalinin's *Bleak Fields* (1958) the hero joins Vlasov's forces only to acquire arms and then desert. He fights with the Russians in Budapest, yet returns to his village in 1957, the implication being that he spent a decade in the Kolyma prison camp. Save for a brief comment in Bondarev's *Hot Snow* (1969) that there may have been political reasons for Vlasov's apostasy, Russian defections are mainly ascribed to German coercion rather than to a change in political allegiance. Writers generally confine their criticism to the Party's dogmatic and undiscriminating approach to *all* Russian prisoners-of-war.

As for the heavy toll which the war exacted in injury and life, anger replaces the stoicism of the forties. Odintsov's *The Breakthrough* (1966) describes the activities of a penal unit which is used as cannon-fodder. Simonov's *People are not Born Soldiers* underscores the waste of manpower involved in the ill-conceived counter-offensive of 1942 culminating in the slaughter at Kharkov where the average lieutenant's "life-span" before death or injury was nine days. Bondarev's *The Battalions Request Fire-Cover* (1957) is perhaps the most terse presentation of this common theme. Two battalions establish a beach-head across the Dnieper. Its maintenance requires artillery support which, although agreed, fails to materialise. Only thirty-six men survive. Although Iverzev, the divisional commander, is a careerist, willing to sacrifice men for the sake of success, his is not the ultimate responsibility. An "omniscient higher power"[66] had decreed a change of plan and the battalions were to be used to create a diversion. The story leaves an impression of remarkable courage and its ruthless exploitation.

Such abundant criticism, however, does not imply that Party members are *ipso facto* inhuman. Many of the stories' heroes are members. Rather, the conflict is between popular patriotism and this "higher power" which, akin to fate, moulds events into arbitrary patterns and whose sole aim seems to be self-assertion and self-perpetuation. In Baklanov's *The Dead Are Not Shamed* (1961) a depleted artillery division is suddenly ordered into battle. Unable to take up position, it is overrun and encircled. The men die bravely. Only one officer, Ishchuk, who deserts his men, escapes. He is interrogated by a team which includes Elyutin, a *Smersh* captain, whose function is to expose and investigate military incompetence. Ishchuk naturally wishes to conceal his cowardice. A coincidence of interests arises which shifts blame for the slaughter to the dead and Ishchuk finds himself relating "not what had taken place ... but what he thought Elyutin wanted to hear him say".[67]

Most writers had served in the war and were aware of the optimism which then obtained. Between the two periods, however, lay eight years of Stalinism. A country, inspired by the belief that the 1930s were over, returned to that dark age. This experience of hope frustrated now leads to a fundamental reappraisal of the war's significance and much bleaker conclusions. Elyutin belongs to a species of character which now becomes a constant, and the shadows which followed Kazakevich's Ogarkov across the plains acquire substance.

Simonov's *Levashov* (1961) presents a classic conflict between two antithetical social types. The first, Levashov, is thrust into prominence by the war. Although a patriot, he is true to the international ideals of the Party. He is a gregarious, popular and practical man who is tired of purely political activity and craves action at the front. Bastryukov is a man of the 1930s. He is a cowardly bureaucrat, a cynical careerist and a rabid nationalist. His closed world seems to be on the point of collapse in 1941–42, but, a master of political nuance and the timely denunciation, he intends to build a military career by employing the same arts. These two types represent major trends in Soviet society and are found in variations in the works of Adamovich, Baklanov, Kron, Bondarev, Bykov and others.

Kron's *The House and the Ship* (1964) establishes the parameters of the conflict. Gorbunov is the commander of a submarine who believes that his crew should be self-reliant and inwardly motivated. His men should never require a Tribunal to stiffen their resolve. The interdependence of a collective unit differentiates it from a "rabble" whose short-lived unity depends upon an externally imposed system of principles. Chance alone saves Gorbunov from the intrigues of his adversary, Selyanin, a Party functionary whose life of duplicity is determined by the attitude – "When authority puts a question ... try to guess just what it is they want to hear you say". Selyanin believes that the country's salvation has been its habituation to cynical, but unquestioning obedience. Russia endured because "at the outbreak of war it was held together, like an enormous barrel, by the iron hoops of the State machine".[68]

Bykov subtly develops the theme in five trenchant and dramatic stories – *The Third Flare* (1962), *A Page from the Front* (1963), *The Dead Feel No Pain* (1966), *Kruglyansky Bridge* (1966) and *Sotnikov* (1970). In all these tales, save the first, the characters who are morally wrong survive and the humanists are worsted. In *A Page from the Front* the cynical Blishchinsky returns to Russian lines, while Shcherbak dies covering his retreat. Sotnikov is hanged: Rybak deserts. In *The Dead Feel No Pain* Vasil'evich is hounded and abandoned by Sakhno, the president of a Tribunal who eventually collaborates. Twenty years later Vasil'evich meets a prosperous legal adviser who in looks and manner resembles Sakhno. He is unable to prove, however, that the man is in fact Sakhno. Kruglyansky bridge is a partisan target. To avoid reprisals, Maskalov and Tolkach try to destroy it without civilian aid. They fail and Maskalov dies. Later, Britvin's unprincipled exploitation of an idealistic local boy works. The bridge is blown and the boy killed. In disgust, Tolkach shoots and wounds Britvin. Judgment awaits the arrival of the commissar.

The outlook for Tolkach is not hopeful. If honour is the lot of the decent, power belongs to the unscrupulous. Such is the spirit of the times, the lesson of total war. Blishchinsky has grasped this harsh truth. Patriotism and heroism are "childish prattle". His aim is survival in order to "fasten like a tick on the new post-war life" and "preach what he does not believe in".[69] Sakhno's role is to unmask non-existent treason. The troops hate him as much as the Germans. The orders he issues lack sense and humanity, but their very absurdity emphasises his unquestioned authority. Indeed, the orders of both sides deny man's humanity. Vasil'evich captures a German whose kindness and musical skills appeal to the Russians. Yet when the latter are captured and Sakhno deserts, the German is instructed to shoot Vasil'evich and does so.

Tolkach becomes aware of "the perfidy of blind circumstance" which resulted in the death of Maskalov, the "best" of the partisans. But there is a logic in fate's caprice. It emerges when Britvin mocks Maskalov's humanism. This war is not about morality and the innocent are pawns: "What relevance has innocence? We are at war! Do the Germans worry who's guilty? They just kill. Fear's the secret of their success."[70] The humanist is caught in cross-fire. A boy is killed, but the bridge is blown. The best must die. A boy's idealism *will* be exploited; Maskalov's conscience *will* lead to his death. They are trapped between two warring forces which are basically similar. Total war teaches the art of survival through ruthless exploitation. Sakhno changes sides and indeed is interchangeable.

Nor are "tactical" compromises possible. To save his life, Rybak serves the Germans. His conversion is naturally insincere. His reasoning resembles Britvin's who despises an idealistic partisan hanged for refusing to acknowledge the Führer's authority. A mere lie would have saved his life. Sotnikov warns Rybak that the German "machine" will brook no such gambits. Rybak will serve it or be ground to dust. The choice, once made, is irrevocable and his destiny depends on which side wins. But Sotnikov's sole "human" gesture of independence from the murderous system is to kick the log from under him on the gallows.

The two sides become almost synonymous. Mezhirov describes the peace which came in 1945: "The same chill no-man's land, / The artillery blasted its own troops, / The sappers crawled back from their recce."[71] A demobilised soldier in Nekrasov's *Home Town* (1954), confronted by the effrontery of evil in post-war Russia, experiences the same sensation of incomprehension and limpness as he did when wounded: "One had a hand and now it's finished. It hangs like a whip."[72] Bondarev's *Quiet* identifies the menace which stalked society in 1949: "It was like a nightmare . . . the shadows of German helmets appearing on the parapet, Germans bursting into the dug-out."[73] A character in Pervomaisky's *Wild Honey* (1963) reels from the fanaticism of a commissar. He is a ten-year-old again, lost in a storm, unnerved by "a natural force, unwilling and unable to consider his plight because of its blind, inherent power".[74] The opposing forces are not dissimilar. Both are elementary and elemental.

Grossman's gaunt *Life and Fate* (1960), which the KGB confiscated and Mikhail Suslov, chief Politburo "ideologist", declared unfit for publication for two or three hundred years, elucidates the innuendoes and lays bare the allusions. Grossman compares the death-camps, social oppression, Caesarism and fanatical nationalism obtaining in both countries and concludes that the two systems of "national socialism" are congeneric. Stalingrad constituted a short-lived challenge to both dictatorships. Grekov, the commander of a doomed observation post behind enemy lines, embodies all that was best in the Stalingrad spirit – independence from and contempt for the Party, a rough humanism and democratic camaraderie, a fatalism based on a readiness to die for the compatriots he loves and a desperate, tired longing for freedom. In the context of the novel's values his death overshadows the destinies of the other main characters. Shtrum, a nuclear physicist, withstands attacks upon his work and refuses to recant until Stalin, alerted by Western interest in nuclear fission, personally offers him every amenity and Shtrum is reabsorbed into the system. Krymov, a coelacanthine Party official, both exhilarated and shocked by the spirit of Stalingrad, is, as he must be, arrested. Novikov, the commander of a tank corps, delays his advance by eight minutes in order to save lives. His commissar, a former Party boss, is awed by his decision but, nevertheless, denounces him and helps his own career. All lack the courage and independence of Grekov, and their fate seems pre-ordained, for Grossman's thesis is that once the Russian counter-offensive of November 19th 1942 had succeeded, the Party re-asserted its authority and pursued its own special goals. The war ceased to be a patriotic battle for freedom. In reality it became a fight for the extension of totalitarianism. The novel plots the erosion of patriotism and liberty, as a chauvinistic, anti-Semitic nationalism is deliberately grafted onto the cynical predatoriness of the 1930s. A German camp-commandant addresses a captured Bolshevik: "But should you win, then we shall perish to live in your victory. It's rather paradoxical: in losing the war we shall win it, we shall live on in a different form, but it will be the same thing in essence".[75]

The works of Grossman, Bykov and Baklanov are of a higher quality than most wartime prose. Only Nekrasov's novel and Kazakevich's *Star* could compare. Yet, as war fiction *per se*, they

are less convincing. The frequently made criticism that their
writings are unhistorical and anachronistic is unfair, but true.
Their fiction does lack the qualities which inform wartime literature. Fear of national extinction and the belief that Russia
had outlived the dark days of the thirties give the literature of the
war years a momentum and tension reflected in its stoical fatalism, its euphoria and sense of national mission. If fear provided
the initial impetus, it had, by the close of the war, been replaced
by an immense, but by no means insular, patriotic pride engendered by an awareness that Russia had repulsed a threat to
humanity and civilisation. The nation felt that it had put the
1930s behind it and had proved itself worthy of a place amongst its
peers. By the 1960s both the fears and the hopes of the forties had
simply been overtaken by time. The "thrust" of the later literature had to be different.

The prose of the post-Stalin period also lacks the peculiar
"context" which wartime fiction enjoyed. The poetry of the
forties enhances the prose. The verse of Berggol'ts, Surkov,
Gudzenko, Sel'vinsky, Inber and others is so vividly graphic and
immediate, so dramatic and emotive, that it becomes the norm or
touchstone which establishes the authenticity of war literature
proper. Wartime prose is inevitably judged by its proximity to the
qualities embodied in this verse and its survival today is
strangely dependent upon poetry.

The literature of the 1960s is totally independent of these
criteria. Twenty years later not only is the element of fear absent,
but the hope which sustained writers in the 1940s had been
frustrated by eight grim years of post-war Stalinism. Later war
fiction, therefore, emerges as a development of a minor branch of
wartime literature; it is an extension of that criticism of the Party,
oblique in published literature and trenchant in such unpublished
works as Dovzhenko's, which had always been an important, but
secondary feature in works of the forties. The focus now switches
from the struggle with Germany to internal conflicts. The novels
become more analytical and insular, and writers concentrate on
the causes of the débâcle of 1941–42 and the reasons why wartime
hopes and aspirations were frustrated. At the risk of over-
simplification, a different conflict generally emerges – that between people and Party. Some writers probe the purely "technical" aspects of the Party's errors and trace the effects of its
misguided policies in the 1930s upon the country's military

capacity. Others explore the moral and ethical implications of these misjudgments, while a few examine the cruel irony whereby that patriotism, which had been the crucial factor in Russian resistance, was exploited to perpetuate a totalitarianism little different from that practised by the invaders. An impression is created less of a nation united against a common foe than of one divided against itself. War literature in the 1960s becomes an integral part of that literature of protest which generally characterises the post-Stalin period. Its theme is not hope, but hope frustrated.

The impact of the war upon Russia was immense. Its wounds still fester and its achievements still inspire. Over half a century after the Napoleonic War Tolstoy wrote *War and Peace*. Although the national awakening of 1812 was also followed by a period of reaction and suppression, by the 1860s Tolstoy could both recapture the patriotic fervour of 1812 and appreciate the historic importance and endurance of that fermentation of ideas which the war inspired. By the turn of this century it may well be thought that the Great Patriotic War played a similar catalytic role in Russian affairs and that the pessimistic, but always challenging and outspoken literature of the 1960s was in fact a re-affirmation of the wartime spirit of independence.

## English Translations of Works Mentioned

Azhaev, Vasilii N., *Far from Moscow*, trans. by R. Prokofieva (Moscow, 1950).

Babaevsky, Semyon P., *Cavalier of the Golden Star*, trans. by Ruth Kisch (London, 1956).

Bogomolov, Vladimir O., *Ivan*, trans. by B. Isaacs in *Flare: The Third Flare . . .* (Moscow, 1964).

Bondarev, Yuri V., *Silence*, trans. Elizaveta Fen (London, 1965).

——, *The Hot Snow*, trans. by R. Daglish (Moscow, 1976).

Bubennov, Mikhail S., *The White Birch*, trans. by L. Stoklitsky (Moscow, 1949).

Bykov, Viktor V., *Sotnikov*, trans. as *The Ordeal* by G. Clough (London, 1972).

——, *The Third Flare*, trans. R. Daglish in *Flare . . .*

Dovzhenko, Aleksandr P., *The Poet as Film-Maker: Selected Writings*. Ed. trans. by M. Carynnyk (Cambridge, Mass. and London, 1973).

Ehrenburg, Ilya G., *Russia at War*, with an Introduction by J.B. Priestley, trans. by Gerard Shelley (London, 1943).

——, *The Storm*, trans. by E. Hartley and T. Shebunina (London, 1949).

Gorbatov, Boris L., *The Undefeated*, trans. as *Taras's Family* by E. Donnelly (London, 1944).

Grossman, Vasilii, *The People Immortal: A Novel* (London, 1943).

——, *The Years of War, 1941–1945*, trans. by E. Donnelly and R. Prokofieva (Moscow, 1946).

——, *With the Red Army in Poland and Byelorussia: First Byelorussian Front, June–July 1944*, trans. by H. Altschuler (London, 1945).

Inber, Vera M., *Leningrad Diary*, trans. by S. Wolff and R. Grieve (London, 1971).

Kazakevich, Emanuil G., *Spring on the Oder*, trans. by R. Daglish (Moscow, 1951).

Kuznetsov, Aleksandr V., *Babi Yar: A Documentary Novel*, trans. by J. Guralsky (London, 1969).

Medvedev, Dmitri N., *Stout Hearts*, trans. by D. Svirsky (Moscow, 1961).

Nekrasov, Viktor P., *In the Trenches of Stalingrad*, trans. as *Frontline Stalingrad* by D. Floyd (London, 1962).

Panova, Vera F., *Travelling Companions*, trans. by E. Manning and E. Budberg as *The Train* (London, 1948).

Pavlenko, Petr A., *Happiness, etc.*, trans. by J. Fineberg (Moscow, 1950).

Pilyar, Yuri E., *It All Really Happened*, trans. by P. Ludwich (London, 1961).

Polevoy, Boris N., *A Story about a Real Man*, trans. by J. Fineberg (Moscow, 1949).

——, *We are Soviet People* (Moscow, 1949).

Sholokhov, Mikhail A., *Hate: Down South* (Moscow, 1942).

——, *One Man's Destiny and Other Stories*, trans. by H.C. Stevens (London, 1967).

Simonov, Konstantin M., *Days and Nights*, trans. by J. Barnes (New York, 1945).

——, *The Living and the Dead*, trans. as *Victims and Heroes* by R. Ainzstein (London, 1963).

Solzhenitsyn, Aleksandr I., "The Incident at Krechetovka Station" in *Great Russian Short Stories* (New York and London, 1969).

Tolstoy, Aleksey N., *My Country: Articles and Stories of the Great Patriotic War of the Soviet Union*, trans. by D.L. Fromberg (London, 1943).

Vershigora, Petro P., *Men With a Clear Conscience*, trans. by M. Parker (Moscow, 1949).

Wassilewska, Wanda L., *Rainbow: A Novel*, trans. by E. Bone (London, 1943).

# 5  United States

**Eric Homberger**

The United States was the last of the major combatants to enter the war, and, except perhaps for the British, experienced the greatest diversity of combat. In effect, the US armed forces fought a half-dozen different wars, on two oceans as well as in five theatres, from the South Pacific to North Africa. The shape of American war literature was imposed by the variousness of war itself. There are American novels set in the Pacific (by Norman Mailer, James Jones, Thomas Heggen), in Italy (Harry Brown, John Horne Burns, John Hersey), in France and Germany (Glen Sire, Stefan Heym, Irwin Shaw), and in England (Hersey, etc.). There are war novels wholly set in America (J.G. Cozzens), and some which do not involve any Americans at all: John Steinbeck's *The Moon is Down*, about German-occupied Norway; Hersey's *The Wall*, which describes the destruction of the Warsaw ghetto; Godfrey Blunden's *The Time of the Assassins*, set in German-occupied Russia; and Albert Maltz's *The Cross and the Arrow*, about German civilian workers in 1942. There are novels of the Marine Corps (Leon Uris's *Battle Cry*), Navy (Heggen's *Mr. Roberts*), Air Force (Hersey's *The War Lover*, Heller's *Catch–22*), and of course, the infantry. There are novels about virtually every kind of military unit; there are pure combat novels (Harry Brown's *A Walk in the Sun*), and novels concerned with military administration of newly-occupied territory (Hersey's *A Bell for Adano*). At least two novels end with concentration camp scenes. There is, in other words, no typical novel of the war.

Americans were actively engaged in the war for less than four years. This was long enough for a small body of war novels to be published during the war, but conditions did not permit an active literary life by soldiers. Journalism was a more characteristic product of the war, and many distinguished writers served as war correspondents: Steinbeck for the New York *Herald Tribune*, Hem-

173

mingway for *Colliers*, Dos Passos for *Life*. Professional journalists like Ernie Pyle, who covered the war for Scripps-Howard, Vincent Sheean, who wrote for *Red Book*, and John Gunther, who went overseas as a broadcaster for the Blue Network, were joined by younger journalists and writers: Richard Tregaskis was sent to Guadalcanal by the International News Service, John Hersey was a *Time–Life* correspondent, Ira Wolfert wrote for the North American Newspaper Alliance. (Wolfert's *Battle for the Solomons* won the Pulitzer prize for journalism in 1943.) Steinbeck and Hersey were authors of early war novels, but combatant-writing generally did not begin to appear in significant quantities until the late 1940s. The high water mark was reached in 1948, when major novels appeared by Mailer, Heym, Cozzens and Shaw. War novels have continued to appear with some regularity ever since.

The cultural context for these novels is not the home front during the war, but the tensions of American culture during the Cold War, the McCarthy witch-hunts, and the 1950s. In an interview in 1948, Norman Mailer explained that he did not initially regard *The Naked and the Dead* as an anti-war book, but it became one as he responded to the mood of America after he returned home:

> every time I turned on the radio and looked in the newspapers, there was this growing hysteria, this talk of going to war again, and it made me start looking for the trend of what was happening.[1]

An unexpected consequence of this was to diminish the presence of the *specific* causes of war, and to see it as a phenomenon which was caused by man's nature: evil and fallen man's innate propensity for aggression and violence seemed responsible for the woes of mankind. There was an inclination in the early 1940s to regard war as a phenomenon transcending history which could only be understood in psychological and ethical terms. Nazism was regarded by most Americans as an unmitigated evil. (Fascism, on the other hand, was not without its devotees on the right and the liberal left.) But the growing influence of Freud's social thought in the 1940s assisted the inclination to empty the war of its political content. The "thinking classes" by and large seem to have accepted the war as a crusade. To understand the American war experience, it is necessary to understand how little this attitude was shared by the man in the street and by the enlisted men in the armed forces. In the literature of the war only a small minority of characters regard the war with enthusiasm. By the late 1940s the enemy had changed, but the fixation upon the "enemy" remained a helpful way to understand the popular mind.

The clearest expression of the way the war was seen by American writers is the prevalence of stark oppositions between characters who endorse a humane and liberal viewpoint and those who either love war and killing, or whose temperament is repressive, conservative and fascistic. The latter are likely to be in positions of authority in the American military; the former to be junior officers – captains and lieutenants – torn between necessity and humane sentiment, or enlisted men like Ackerman in *The Young Lions* (1948) and Prewitt in *From Here to Eternity* (1951), bursting with individualism and conscience. In Hersey's *The War Lover* (1959) the dichotomy is suggested by the conflict between Boman and Buzz Marrow; in Martin Abzug's *Spearhead* (1946) in the conflict between Hollis and Knupfer; in Heggen's *Mr. Roberts* (1946) between Lieutenant Roberts and Captain Morton; in Alfred Coppell's *Order of Battle* (1969) between Devereux, who reads the *Oxford Book of English Verse*, and Porta, who loves to kill; in *The Naked and the Dead* (1948) between Hearn and Cummings, and Valsen and Croft. James Gould Cozzens reverses the liberal bias of the war novel in *Guard of Honor* (1948), but finds the same structure of polar opposition congenial to his purposes: the symbol of order (Colonel "Judge" Ross) is emphatically opposed to that of political and racial disorder (Lieutenant Edsell). In comparatively few American novels does the Fascist enemy actually turn out to be a cunning, brutal, wily Nazi: Pettinger in Heym's *The Crusaders* (1948) is opposed to Lieutenant Yates; Lieutenant Raeder in Glen Sire's *The Deathmakers* (1960) is opposed to Captain Brandon; and Lieutenant Hardenburg and Sergeant Diestl in Shaw's *The Young Lions* are carefully opposed to the liberal intellectual Michael Whitacre and the New York Jew Noah Ackerman. (The "enemy" first showed his face in *The Young Lions* in an army training camp in the American south: the southern racists, bigots and anti-Semites who made up the majority of Whitacre's and Ackerman's company.) These patterns are insistent; authorial loyalties are involved. Such elaborate dichotomization is less typical of the interwar years, when this patterning appealed mainly to authors of proletarian novels, than of the harsher political climate which followed the war and the opposed categories (East/West, democracy/dictatorship) which characterised Cold War thought. The very structures of the American war novel bear the stamp of the mental climate in which they were written.

There is a paradoxical point here about literary history. The generation of American writers who served in the Great War left an important legacy. Dos Passos's early novels, especially *Three Soldiers* (1921), Cummings's *The Enormous Room* (1922) and Hemingway's *A Farewell to Arms* (1929), to say nothing of the minor classics of the 1930s, *Company K* by "William March" (1933) and Humphrey Cobb's *Paths of Glory* (1935), established the war novel as an important contemporary genre. To some extent these books influenced attitudes towards the army and patriotism. It would be hard not to conclude, after a reading of the American fiction of the Great War, that the army was a vicious, repressive and totalitarian microcosm of American society, that war was dehumanizing, and that heroism and patriotism were things which serious people could no longer believe in. (Such attitudes were far more likely to be found among American intellectuals, and the liberal middle-class, from which class the writers were drawn, than elsewhere in American culture.) It is striking, however, that even among the war generation there was little interest in war literature. The great European novels and poems of the First World War seem to have left no trace on American writers. Fitzgerald is in this something of an exception. Shane Leslie introduced him to Scribner's Sons in 1918 as an American prose Rupert Brooke.[2] The comparison is not wholly frivolous: Fitzgerald took the title of *This Side of Paradise* from a Brooke poem. Perhaps because he did not manage to get overseas in 1918, Fitzgerald was one of the few American writers who remained actively interested in war writing. He did a screenplay in 1937 for Erich Maria Remarque's *Three Comrades*. Those who grew up in the interwar years in Europe may have lived with the shadow of the Great War – Christopher Isherwood is an interesting example – but their American contemporaries, the writers of Second World War novels, do not seem to have much familiarity with Remarque, Sassoon, Owen and the others. American isolationism had an important cultural dimension. If anything, American writers seem to have been influenced more by movies about the Great War than by its European literature.[3]

The specific image of the war on the Western Front, whether

derived from films or war literature, with its rituals, elaborate patterns and precise structures, remained in most people's minds as *the* shape of war. War meant knowing with some precision that the enemy was in trenches which closely mirrored our own. Like ourselves, they had to live underground, and follow the same daily rituals of stand-to at dawn and dusk. When they attacked, they had to go over the top and pass through nearly identical patterns of barbed wire, and face our machine guns; and the same applied to ourselves. The characteristic flavour of despair in war literature seems to have faded; what survived was a formal pattern of combat, with its own etiquette, vocabulary and mythology.[4]

Despite the overwhelmingly anti-heroic nature of the war literature of the 1920s and 1930s, writers continually felt the need to debunk the fantasies of heroism which have for so long cast an aura around militarism. Novelists of modern warfare, certainly since Stendhal, have found something decidely useful in romantic dreams of heroism. The conjunction of dream and reality makes available the traditional forms of irony. There is a long passage in *The Naked and the Dead* in which Wyman, Toglio and Goldstein haul a heavy anti-tank gun through the jungle. One layer of irony is revealed when we learn that the effort has gone for nothing: there never had been any chance of a Japanese counter-attack. Mailer enhances the irony by contrasting the foul-smelling and exhausting work (no other writer on war has so devastatingly caught the depths of physical tiredness) with Wyman's vague dreams of military glory: "He dreamed of himself charging across a field in the face of many machine guns; but in the dream there was no stitch in his side from running too far while bearing too much weight." Journalists, no less than novelists, felt in themselves lingering traces of romantic expectation about going into combat. "This generation", wrote the liberal journalist Ralph Ingersoll,

> has been brought up on the novels and the histories of the last war which told of weeks in the trenches under continuous fire, of 36-hour barrages and 'going over the top,' of mass charges to cut your way through wire while enemy bullets burned around you. Maybe it was like that all the time. . . . . Nothing could be more violent than the most violent moments, but these moments were spaced out. Between them there were long spells of waiting, walking, and waiting.[5]

War, in other words, had its boring moments. Harry Brown, writing in *A Walk in the Sun* (1944) of the Italian campaign, said that "the soldier waits for food, for clothing, for a letter, for a battle to begin. And often the food is never served, the clothing is never issued, the letter never arrives and the battle never begins". Even though every war was mostly like this, the fact was soon forgotten. It is almost more important to study the ways war is forgotten than to study the ways it has been remembered.

Memories of the Great War hover above the war literature of 1939–45, through a selective and distorted memory, even to the point of nostalgia. The Great War seemed somehow coherent and *organized* by comparison to the jungle warfare in the Pacific, or the fighting on the deserts of North Africa. Irwin Shaw suggests such a nostalgia in *The Young Lions* when a German Sergeant, Christian Diestl, compares the irregular and fluid fighting in the desert, in a landscape which lacked definition, to the Western Front in the Great War:

> The slaughter was horrible in the trenches, but everything was organized. You got your food regularly, you had a feeling that matters were arranged in some comprehensible order, the dangers came through recognizable channels.

The jungle warfare of the Pacific seemed to American writers particularly terrifying because it lacked clear demarcations and sides. Hence Mailer's description of the initial landing and advance on Anopopei in *The Naked and the Dead*:

> There was no front line for several days at least. Little groups of men filtered through the jungle, fought minor skirmishes with still smaller groups, and then moved on again. Cumulatively there was a motion forward, but each individual unit moved in no particular direction at any given time. They were like a nest of ants wrestling and tugging at a handful of breadcrumbs in a field of grass.

Peter Bowman, in his verse novel *Beach Red*, emphasised the same point:

> In front of you is a fringe of matted vegetation, and the push slows down. There is no precision here, no formation of steadily

advancing men. Just an unhealthy mixture of friend and foe stirred vigorously in seething cauldron.

At one point on Guadalcanal Richard Tregaskis heard mortar shells burst in the direction of the Tenaru river front. Someone wondered if they were theirs or ours.

'I don't know,' said Col. Gates, taking a puff from his long cigarette holder. 'That's the trouble with this war', he said with a smile. 'You never know.'

'In the last war we used to know where the enemy was . . .'[6]

Newsreels of the first part of the war suggested a new pattern of rapid movement, the *Blitzkrieg*, and were especially particularly effective in presenting the devastating impact of air power. But the newsreel paled in comparison to the feature film as a medium of propaganda and information.[7] Novelists who served in the war and who generally had to wait until the war ended before they could begin work, found themselves struggling against the Hollywood version of the war. It was so pervasive, and in the eyes of returning veterans, so dishonest, that "the movies" became synonymous with the falsification of war. "Instead of trying to show the distressing complexity and puzzling diffusion of war", wrote James Jones,

they pulled everything down to the level of good guy against bad guy. Instead of showing the terrifying impersonality of modern war, they invariably pulled it down to one-on-one situation, a man-against-man, like a tennis match. At best they made it like a football game. And modern war was not men against machine. It it was industry against industry. And we had the best machines.[8]

Jones felt that the nature of popular entertainment, with its tidy and reassuring structures, was at the heart of its dishonesty. "If this were a movie", Sergeant Bell mused in *The Thin Red Line* (1962),

this would be the end of the show, and something would be decided. In a movie or a novel they would dramatise and build to the climax of the attack. When the attack came in the film or novel, it would decide something. It would have a semblance of meaning and a semblance of an emotion. And immediately after it would be over. The audience would go home and think about the semblance of the meaning and feel the semblance of the emotion. Even if the hero got killed, it would still make sense. Art, Bell decided, creative art – was shit . . .

Here there was no semblance of meaning. And the emotions were so many and so mixed up that they were indecipherable, could not be untangled. Nothing had been decided, nobody had learned anything. But most important of all, nothing had ended. Even if they had captured this whole ridge nothing would have ended. Because tomorrow, or the day after, or the day after that, they would be called upon to do the same thing again – maybe under even worse circumstances. The concept was so overpowering, so numbing, that it shook Bell. Island after island, hill after hill, beachhead after beachhead, year after year. It staggered him.

The sensitive soldier-novelist might perceive the profound incomprehensibility and disorder of modern warfare, but the demands of art, and of contemporary readers, do not allow the fallacy of imitative form: even though Jones saw the meaningless-ness of war, his war novel cannot be without structure or meaning. In a more complex fashion the novelist (no less, it must be said, than the Hollywood film maker) imposes coherence, meaning and structure.

Contempt for Hollywood, for its artificial tidiness, often sur-faces in war novels. British films made a substantial impact in the early phase of the war, and gave a measure of the ways in which life was seen to imitate (bad) art. Sailing on an American mer-chant marine vessel entering a combat zone in the South Pacific, Ira Wolfert complained that the crew were "so damned casual" that "you'd think they were a bunch of limeys in some movie with Leslie Howard".[9] John Gunther, on board a British destroyer in the Mediterranean in July 1943, was mightily impressed by the calm in which the captain responded to unidentified aircraft: ". . . for a few minutes the scene was remarkably like Noel Coward's [1942] movie 'In Which We Serve'".[10] A soldier in Peter Bow-man's *Beach Red* overhears Japanese soldiers singing: "What do the Japs think this is – Gilbert and Sullivan?" (There were other

ways in which life imitated art: a character in John Horne Burns's
*The Gallery* (1948) noted the GIs who "deliberately tried to look
like Bill Mauldin cartoons".

War movies provided the war novelist with good examples of
hollow, clichéd, insincere speeches, and stagey gestures. In October 1942, John Hersey noted that a Marine captain was showing excessive caution. The soldier's vigilance seemed "just a little
exaggerated, like something out of an unconvincing movie".[11] In
Joe David Brown's *Kings Go Forth* (1956), Major Blaine shakes
his men's hands before a dangerous mission. "'Good killing,
men,' he said. Major Blaine had seen too many movies." An
American platoon leader in Harry Brown's *A Walk in the Sun* gets
"that old Lost Patrol feeling". Memories were still fresh enough
during the war to recall John Ford's 1934 film starring Victor
McLaglen about an isolated British patrol under Arab attack.
Reassuring his men ("We'll get through") only makes the
American officer feel like a "damned fool": "This wasn't the
movies." When Minetta in *The Naked and the Dead* attempts to fake
madness to avoid being returned to his platoon after a minor
injury, the movies show him how: "He began to tremble and
allowed some spittle to form on his lips. That'll work. He had a
picture of a madman he had once seen in a movie who had foamed
at the mouth." Michael Whitacre in *The Young Lions* parodies the
wartime spy fever on the West Coast:

> Perhaps this aged gardener in his ragged clothes was really a
> full commander in the Japanese Navy, cleverly awaiting the
> arrival of the Imperial Fleet outside San Pedro harbor before
> showing his hand. Michael grinned. The movies, he thought,
> there is no escape for the modern mind from their onslaught.

Movies powerfully reinforced romantic attitudes to war. Students of literature are apt to exaggerate the impact of anti-war
novels and memoirs of the Great War, and ignore the way
Hollywood between the wars contributed to the popular associa-
tions of war with personal courage, and heroism with patriotism.
The isolated anti-war films represent an honourable exception to
the general tendency.

The reality of war, and of the US Army, did not encourage
romantic fantasies of heroism, but contemporary observers often

wrote as though such expectations survived intact. "In the imagination of every soldier who expects to fight", according to Ralph Ingersoll,

> the word 'battle' grows until he expects the real thing to call for continuous heroism, unbelievable fortitude and a superman's skill at arms. He is just a little surprised then, when he finds that so much of a battle is no more strenuous than the maneuvers he's been on . . .[12]

If many die in battle, even more unheroically survive. Dr. Karandash, the tragic Ukrainian intellectual in Godfrey Blunden's *The Time of the Assassins* (1952), records in his notebook that "the truth about war is that it is never quite Homeric; that humanity survives. Though the villages are empty, and many dead are to be counted in the ruins, there is life in the country". "Never quite Homeric": a nice understatement for the war in Russia, and scarcely less appropriate for the war in the Pacific, where nothing survived of chivalric codes of conduct. Few writers have been as systematically devoted to the discrediting of romantic conceptions of war as James Jones. Consider, for example, his description of a soldier under mortar attack in *The Thin Red Line*:

> Slowly he stopped weeping and his eyes cleared, but as the other emotions, the sorrow, the shame, the selfhatred seeped out of him under the pressure of self-preservation, the fourth component, terror, seeped in to replace them until he was only a vessel completely filled with cowardice, fear and gutlessness. And that was the way he lay. This was war? There was no superior test of strength here, no superb swordsmanship, no bellowing Viking heroism, no expert marksmanship. This was only numbers. He was being killed for numbers.

This would have been better prose if Jones had not simply named the emotions but tried to show them in the sequence of events, in consciousness itself. Jones's point is that the conditions of modern war do not permit exercises in heroism. The war as a whole never seems to have become an heroic or uplifting cause for American GIs. Popular wisdom decades after the war concludes that it was a Good Thing, that the defeat of Hitler redeems the war as a whole. But the war novels suggest no such conviction. "I just don't know

whether our soldiers think much about causes", remarked Major
Victor Joppolo in John Hersey's *A Bell for Adano* (1944): "That's
one thing that worries me about this war." Liberals like Hersey
and Ralph Ingersoll were bothered by a lack of serious commitment both in the army and on the home front (where Ingersoll
pointed to "the thousand daily evidences of our lack of determina-
tion"). Lieutenant Roberts in Thomas Heggen's novel, who has a
long record as a "frustrated anti-fascist", is the only one on board
the *USS Reluctant* to be actively concerned about the war: "'I feel
left out', he said to Doc. 'I wanted in that war, Doc. I wanted in it
like hell'." Doc's reply comes closer to what seems the common
view: "I see it as a war of unrelieved necessity – nothing more.
Any ideology attaching is only incidental. Not to say accidental."
Martin Abzug reverses these attitudes in *Spearhead*, in which a
humane and liberal captain regards the war as ". . . nothing more
or less than an unpleasant job that has to be done", while his
German-born lieutenant, who hates Nazis, is perceived to be a
dangerous fanatic. The reversal of attitudes, in which liberals are
portrayed as both believing and not believing in the war, adds to
the confusion and moral ambiguity of the war as portrayed in war
novels. Warfare in the desert or jungle heightened uncertainty
over where the enemy was. The failure to believe in the war as a
cause left a blankness at the heart of the American involvement in
the war, and, of course, in war novels.

In the missing place of public values and purpose, which
Archibald MacLeish and the Office of Facts and Figures gamely
tried to instil in the nation, James Jones's soldiers fought only for
personal respect, for each other, and for survival. Fife, so often the
voice of Jones's thoughts in *The Thin Red Line*,

> could not believe he was fighting this war for God. And he did
> not believe he was fighting it for freedom, or democracy, or the
> dignity of the human race. When he analyzed it . . . . he could
> find only one reason why he was here, and that was because he
> would be ashamed for people to think he was a coward,
> embarrassed to be put in jail.

In *Whistle* (1978), the third volume of Jones's war trilogy, Private
Landers is asked to give a talk on the soldier's responsibilities to
draftees at this hometown Elks Club:

the soldier's first responsibility is to stay alive ... I can't in honesty tell you that you will be fighting for freedom, and God, and your country – as all these other gentlemen have told you. In combat you don't think about any of that. But I can assure you that you will be fighting for your life. I think that's a good thing to remember. I think that's a good thing to fight for.

"Responsibility", during the war, was a code-word used in a vociferous attack on the politics of American intellectuals and writers. Archibald MacLeish's polemic in 1940, *The Irresponsibles*, and Van Wyck Brooks's lectures on contemporary letters delivered at Columbia University in 1940 and 1941, suggests the flavour of the attack on intellectuals, modernism, and avant-garde cultural attitudes. Many old scores were being settled.[13] Private Landers in *Whistle* was an "irresponsible" in MacLeish's phrase, who remained quite indifferent to the ideals and "inherited culture of the West". None of the draftees came over to thank Landers for his speech. The tough and realistic 1st/Sergeant Mart Winch, in an impulsive address at an outdoor political rally in San Francisco, shows that he, too, is an "irresponsible": "... I'm more like a Jap first sergeant or a German first sergeant than I am like these civilian sons of bitches."

James Gould Cozzens, who would certainly have been among the "responsibles", assumes in *Guard of Honor* that the ideals and high principles of the army were little more than a necessary fiction, useful to preserve the outward seemliness of military affairs, but which had nothing to do with people's behaviour and beliefs. Cozzens gives a further conclusion to "Judge" Ross: the war aims of the average man "was to get out as soon as possible and go home":

Though the level of intelligence in the average man might be justly considered low, in very few of them would it be so low that they accepted notions that they fought, an embattled band of brothers, for noble 'principles'. They would howl at the idea; just as, in general, they despised and detested all their officers; hated the rules and regulations and disobeyed as many as they could; and from morning to night never stopped cursing the Army, scheming to get out of it, and hotly bitching about the slightest inconvenience, let alone hardship.

Cozzens's nihilism is even bleaker than Joseph Heller's. The change of sensibility between *Guard of Honor* and *Catch-22* is clearest in Heller's open recognition of the meaninglessness of the "official" purposes of the Air Force and the war. For Cozzens that kind of truth is best repressed in the name of military discipline, and of the public values of duty, honour and country, no matter how little one may privately believe in them. The commanding officer at an Air Force base may have been a drunk and a suicide, but a guard of honour, and all that it implies, is provided for the funeral. It is a matter of taste which of these nihilisms is preferred.

The official mind in the Pentagon recognized that morale in the armed forces was not well. The Assistant Secretary for Air noted that there was "very little idealism" in the armed forces. The general attitude towards the war was to regard it "as a job to be done and there is not much willingness to discuss what we are fighting for". John Morton Blum has pointed out that in 1942 only one American in ten could name even one provision of the Atlantic Charter, and a majority had no "clear idea what the war is all about". By 1945 only a minority remained openly puzzled by the war. America had not been bombed, except at Pearl Harbor, nor had it experienced invasion or military occupation. As Blum interestingly notes, alone among the great powers America was "fighting this war on imagination alone".[14] At certain deeper levels of national life, the war remained remote and irrelevant. War novelists showed a good understanding of the limits to the American participation in the war. Few Americans, and few novelists, exercised themselves over the question of war aims. It was simply there, and needed no further explanation. An unusual exception is Stefan Heym's *The Crusaders*. (Heym's work is also discussed in Chapter 3.) As much a political thriller as a war novel, Heym dramatizes the issue of war aims through conflicting attitudes towards a propaganda leaflet. Captain Yates believes the only credible appeal to German soldiers lay in ". . . corned beef hash, Nescafé and the beauties of the Geneva Convention". His chief interrogator of POWs, the German-born Private Bing, appreciated the need to appeal to higher principles and ideals. Bing's leaflet works, but his struggle to define American ideals, even on so limited a scale, reveals a cynicism and naïveté which Heym takes to be characteristically American. Captain Yates, with frequent prodding from Private Bing, comes to suspect that his superior officer, Major Willoughby, is actively pursuing his private financial advantage in the reconstruction of a steel cartel after the war. Willoughby's deal with the von Rentelen steel interests, which had been actively mobilized in support of the Nazi war effort, typified the cynical and corrupt capacity of the American military administration to line its own pockets at the expense of the postwar hopes of the German people. Here is another case in which the powers of selective forgetting need correction. The common assumption takes the victorious Yanks to have been generous, perhaps a little innocently so, but motivated by idealistic and humanitarian concerns. But American war novels suggest, in Malcolm Cowley's phrase, that the military administrations were "irresponsible and corrupt".[15] Hersey's *A Bell for Adano*, John Horne Burns's *The Gallery*, and Heym's novel contradict some of the basic assumptions of American character and motivation. There are in all three novels "good" characters moved by decency and integrity; but the overwhelming impression is of cynicism and self-seeking. The symbolic resolution of the issue in *The Crusaders*, in which the von Rentelen family estate was turned over to the survivors of the Paula concentration camp is not persuasive. But Heym's novel, written by a German antifascist emigrant who attended the University of Chicago and served in the psychological warfare branch of the US Army (and subsequently returned to live in East Germany), assumes that the enemy is not only on the other side, but that evil exists within the American Army and within American values.

This was not the self-image which most Americans had of themselves, or why they were in the war. John Hersey asked a group of young Marines on Guadalcanal in October 1942 why they were fighting. After a long, uneasy pause, one Marine remarked, "'Jesus, what I'd give for a piece of blueberry pie.'" Another preferred mince pies, a third apple: pie was a potent symbol of home. Other men had other symbols, but the meaning was clear. They were fighting "to get the goddam thing over and get home": "Home is where the good things are – the generosity, the good pay, the comforts, the democracy, the pie."[16] Peter Bowman assembles a different catalogue with a similar intention:

> Here's what really matters to him: a paved street lined
> with familiar trees and a grassy lawn and a car
> and a girl and a hamburger joint and a crowd
> coming out of a movie and a hot bath and

> a gay necktie and the labor of a trolley going
> uphill and a glossy pond and peanuts behind third base.
>
> (*Beach, Red*)

Normality defined itself in comfortable ways. The one class of characters in American war novels to be uncomfortable with apple pie and hamburger joints as symbols of American values were the intellectuals and liberals. There is a surprisingly large number of them: Milton Norton in *Battle Cry* (1953), Tyler Williams in *The Steel Cocoon* (1958), Jim Edsell in *Guard of Honor*, Terence Reardon in *Wolf Pack* (1960), Doug Roberts in *Mr. Roberts*, Hollis in *Spearhead*, Michael Whitacre and Noah Ackerman in *The Young Lions*, and Robert Hearn in *The Naked and the Dead*. Very few survive the war with their liberalism intact. Norton, Roberts, Ackerman and Hearn die in the war; many of the others lose their liberalism in collision with reality; Edsell, the radical in Cozzens's novel, is shown to be a liar and a loud-mouthed troublemaker. One might write the history of post-war liberalism through their fates.

Mailer's Lieutenant Hearn is the most fully-realized portrayal of a liberal in the American war novel, and will repay closer attention. Hearn does not simply embody a series of abstract propositions or political opinions. His liberalism is uneasy, and is without the destructive confidence of Lieutenant Edsell in *Guard of Honor.* Mailer roots Hearn's politics in his childhood rebellion against the philistine prosperity of his father. Marked by "guilt of birth", Hearn's rebellion extends to the Army, and to the privileges of the officer class. He has earned his commission the hard way, through Officer Candidate's School; but, as Mailer indicates, it has not been easy for Hearn to sustain his anger at the injustices of society, especially when he was himself the direct beneficiary of injustice. A partial explanation of Hearn's outburst at Lt. Col. Conn's "labial interpretation of history" (the near-universal belief among Republicans and Southerners that Roosevelt had a black mistress. In fact, she was white.) was his fear that he did not really care if such ignorant racism was openly displayed in Headquarters Company, or whether rations were unfairly distributed between officers and men. Mailer emphasizes the conflict between Hearn's objective interests (a larger meat ration, avoiding conflict with a superior officer) and his sentimental inclinations. When he is asked to leave the John Reed Society at Harvard, Hearn is reminded that "You're independent of economic considerations, and so you're without fear, without proper understanding." This emphasis on the economic paradoxes of middle-class liberalism is unsubtle; it is also necessary for the understanding of the basically frail and, in Mailer's view, undependable nature of liberalism itself. It is a nice touch on Mailer's part that those with the requisite "economic considerations" such as Martinez, Gallagher and Valsen were hardly liberals: there is nothing like Marxist orthodoxy in Mailer's criticism of liberalism.

Hearn's conversations with General Cummings are rightly felt to contain the heart of the book's politics. Cummings sees in Hearn a proper adversary and an educated man; he alone in Headquarters Company is capable of understanding the political and philosophical implications of the general's thought. Their relationship is objectively unequal, and something central to Cummings's personality is revealed in the evident pleasure he takes in baiting Hearn, and then slapping him down. The strong undercurrents of sexual tension between Cummings and Hearn have often been noted. Cummings would like to see the aloof, Harvard-educated liberal humiliated, to see him "afraid, filled with shame if only for an instant". His relationship to Hearn is a long, aggressive prelude to buggery. Hearn on the other hand knew, while attacking Lt. Col. Conn, that Cummings would intervene to save him. The general is more a father-figure, someone against whom he can safely rebel, than a real object of fear. There is another aspect of Cummings which attracts Hearn: he is a man who exercises power, whose will, at its deepest level, seeks the domination of others. Cummings's Faustian urge for power touches upon a similar impulse within Hearn; the "peculiar magnetism" of power attracts him, and dissolves the clear political difference between the two men:

> There were times when the demarcation between their minds was blurred for him.... Divorced of all the environmental trappings, all the confusing and misleading attitudes he had absorbed, he was basically like Cummings.... They were both the same, and it had produced first the intimacy, the attraction they had felt toward each other, and then the hatred.

When Hearn is sent off on a dangerous patrol by Cummings, he discovers that the experience of leading men was deeply satisfying. He recognizes in himself that he was, in the desire to lead, "just another Croft" (the sergeant who was the previous leader of the Intelligence and Reconaissance platoon). The recognition that he was like Cummings and Croft humanizes Hearn, saves him from liberal priggishness. But it does not save him from sentimentality, a far more serious failing in Mailer's eyes. Hearn struggles to reconcile his liberal instinct to be a nice guy (qualified by the "casual truth" which Hearn grants that he cared for others only in the abstract) with the objective reality (again!) that he must dominate his new platoon, and its highly competent and vicious sergeant, or lose control of the patrol altogether. The separation of Hearn and Cummings deprives *The Naked and the Dead* of some of its political energy. Croft is too instictive and inarticulate to engage in a dialogue with Hearn; all he can do is kill him. Hearn was isolated in Headquarters Company, and even more so on the patrol. His overtures are rebuffed by the men, contemptuous of officers trying to buddie up with them, and he is deceived by Croft. The odds have been stacked against Hearn, and his sentimental liberalism, but not with contempt. The political alternatives present elsewhere in Mailer's book leave room mainly for qualified pessimism. Cummings's vision of a totalitarian future ("... the only morality of the future is a power morality...") is not answered by liberalism: for reasons of temperament and *force majeure*, Hearn must "crawfish" before authority. Ironically, it is the anonymous American soldiers on Anopopei who successfully resist Cummings's will. When the difficult wheeling manoeuvre to face the Toyaku line was completed, the offensive stalled. The soldiers settled down in their positions, attended to improving their creature comforts; inertia, not political principle, resisting the Faustian will:

> ... apparently without cause [the general thought], or at least through causes too intangible for him to discover, he had lost his sensitive control. No matter how he molded them now the men always collapsed into a sodden resistent mass like dishrags, too soft, too wet to hold any shape which might be given them.

The central drama of General Cummings's existence was the sheer exertion of power, the struggle of the will against the mass. His temporary defeat before the Toyaku line has a biological basis: however imperiously the will asserts itself, there is always that other, "intangible" limitation in man's nature which constrains his reach. As much as Hearn's liberalism was an act of will, qualified by objective interests and his "guilt of birth", Cummings's Faustian vision of a world responsive to the will of an individual arrives at its own limits. Hearn and Cummings represent opposite positions politically, but come to resemble each other in ways by now characteristic of the American novel of the war. Opposites lose their distinctness; clarity of definition fades; the grey fog of history looks more and more impenetrable.

In *Battle Cry* a trouble-maker is, after much provocation, beaten up by L.Q., Danny, Ski, Norton and the rest of the guys – but he refuses to rat on them to the drill instructor. Danny would rather flunk his radio test than leave his pals behind: "Just that you make a buddy – and, well, I think it's more important we stick together than we make it alone." Buddies look after each other when they fall ill, and when they are betrayed by women: ". . . a smile and the voice of a buddy meant something that none but us could understand". The feeling that soldiers learn to have for each other is a glowing, precious thing which flies in the face of the demoralized and cynical routine of army life. The platoon or company, the crew of a bomber or a submarine, are natural communities, dependent upon each other for survival. If the characteristic malaise of twentieth-century life is anomie and alienation, it is no wonder that, in J. Glenn Gray's phrase, the feeling soldiers have of caring and depending upon each other constitutes an important part of the "enduring appeal" of battle.[17]

"If one died," writes Alfred Coppel in *Order of Battle*, "the chances were that all would die, and so each became very precious to the others. Together they were more than the sum of their individualities. They were a team, a unit. Only war could do that to a group of men." For those who did not experience combat, the feeling of mutual dependence and solidarity was rare and to be savoured for its uniqueness. "The fresh breeze blew on the faces of the crew", writes Heggen of the *USS Reluctant* after liberty on Elysium:

> They felt good in the same way . . . that any group with the bright bond of communal achievement feels good. The crew was a unit at last, and the common artery of participation ran through and bound together such distant and diverse characters as Costello and Wiley and Ringgold and Schlemmer. They stood along the rail in little groups; but those were accidental

groups with interchangeable membership, and not the tight, jealous cliques of old.

The feeling of mutual dependence is seen with greatest clarity when danger threatens. Peter Bowman writes in *Beach Red*:

> You walked through the jungle and Lindstrom and
> Egan and Whitney were in front of you and you were
> behind them, and between you there was connecting tissue.
> It was not because of any similarity you may have
> had in thought or behaviour or habit or belief, but
> because you had groped for it and found it and
> it had drawn you close. One of you fell and another
> picked him up and carried him in the simple compulsion
> of linked survival, and that is the parallel
> transcending tribe and race in the utter need of existence.

William M. Hardy in *Wolf Pack*, a popular adventure novel about submarine warfare in the Pacific, assumes that for the crew survival was a collective instinct: "The boat must survive, and, if it did, then every man aboard had the right to expect that he would survive also." The crew of a B-17 had an identical sense of mutual dependence. "All ten of us were linked to the ship," writes John Hersey in *The War Lover*, "and to each other by those life-keeping hose lines, and we were like an unborn litter of young in the belly of our common mother. Never before had I – nor since have I – had such a feeling of being part of a brood in a plane." The "common artery of participation" (Heggen), "connecting tissue" (Bowman), "instinct" (Hardy), and the feeling of being in the belly of "our common mother" (Hersey), suggest a solidarity which transcends other kinds of shared purpose, and which is firmly rooted in a naturalistic perspective.

Mailer suggests the naturalistic lineage of *The Naked and the Dead* in similes emphasising the insignificance of human effort:

> ... they ground the guns forward blindly, a line of ants dragging their burden back to their hole.
> They had the isolation, the insignificance of insects traversing an endless beach.
> Their minds scurried about inside their bodies like rodents in a maze ...

Mailer was more deeply influenced by naturalism than any of the other writers of the war; at a certain fundamental level naturalism pervaded the common culture. Mailer found in the biological pessimism of Jack London political overtones which made sense in 1946 – 7; others may have seen in the example of the Joad family in Steinbeck's *The Grapes of Wrath* (1939) a more optimistic way of understanding the communal instinct.

Where the American novels of the Great War powerfully asserted the rights of the individual against the state, embodied in the army, and against the threatening claims of society (and in this were very *American*), by the 1940s Romantic individualism did not make sense on Anopopei or elsewhere. The gesture of a Frederic Henry, declaring a "separate peace" between himself and history, is not possible in the conditions of the Second World War. Maggio, Prewitt's friend in *From Here to Eternity* (1951), declared his own separate peace in the war between himself and the army – and received a dishonourable discharge. At one point in Jones's *The Thin Red Line*, Fife and Storm analyse the prospects for evacuation:

> It was easy to see, when you looked at it from one point of view, that all prisoners were not locked up behind bars in a stone quadrangle. Your government could just as easily imprison you on, say, a jungled island in the South Seas until you had done to its satisfaction what your government had sent you there to do. And when one considered it – as all the wounded had – this matter of evacuation might well be actually and in fact a life and death matter.

There was no convenient Switzerland for Americans fighting in the Pacific, nor the chance to play snooker with Count Greffi before escaping by rowboat at midnight. Hemingway in *For Whom the Bell Tolls* suggests a more complex understanding of the conflict of loyalties. Robert Jordan, unlike soldiers in most American war novels, had a cause to fight for: "... you fought that summer and that autumn [1936] for all the poor in the world, against all tyranny, for all the things that you believed and for the new world you had been educated into".[18] The "things" he believes in, as the war goes on, become meaningless; his faith in "the new world" does not remain innocent or even hopeful. (Jordan has seen too much at Gaylord's Hotel, seen too many lies and too much deception; he has even come to enjoy the machinery of deceit for its own sake.) Yet the cause, the Republic and the Spanish people, is strong enough to sustain his loyalty. However drastically the cause has been corrupted, defeating Fascism is important enough for Jordan to accept his own death. His loyalty is to an idea, a metaphysical hope, for which he is willing to sacrifice himself and everyone in El Sordo's and Pablo's band. Romantic gestures and political commitments like Robert Jordan's have little place in the mechanized and collective war in American novels.

The fate of Robert E. Lee Prewitt, a miner's son from Harlan County, Kentucky, hero of James Jones's *From Here to Eternity*, is a case in point. Prewitt enlisted in the army to escape the coalmines. (Harlan County was the scene of a desperate conflict in the early 1930s between miners and coal operators: the name was synonymous on the American left for repression and violence against workers.) He thinks of himself as a thirty-year man who loves the army, and what he believes it stands for, with passionate conviction. He has a lonely, courageous integrity, a belief in ethical imperatives and the honourableness of institutions, which older and wiser heads among the noncoms try to bring down to earth. One old soldier tells him that a man can no longer do what he wants to do:

> 'Maybe back in the old days, back in the time of the pioneers, a man could do what he wanted to do, in peace. But he had the woods then, he could go off in the woods and live alone. He could live well off the woods. And if they followed him there for this or that, he could just move on. There was always more woods on up ahead. But a man cant do that now. He's got to play ball with them.'

Prewitt is an heir of the frontiersman and pioneer, with the integrity of someone for whom "words meant what they said".[19] He believes in the the letter of Army Regulations, and hopes that by avoiding any infringement in the law, he cannot be impelled to violate his own code of integrity:

> '... I don't think they got the right to order me what to do outside of duty hours.'
>
> 'It aint a question of right or wrong [replied Chief Choate],

its a question of fack. But there is awys been a question if there is any outside duty hours for a soljer, whether the *soljer* has the right to be a man.'            ⸺

Prewitt would like, in some vaguely-understood way, to change the world. He seems a "Kid Galahad" to his friend Angelo Maggio. The company commander wants Prewitt to box in the regimental tournament. Prewitt, who has killed a man in the ring, does not want to box again. The choice confronting him is stark enough: he can either go out for the boxing team, or else refuse and receive "The Treatment", a systematic and brutal Army coercion, ending as he saw with "company punishment for inefficiency plus extra duty plus restrictions plus, eventually, the Stockade". In a rueful moment of introspection Prewitt grants that he had suffered "from an overdeveloped sense of justice". Pride, even more than a belief in justice, has shaped Prewitt's character: "I can take everything they can all of them hand out, and come back for more . . ."

What sustains Prewitt through his ordeal is the comradeship of men he respects: Maggio, Jack Molloy, and, from a distance, 1st/Sgt. Warden. Each in a different way breaks through the shell of self-protective pride which Prewitt has erected about himself, and touches him as a man. In Jones's world such allegiances form isolated moments in a military system dominated by fear and violence. Brigadier Slater develops this theme in a discussion with Captain Holmes. In the past, he argues, the fear of authority was only the negative part of a moral code emphasising Honour, Patriotism and Service. Now the world has changed, the positive code has been destroyed by "the machine": "In the Civil War they could still believe they fought for 'Honor.' Not any more. In the Civil War the machine won its first inevitable major victory over the individual. 'Honor' died." Prewitt, like Guy Crouchback in Waugh's *Men at Arms* (1952), felt the "sickening suspicion . . . that he was engaged in a war in which courage and a just cause were quite irrelevant to the issue."

After hearing a song ("The Truckdriver's Blues") Prewitt lapses into reverie on the human condition:

he saw himself and Chief Choate, and Pop Karelson, and Clark, and Anderson, and Warden, each struggling with a different medium, each man's path running by its own secret route from the same source to the same inevitable end. And each man knowing as the long line moved as skirmishers through the night woodsey jungle down the hill that all the others were there with him, each hearing the faint rustlings and straining to communicate, each wanting to reach out and share, each wanting to be known, but each unable, as Clark's whining nasal was unable, to make it known that he was there, and so each forced to face alone whatever it was up ahead, in the unmapped alien enemy's land, in the darkness.

The whole of Jones is in this passage. Men must live their lives in an inner isolation. While hoping to make contact with other men, they must face the prospect that their efforts will fail. At one moment in *From Here to Eternity*, when Prewitt plays taps at Schofield barracks, there is a revelation of "sympathy and under-standing":

The notes rose high in the air and hung above the quadrangle. They vibrated there, caressingly, filled with an infinite sadness, an endless patience, a pointless pride, the requiem and epitaph of the common soldier, who smelled like a common soldier, as a woman once had told him. They hovered like halos over the heads of the sleeping men in the darkened barracks, turning all grossness to the beauty that is the beauty of sympathy and understanding. Here we are, they said, you made us, now see us, dont close your eyes and shudder at it; this beauty, and this sorrow, of things as they are. This is the true song, the song of the ruck, not of battle heroes.

As the notes reverberate across the quadrangle, men come to the porches "to listen in the darkness, feeling the sudden choking kinship bred of fear that supersedes all personal tastes":

They stood in the darkness of the porches, listening, feeling suddenly very near the man beside them, who also was a soldier, who also must die. Then as silent as they had come, they filed back inside with lowered eyes, suddenly ashamed of their own emotion, and of seeing a man's naked soul.

A few such beautiful moments in *From Here to Eternity* intimate the yearning for community, and its frustration. The stark choice before Prewitt, whether to box or go to the Stockade, is no longer available when, in Jones's *The Thin Red Line*, the company lands on Guadalcanal late in 1942. Corporal Fife experiences "... a terror both of unimportance, his unimportance, and of powerlessness: his powerlessness. He had no control or sayso in any of it". Sergeant Bell comes to the same realisation. "Free individuals?" he wonders:

> Ha! Somewhere between the time the first Marines had landed here and this battle now today, American warfare had changed from individualist warfare to collectivist. . . . But free individuals? What a fucking myth? *Numbers* of free individuals, maybe; *collections* of free individuals.

Confronted by the prospect of their own death, Jones shows the soldiers appreciatively agreeing with S/Sgt. Skinny Culn, the company's folk philosopher: "Whatever they say, I'm not a cog in a machine." Jones's point, and the naturalistic perspective, contradicts this hopefulness. The more reflective men, like Fife and Bell, grasp the "total isolation and helplessness" of their situation. Their nightmares are of total entrapment. The autonomous individual of Western humanist cultures reaches its nadir in Jones's *The Thin Red Line*. This kind of exhausting battle turns men into unfeeling, unthinking automatons. The soldiers become indifferent to their tiredness, and this itself was an essential tool for survival:

> Exhaustion, hunger, thirst, dirt, the fatigue of perpetual fear, weakness from lack of water, bruises, danger had all taken their toll of him until somewhere within the last few minutes – Bell did not know exactly when – he had ceased to feel human.

Even fear was dulled by this emotional apathy. Bell no longer cared about anything. But Jones emphasises that this did not impair Bell's ability to function as a soldier. There is, as Jones sees it, a biological basis to this emotional closure:

> Their systems pumped full of adrenaline to constrict the peripheral blood vessels, elevate the blood pressure, make the heart beat more rapidly, and aid coagulation, they were about

as near to automatons without courage or cowardice as flesh and blood can get. Numbly, they did the necessary.[20]

(Orwell's splendid 1940 polemic, "Inside the Whale", concludes with the advice that one must "Give yourself over to the world-process, stop fighting against it or pretending that you control it; simply accept it, endure it, record it." Other contemporary sources might be cited to similar effect: the war, whether for civilians or soldiers, was too immense an experience to be endured with anything other than the wise passivity of quietism.[21]) During combat, sympathy and concern for others narrowed: ". . . while B's middle platoon shot and were shot, fought and sobbed thirty yards away beyond the ledge, Gaff's group talked". (Auden in "Musée des Beaux Arts", written in December 1938, has made this point in a different context.) Combat numbness could, with experience, be recognised and even anticipated. Private Doll welcomes the return of numbness: "It left his mind clear, and cool, suffused with a grinning bloodthirstiness. It spread all through him, making a solid impenetrable layer between himself and the choking fear which would not allow him to swallow as he hugged the ground." After being relieved, the "universal numbness" took two or three days to go away. This kind of collective experience brought the company together; at the same time the personnel of the company changed. Some of the younger officers had been killed; the original noncoms of C-for-Charlie were dead; promotions and the arrival of replacements changed the old company pecking order. Fife was promoted to sergeant, Bell received a battlefield commission. "It was a totally different organisation, with a different feel altogether now." The inevitable tragedy of change was taking place.

Despite the many alterations in C-for-Charlie, the *idea* of the company remained fixed in the minds of those who, in *Whistle*, have been sent to convalesce in Army hospitals in America. Their names have changed (1st/Sgt. Welsh is now Mart Winch, Witt is Bobby Prell, Mess/Sgt. Storm is now John Strange) but their group loyalty is still intense. It is the strongest thing they have left. Landers and Winch are the only ones to understand that they are alone with themselves, and their debilitating wounds; they must learn to live with their isolation. Prell, whose legs had virtually been smashed by a Japanese machine-gun, had no other life or identity to turn to. "Without the old company, Prell did not really feel he belonged anywhere." They each fail to make contact with their old civilian selves. Strange's wife has fallen in love with another man; Landers cannot get along with his family; Winch feels nothing but contempt for his unfaithful wife. They are together in a hospital in Luxor (i.e., Memphis), Tennessee, and form a closely-knit group:

> 'It's not so much that we think a lot of Prell. It's like we were investors. And each of us invested his tiny bit of capital in all the others. When we lose one of us, we all lose a little of our capital. And we none of us really had that much to invest, you see.'
> '"Do not ask for whom the bell tolls,"' Curran quoted.
> 'John Donne, sure,' Landers grinned wolfishly. 'But that's shit. And that's what it is with us. That's abstract. And it's poetry. That's all of humanity. We're not all of humanity. And we don't give a shit about all of humanity. We probably don't give much of a shit about each other, really. It's just that that's all the capital we have.'

The allusion to Donne enables the real point of the comparison to surface: Jones is thinking of Hemingway's use of the passage from Donne as epigraph (and title) of *For Whom the Bell Tolls*. Jones opposes the personal ethic of Robert Jordan with a tragic, intensely-felt group loyalty. As news reaches them of changes in the company, each reacts differently. Sergeant Winch is a supreme realist who knows that no matter how important he once was in the company, he now must be forgotten. He has no lingering hopes of reconstructing the past. Strange regards the news from the South Pacific as a calamity. He had a secret hope ". . . that some day when the war was over they would all of them get together again somewhere". In the middle of a drunken party, Prell has an apparition. The members of his old platoon appear before him, like the sequence in Lewis Milestone's 1930 film adaptation of Remarque's *All Quiet on the Western Front*: "Slowly, each hollow-eyed face turned back to smile wistfully, sadly, before it moved on and faded."

Each in turn were inevitably drawn into their own private lives. Prell, the rebel and individualist, is awarded the Medal of Honor and tours the country selling war bonds. This is an unexpected fate for Prewitt-Witt-Prell, and a sad one. Strange is assigned to a new company, but feels no loyalty to anyone about him. Despite his physical decline, Winch is assigned to a new posting. His attempts to help Prell and Landers are rebuffed and misunderstood. His emotional decline ends in collapse and insanity. Landers cannot face life in the army or outside it, and kills himself in an accident with a car. On his way back to combat in Europe, Strange, like Jack London's Martin Eden, commits suicide by jumping off his ship. *Whistle* portrays the disintegration of the collective loyalties which held these men together. Their solidarity has faded, but there is nothing to put in its place. Strange now suffers "... from feeling naked and alone and orphaned with a severity he'd never experienced before". At the heart of their tragedy, as Jones sees it, is the inevitable disintegration of the feelings which these men had for each other.

As group solidarity takes on a new meaning in war novels, the perceived role of individual soldiers diminished. It was part of the accepted wisdom, in Jones's words, that an infantryman "was about as note-worthy and important as a single mosquito in an airplane-launched DDT spray campaign ...".[22] Guerilla warfare on Leyte in the Philippines was described by Ira Wolfert in similar terms: "We are a tick in their [the Japanese] hide. All the building we do, all the work ... is just to build ourselves up to a tick in their hide. Then the minute they feel the itch of us, they reach with their two fingers and squash."[23] The scale of war intimidated ordinary soldiers, and produced a cynicism well-expressed by Red Valsen in *The Naked and the Dead*: "No one's gonna ask you what to do. ... They just send you out to get your ass blown off.... Don't kid yourself ... a man's no more important than a goddam cow." This is a theme preoccupying General Cummings, who notes in his journals:

> in battle, men are closer to machines than humans. ... We are not so discrete from the machine any longer. ... A machine is worth so many men; the Navy has judged it even more finely than we.

The tendency of wartime journalism, and the Hollywood war movie, was to emphasise the individual's role in the war, and to stress that GIs were ordinary Americans with values recognisably emerging from American culture. Journalists tried to humanise the face of war.[24] Soldiers in their reports were not mosquitoes or ticks caught up in an experience that defied understanding: they were hometown boys, athletes with sweethearts, whose image of home was a compound of soda shops, tinkering with the jalopy, and blueberry pie. In the first part of the war – through 1943 – novelists were competing for a contemporary audience with journalists, and it is true that some of the interest of the early war novels is more documentary and journalistic than anything else. The frequent use of details from journalism in this chapter, side by side with the fiction, has tried to emphasise their affinity. Some of the finest prose of the war is to be found in the wartime journalism of Pyle, Gunther, Tregaskis and Hersey.

It is hard not to feel that the American novel of the Second World War has passed into an almost total neglect. Mailer is still read with attentiveness, but Jones, so powerful a presence in the 1950s, scarcely exists for students of the contemporary novel; and there are few others. Two writers of undoubted promise died young (Thomas Heggen and John Horne Burns), others have become, or more precisely remained, hacks. It is perhaps too easy to exaggerate the importance of academic opinion in the current neglect of the war novel. But the shift in critical enthusiasm away from realism has helped to relegate the war novel to its present cul-de-sac. Having lost its topical interest, and belonging in literary technique to an unselfconscious realism, one might as well be exploring the popular fiction of the civil war for all the currency this literature possesses today. And yet many of these books are interesting, and some are capable of gripping a reader. A few can shock and move. With the exception of Leon Uris, no war novelist filled me with contempt. Even *Battle Cry*, with its cult of the Marine Corps, and comic thinness of characterisation, has its moments of vivid interest. Uris's description of the pursuit of the Japanese through the Tarawa atoll is, perhaps, the finest thing he has ever written.

There is a claim, however, which this literature taken as a whole makes on us. The war killed so many millions of people that the sheer numbers mean nothing, cannot be held in the mind no matter how easily they roll off the tongue. New terms such as "genocide" and "holocaust" have entered our vocabulary, but the reality of individual death, to say nothing of forty million dead, leaks out of western culture. Philippe Ariès has argued that death has been progressively alienated from our lives. People die in hospital, or nursing home, and not with their families; unlike any earlier period in history, it is possible in our society to grow into middle age and beyond without seeing a dead person or having any close relatives die. Overt displays of mourning are likely to make others uncomfortable. Ariès suggests that there is a powerful tendency in western culture towards "the almost total suppression of everything reminding us of death".[25] Ariès does not analyse popular entertainment, however. If he had done so, a puzzling contradiction would have emerged. As we very well know, the representation of death, along with violence and crime, is overwhelmingly present, but the physical reality of death is studiously avoided. The old Hollywood conventions apply with virtually unabated strength. Physical wounds are generally tasteful and people do not make an excessive fuss over their pain. No screaming or tears, and for the most part no gore or smashed limbs.

War writing is not without its own version of these conventions, as may be seen in Richard Tregaskis's account of the aftermath of the battle of Tenaru in *Guadalcanal Diary*. "I watched our men standing in a shooting-gallery line, thumping bullets into the piles of Jap carcasses. The edge of the water grew brown and muddy. Some said the blood of the Jap carcasses was staining the ocean."[26] The "Jap" was a wily and dangerous opponent. Among the dead there may have been wounded men, or those only pretending to be dead. American soldiers had died in the Pacific when Japanese suicidally rose to stab or shoot one last enemy. It was a symbol of the mental and cultural gap separating the adversaries. So the dead must be re-butchered. The erect posture of the soldiers suggests to Tregaskis a shooting-gallery, with its kewpie-doll prizes and fairground atmosphere. The dead have been transformed into "carcasses", the Japanese into "Japs", re-butchery into a shooting-gallery: each transformation subtly alters the human meaning of the scene. Tregaskis indicates that a later count of the dead revealed 871 Japanese corpses, enough for their blood to turn the edges of the river "brown and muddy". The scale of human death is transforming nature, although Tregaskis withdraws from such a conclusion. It was not he who saw the ocean stained by Japanese blood, but unnamed others.

The battle of Tenaru was over, and the American perimeter around Henderson Field on Guadalcanal was secured. A day later Tregaskis revisited the scene. By then the bodies on the spit were "puffed and glossy, like shiny sausages"; one soldier's chest had expanded and been peeled back "like the leaf of an artichoke";

another, wearing tortoise-shell glasses, lay on his back "with his chest a mass of ground meat". The truth about violent death is forced upon us, but domesticated in simile. Tregaskis's description of the Tenaru battlefield is easily among the most powerful passages in *Guadalcanal Diary*. Only Norman Mailer's description of Japanese dead on Anopopei in *The Naked and the Dead* compares with it in impact. Mailer's prose is as heavily figurative as Tregaskis's, and in part serves a similar function. The head of the driver of a Japanese half-track, crushed, lay sodden as if "it were a beanbag". Another corpse lay with its intestines bulging out "like the congested petals of a sea flower"; a body has swollen "like a doll whose stuffing had broken forth". Japanese entrenchments, heavily bombed by the Americans, had partly caved in "like a sand hole on the beach after the children have deserted it and people tread over its edges". Beanbags, flowers, dolls, children playing on the beach: the over-whelming incongruity of the comparisons is, even more than in Tregaskis, calculated and daring. Mailer allows the resonances of violent death to mingle with a whole series of emotions introduced through simile and metaphor which pertain to peace, life, normality. He has attempted to go beyond this in re-humanising the "carcasses": the men in Sergeant Croft's platoon see Japanese dead who "lay very far from repose, their bodies frozen in the midst of an intense contortion"; another's "hands in their death throe had encircled the wound. He looked as if he were calling attention to it". The gestures remain, after death, as reminders of life unwillingly lost. When seen in narrative context (the platoon had been heavily drinking, and on Red Valsen's suggestion went to the site of a recent battle to look for souvenirs), with the brutally unsentimental comments of the platoon, the full force of Mailer's prose is abundantly clear. The tensions created by domesticating the corpses, and then restoring their human and emotional reality, touched the men in the platoon differently, and in ways which the reader can expect if not share. The effect is sombre and complex, and suggests layers of meaning not to be found in superficially similar passages in *Guadalcanal Diary*. Only writing of this quality can make the ultimate meaning of war accessible to our understanding.

Of all the many images of war in American war novels, it is not descriptions of the dead which haunt the memory, but of transformation, the passage out of life, in which war reveals its true face.

The central character in Glen Sire's *The Deathmakers*, a tank commander, recalls early in the novel something he saw during the Battle of the Bulge:

> In the right-hand lane of the road stretching in toward Bastogne, and for as he could see, there were the six-by-sixes, loaded with the orderly rows of sitting men, living men, whose bodies breathed, and who were warm with life and dreams.
>
> And in the left-hand lane, the other column of trucks, coming back out of Bastogne, and for as far as he could see – coming away from the great machine of the war, in their six-by-sixes, were the cadavers of men who, only a few hours before had been in column going up. And now, as they returned the dignity was gone out of them. They were piled high in the trucks like cordwood – no, not like cordwood; more like garbage. Tumbled, pushed, jammed, crammed, contorted; arms, legs, faces, hands jutting out the sides of the trucks – yes, like garbage, he thought, remembering. The orderliness was gone, the sitting side by side. It was a crowd of death, and the dead need no comfort.

Mechanisation has indeed taken command. There were small hints of this process embedded in the linguistic quirk of weapons being endowed with their own voice:

> machines guns cry out, 'Da-da-dat! Da-da-dat!'
> The Garand exclaims 'Kapow!' and the 4.2 mortar adds 'Palot!'
> while the bazooka terminates the discussion with an
> irrefutable 'Phoosh!' (*Beach Red*)

The same idea, of weapons speaking to each other, occurred to Tregaskis: "It was 11.40, and we were working our way down the beach at the fringe of the jungle, when there came a sudden splattering of sharp rifle reports. ... Deeper-toned rifles took up the chorus, machine guns joined in, and the shower of sound became like a rainstorm."[27] The trucks roll to and fro from the battle, carrying soldiers and returning with disorderly "garbage"; guns speak out, seemingly with a volition of their own: war is carried on increasingly without the need for further intervention by soldiers. There is a bleak comedy in warfare taken over by weapons, and perhaps also a preview of a battlefield mainly

consisting of computers, weapons-systems and electronic count-
er-measures. The transformation of the soldier from central importance in war to an adjunct of diminishing interest hints at a
host of other reversals and transformations which now characterise modern warfare. The writer who grasped the ironic possibilities of such fluid meaning was Joseph Heller. *Catch-22* (1961)
caught the temper of the 1960s, at a time when the other novels of
the war had begun to fade from memory (and when the cycle of
adaptations of major novels for the cinema had been completed).

None of the meanings of normality or sanity survives in Yossarian's world. He alone is the one who cares, who is outraged at
the moral wilderness which constitutes the Air Force on Pianosa.
There is no shred here of purpose, group loyalty or idealism.
Every value comes under Heller's skeptical scrutiny:

> 'The hot dog, the Brooklyn Dodgers, Mom's apple pie.
> That's what everyone's fighting for. But who's fighting for the
> decent folk? Who's fighting for more votes for the decent folk?
> There's no patriotism, that's what it is. And no matriotism,
> either.'
> The warrant officer on Yossarian's left was unimpressed.
> 'Who gives a shit?' he asked tiredly, and turning over on his side
> to go to sleep.[28]

The verbal energy, and Heller's openness to nonsense while in
search of fresh meaning, suddenly run up against a discourse
from a different novel. The warrant officer is closer to Sergeant
Croft's world than Yossarian's. Heller gaily allows his considerable verbal gifts free rein, and is not afraid to negotiate the distance
from tragedy to black comedy in successive paragraphs. He
adores the snappy one-liner, the stand-up comedian's wisecrack,
the pun and verbal misunderstanding. Heller is the first novelist
to show the influence of the Marx Brothers. He seems also to have
realised that there was a new audience to write for, a college-
educated readership able to appreciate literary allusions of an
accessible sort: the Chaplain finds himself echoing Shylock; ex-
Pfc Wintergreen makes a nice joke with T.S. Eliot's name; and
there is an allusion to "Raskolnikov's dream".

At a deeper level, Heller's humour is serious, indeed even
political. It is firmly based upon the perception (so widely to be
observed in American war novels) that the old clarity between

enemy and friend, them and us, was no longer meaningful in the conditions of modern warfare. *Catch-22* submerges its bitterness in humour and irony, but its meaning is not to be mistaken: the old claims of patriotism and loyalty have, for the *Catch-22* generation, lost their power, have indeed become an obscene charade. The novel bids a plague on both sides. Indeed, in Heller's world causes are immediately recognisable as deceits and frauds. We see nothing of the Nazis in the novel, but "our" side was as blandly bureaucratic, as inhumane, as uncaring, as we know "they" were. The politics of the novel are from the Cold War, but belong more to an undercurrent of suspicion which gained ground in the 1950s that the rival states were far more akin to each other, were being reciprocally deformed by their conflict, than the proclaimed official ideologies would suggest. Heller tapped a subterannean current of feeling on the American left, which was looking for a way to escape the Cold War dichotomies. He gave brilliant comic expression to a minority, fugitive sentiment, and helped persuade a generation that they agreed. The novel ends – shades of *Huck Finn* – with flight and escape, a psychologically accurate and sympathetic response to the dilemmas it poses. The irony of ironies is that, unnoticed by the millions of young readers of *Catch-22*, anxiety was growing in the Pentagon and the State Department in Washington over the deterioration of the position in South Vietnam. A few soldiers and politicians were beginning to wonder in 1961 whether it might be necessary to send American advisers to bolster up the Saigon regime.[29] As one nightmare began to lift, another swiftly loomed upon the horizon.

# 6 Japan: a Perspective

**Harry Guest**

Party government in Japan came to a violent end when members of an extremist organisation assassinated the Prime Minister on 15 May 1932. This was only one of a series of bloody events during the 1920s and 1930s as fanatical patriots sought to turn the clock back and rid Japan of all contaminating influences that had been introduced from the West during the previous eighty years.

National pride had been offended by the White Australia Policy as well as new American immigration laws which were specifically aimed to curb Japanese economic expansion. The London Naval Treaty in 1930, too, helped to reinforce the sense of deliberate international persecution.

Japan had been hard hit by the Depression. Agricultural communities suffered most and young army officers, who were recruited largely from farming stock, increasingly believed that it was the alliance between big business and party politicians that was responsible for the immense discrepancies in wealth.

Communism was tainted because it offered a non-Japanese solution. The Japanese Communist Party, secretly inaugurated in Hiroshima in July 1922, was outlawed eleven months later, and leftists were persecuted both under "democratic" and "military" rule. Several hundred left-wing sympathisers are estimated to have been liquidated during the 1930s and 1940s. In *Runaway Horses* – the second volume of the tetralogy which, with a consciously melodramatic gesture, he completed at dawn some eight hours before his gory suicide in 1970 – Mishima Yukio[1] gives details of a right-wing brotherhood who are intending, in 1933, to purge Japan of its capitalists in the hope that the people will see the errors of their ways, turn to the emperor again and get rid of any debilitating Western influences. Young members of this secret society are arrested before they are able to assassinate various key industrialists. While in the police cells they hear the screams of young Communists being beaten up and, when a right-wing prisoner asks why he and his friends are not being treated similarly, the policeman tells him that he and his colleagues sympathise with the aims of the brotherhood – the leftists are foreign-influenced whereas the right-wing society is patriotic in its desire to break the law.

Outbreaks of violence from extremist organisations gave increasing power to the military who could always use the threat of insubordination as blackmail. The professional politicians found it impossible to curb the influence of the army and, by the mid-1930s, Japan was virtually run by a military government.

Japanese expansion had begun of course with the annexation of Korea in 1910; but in 1932 the invasion of Manchuria heralded a war with China which flared intermittently after Japan left the League of Nations in 1933 until, in 1937, war was formally declared and the horrifying massacres in Nanking and elsewhere indicated to the world that Japan had openly embarked on a policy of forcible colonisation of the Asian mainland – using, with increasing frequency, the argument that they were liberating Asia from the Western colonial powers. Cinematic fiction was tailor-made for the expanding market. In 1940, *China Night* – the story of a love-affair between a Japanese naval officer and a Chinese orphan – was given three separate endings: for Chinese distribution they were happily wed; for the Southeast Asian market he saves her from suicide; for home audiences the girl kills herself.

In 1940 all former political parties were dissolved and the Tripartite Pact of Mutual Assistance was signed with Germany and Italy. Japan advanced further and further southwards on the Asian mainland and, in the summer of 1941, forced the French to allow Japanese forces to occupy the whole of Indochina. In December that year came the attack on Pearl Harbor.

Intellectuals and creative artists (among whom was the great director Ozu Yasujiro) were conscripted as a matter of deliberate policy and sent to the battlefield – not only so that they should not be regarded as special cases but in order to encourage them to collect facts of Japanese heroism for distribution at home. Hino Ashihei's three volumes of war diaries *Troops Among Barley, Troops on Bare Earth, Troops Among Flowers* published in 1938 and 1939 were immediate best-sellers. They got across the authentic flavour of the Chinese War while at the same time enlivening the reader at home with the sense of Japanese bravery and Japan's divinely inspired mission to free the Asian mainland from the yoke of the West. One of the anecdotes Hino recounts is of a villager he knew whose horse was commandeered for the army – a theme expanded in Yamamoto Kajiro's film *The Horse* (1941) on which Kurosawa Akira worked as assistant director. The pathos of this film in which a colt reared by a young girl is taken for the army did not find favour with the authorities: all sacrifices were to be made gladly, indeed were not to be counted as sacrifices at all.

In 1938 Ishikawa Tatsuzô brought out his novel *Living Soldier* which criticised the war. It was immediately banned and became something of a test case as thereafter authors were actively encouraged to produce pro-war literature. A new school of writing emerged, "novels that followed the colours" like Ozaki Shiro's *Late Autumn Wind* (1939), Hayashi Fusao's *Shanghai Battle-Line* or Kishida Kunio's *50 Days with the Army* (both 1940). Moreover, watch committees were set up in every town and village to monitor reading habits – members of these committees were to be branded as criminals after 1945.

Censorship under the military régime became extremely strict. Everything from magazines to school textbooks had to be submitted to the most rigorous vetting before publication was allowed. As early as 1937, the film industry was given the most specific instructions as to what was expected. First and foremost, military matters were not to be treated lightly. However, realistic horror in battle was to be avoided as having a bad effect on morale. Individualism as portrayed and praised in European or American films was to be shunned. The Japanese family spirit and the sense of duty and sacrifice were to be stressed. Puritanism prevailed in sexual matters and any evidence of "loose" morality was labelled decadent. Romantic love was a Western invention and ipso facto undesirable. Fanatical "Japaneseness" went so far as to ban foreign words from the language, an experiment in turning back the linguistic clock that Goebbels was attempting to perform in Germany. Neologisms were coined to replace words such as "baseball" borrowed from English, and their use was made obligatory.

In 1937, the first year of the "official" Chinese War, a novella by Kafû, then in his late fifties, found disfavour with the authorities. It may in fact be his masterpiece, *A Strange Tale from East of the River*. With a kind of dreamy squalor he imagines a writer very like himself "stuck" as it were with a story he is engaged on and seeking to find creative release by wandering in a sleazy half-world of cheap brothels beyond the River Sumida, Tokyo's traditional northeastern boundary. The narrator forms a half-hearted relationship with a prostitute and, anonymous both from a desire to cast off his social role and to avoid suspicion from the police, he pretends to be poor – indeed, to her, he goes so far as to claim he is a peddler of dubious books and thus to identify himself with a world where crime and fallen women form an alliance against strait-laced society.

Not only the twilit morality of the area of Tokyo described in the most sensuous detail but the fact the "hero" is engaged in the translation of French literature meant that it was an undesirable text for those supposedly stirring and heroic times. After it Kafû published nothing until after the war. However, in 1942 he wrote *The Decoration*, set mainly in the slatternly dressing-room of a theatre where the girl dancers sprawl and smoke and gossip between performances. An old man earns a pittance bringing food to the girls and, talking to a young actor in a fake soldier's uniform, he boasts of his own military glories – in 1904, during the Russo-Japanese War, of special significance being the first occasion in modern history when an Oriental nation defeated a Western power. The following day he is persuaded to bring along the medal he won. The girls are thrilled, make him put on a stage-uniform and get him photographed. When the picture is developed it is seen that the medal was sewn on the right pocket, not the left. So the photographer reverses the negative "to make things seem in order". In this shabby, believable setting Kafû takes us to the heart of ostentatious militarism and shows the hollowness, the ultimate pathos and, by photographic sleight-of-hand, the way even apparent evidence is suspect.

Civilian life was unimportant to the authorities. It was the expansion during the first years after Pearl Harbor that was acclaimed and regarded as being the true subject of heroic fiction. By February 1942, because Siam after a token resistance of twenty-four hours had allowed Japanese troops through her territory, Japan controlled the whole of Malaya as far as Singapore. Burma and the Philippines were taken in May. In the same year Yamamoto more than made amends for his gently defeatist *The Horse* with an immense epic *The War at Sea from Hawai to Malaya*. So brilliant were the effects that the US Occupation forces assumed it was a documentary, though in fact the entire film was shot in the studio. The war heroes were the embodiment of Japanese fighting spirit – something no effete Westerner could either understand or withstand. To keep this spirit going martial songs were written and circulated – songs that are still sung in upstairs rooms above certain cafés in Tokyo today when veterans foregather.

The "Spirit of Yamato" was extolled – Yamato being the name of the province ruled by the legendary first emperor of Japan in 660 B.C. and a name that has become synonymous with all the most desirable qualities in Japanese tradition. Contemporary Japanese were conscious of being a superior race, but flowers of such splendour must be shown to have strong roots. More and more the authorities encouraged historical or pseudo-historical fiction that would prove how native to Japan are such virtues as self-sacrifice, stoicism and abiding love of the fatherland. Yoshikawa Eiji – significantly a member in his student years of an extremist patriotic movement – has been called the inventor of pre-20th century Japan and certainly his highly-coloured, carefully tailored novels demonstrated to his contemporaries exactly what they had imagined Japan's heroic past to have been. It was expedient to re-interpret, or rather to traduce, three epochs in particular. The 12th century civil war that raged between the major clans not only brought about the rise of the samurai with their code of loyalty and asceticism. The conflict also had as a direct result the establishment of the Shogunate – a system whereby the all-powerful samurai government controlled and protected the imperial throne. This could now be seen as the historical precedent for the current situation – a Fascist government running Japan "in accordance with the wishes of the Divine Emperor". The Tokugawa era (1603–1868) was a period during which Japan, uncontaminated by the West, saw the common people gaining sufficient status to be themselves loyal retainers of the emperor. In this age the "aristocratic" arts of poetry and theatre became more available as traditional themes and legends were moulded into Kabuki plays or Bunraku puppet-dramas – both genres aimed at the emerging town-dweller class. The Meiji Restoration (1868–1912) was a time when Japan took from the West what was to prove useful to her while never abandoning the true national qualities of frugality and obedience to the emperor. Tomita Tsuneo pleased the authorities with his novel *Sugata Sanshiro* (1943). The period is the 1880s and the martial art of ju-jitsu has become lifeless and set uncreatively in its ways. A new version, called judo, based on meditation, asceticism and utter dedication, has found a new devotee in the eponymous hero. Kurosawa read it and made it into his first feature film.

As an antidote to the slapdash propaganda of Yoshikawa's immensely successful historical novels, Tanizaki Junichiro, Japan's greatest contemporary writer, embarked on a version in modern Japanese of Lady Murasaki's *The Tale of Genji*. It should perhaps be said that this rich and densely lyrical work which has been hailed with much justification as a genuine harbinger of Proustian techniques and is in any case one of the earliest examples in the world of what can be classified as a "novel" is far more remote from 20th-century Japanese than, say, Chaucer is from modern English. (The work has been superbly translated in our own time both by Arthur Waley and by Edward Seidensticker.)

Tanizaki worked, officially, at this self-imposed task from 1939 to 1941. Then, frustrated by the restrictions and totally out of sympathy with the régime and its hysterical praise of war, he withdrew from the strident lies around him to study, in *The Makioka Sisters*, pre-war Japanese society with deep affection, lyrical irony, and a sense of a lovely epoch gone for ever. Comparisons are possible both with the plays of Chekhov and with Thomas Mann's *Buddenbrooks*, yet, in its oblique narrative, it is uniquely a Japanese work. The work was serialised (as is often the case with Japanese fiction) and he was forced to discontinue its publication on the grounds that it was incompatible with wartime discipline. It did not appear in its entirety until the war was over. In his speech accepting the Imperial Prize for literature in 1949 he himself said he reached out across the gulf of war in an attempt to re-create a beautiful world that had vanished. "I tried to limit myself to what was attractive, but I was unable to withdraw completely from the enveloping storm. This was the necessary fate of a novel born of war and peace."

The Makioka family – once important merchants in Osaka – has declined in its fortunes. There is no son to carry on the name and so the husbands of the two eldest daughters take on the surname of Makioka – not, in fact, an uncommon Japanese practice. Through over-caution the fortunes of the family gradually ebb still further and much of the book is a threnody for the lost splendours of civilised life in Osaka – the traditional commercial centre of Japan since the 1600s and possessing a reputation for ease and gentleness compared with the brasher, more ruthless atmosphere of Edo later to become Tokyo, capital of the east.

The plot centres on the two youngest sisters. Yukiko is at 30 still unmarried and the family find a succession of suitors whom, one by one, she passively refuses. Although at the end of this long novel preparations are at last well under way for Yukiko's wedding, the reader feels it not unlikely she will still find a way to evade the final commitment. If Yukiko can be said to represent the Japanese girl of the past, doomed, probably, to a quietly sterile life, Takeo, the youngest sister, is a rootless, pleasure-seeking example of the modern Japanese woman. Equally self-centred, though in a more active fashion, she has an illegitimate child and ends up as the wife of a barman – it is emphasised that the bar will cater especially for foreigners. The sisters are contrasted, but Tanizaki's mind works in a complex way. For example, all Yukiko's suitors are found for her whereas Takeo goes out and gets her own men. Takeo also actually earns a living – ironically by making traditional Japanese dolls – whereas Yukiko never does anything. Tanizaki stresses his sense of change and loss as the eldest sister is forced to move her family to Tokyo where they have no friends, no identity, no reputation. It is the beginning of the Pacific War. Rice rationing has been imposed and, because of the austerity edicts, they are unable to have new kimonos for Yukiko's apparently imminent wedding. In early days the Makioka family know some White Russian émigrés who refuse to refer to Petrograd by its post-revolutionary name. Later some Germans they meet return to Berlin and chatty letters are received mentioning the Hitlerjugend. The last letter they receive is dated 1941. An age has come very grimly to an end.

By any standards, *The Makioka Sisters* is a great novel. The three-dimensional characterisation, the humour and the narrative control make it more than an enjoyable experience for the non-Japanese reader. But its special quality for the Japanese lies in its evocation of a society in flux – traditional ceremonies lovingly described and seen as vanishing as a world descends into war. In the last pages, the family go and view the last of the cherry-blossom in Kyôto and, as they drink cold saké from lacquer cups, realise poignantly that, because of their worries, they have not taken in any of the beauty they have seen. Tanizaki, like many authors of his generation, had begun by being frenziedly "Western" in his enthusiasms. By the time he wrote *Some Prefer Nettles* in 1928 he had come, at the age of 42, to concentrate on the perfection of a purely Japanese style.

Kawabata Yasunari, on the other hand, has always been regarded as a "traditionalist". Indeed, his Nobel Prize in 1968 was to celebrate "a uniquely Japanese achievement". His novels are allusive, even cryptic. The prose he uses has echoes of haiku, and the oblique dialogue between two characters often resembles the exchange of poems between the heroes and heroines of earlier Japanese romances. *Snow Country*, written and published intermittently between 1935 and 1947, is regarded by many as his most typical and successful work.

A man of independent means called Shimamura visits a small spa on the west coast – the "snow country" where for several months each year the countryside is blanketed with impassable snow. He has a wife and family whom we never encounter and his dilettante passion fixes itself on Western ballet which he has never seen, has no intention of ever going to and knows about merely from books on the subject. Kawabata specifically relates the odd charm of this kind of knowledge to a love-affair with a woman one has never seen. Shimamura lives at one remove from his hobby – as he remains at one remove from all human feelings. He has an affair, off and on, with an amateur geisha who ekes out a living as an "entertainer" at the spa, drinking too much and going rapidly to seed. She loves him but he is incapable of responding and, at the end of this short novel, we glimpse the shabby future in store for her when her physical charms have gone. There is another, younger, girl, first seen by her reflection in the train window – much play is made of the way Shimamura tends to find life in mirrors or in panes of glass, at one remove each time from the "real thing". At the climax of the novel the first woman plunges into a burning building to rescue the second girl while Shimamura stands passively by. She emerges with the girl in her arms but the book ends without our knowing whether she is alive or dead. All that is definite is that Shimamura will drift on, atrophied, of no use to the geisha or indeed anyone. Whereas both Kafû's novella and Tanizaki's saga of Osaka life were linked in detail to the outside world, *Snow Country* hangs, as it were, anywhere in time. The seasons are as delicately and correctly described as in any haiku but the events of the novel are not connected with history.

The atmosphere under the military government was not conducive to good writing. Certain themes were actually given out to authors to work on – for example, to write a book that would encourage students to volunteer for the armed forces. Only, perhaps, a fatalistic Oriental turn of mind could have interpreted Tamba Fumio's 1939 novel *The Regiment That Will Not Return* as a call to arms. It is hardly surprising that the few major works of literature produced during the war years were not in fact published until after the war was over. The paranoia and narrow-mindedness of the authorities is shown by the fact that such an innocuous novel as *First Journey* by the popular woman writer Hayashi Fumiko was banned in 1941 because it did not encourage the war effort.

The experiences of Japan's two greatest film-directors are of relevance here. Mizoguchi made four important films during the period 1939–45. Two of them were set in the Meiji era and concerned Kabuki actors and Bunraku puppeteers respectively. These were acceptable because they only celebrated purely Japanese achievements though neither *The Story of the Last Chrysanthemum* nor *Woman of Osaka* was overtly patriotic. In 1942 he was ordered to make his version of the hardy Japanese perennial *The Tale of the Loyal Forty-Seven Ronin* who, in 1703, avenged their master's death and then all took their own lives. In 1944, having thus placated the authorities, he was able to make a highly personal film *The Life of an Artist* set in the Tokugawa period.

Although later films of Mizoguchi's like *Ugetsu Monogatari* have won well-deserved acclaim in the West as examples of Japanese cinema at its best, it is perhaps in the work of Ozu that the spirit of Japanese art is most perfectly conveyed. Quiet, eschewing drama-tic effects, he is usually content to set his camera low and just observe people – because it is after all on the floor, on the tatami mats of the traditional Japanese house, that ordinary domestic life takes place. When he was allowed to return from China in 1939 he wrote a filmscript: a man is about to leave for the front and he and his wife discuss what to have at the customary final meal together. They choose the most simple, the most Japanese – green tea over rice, the title of the piece. The censors rejected it out of hand as "lacking seriousness" and the film was never made, though Ozu used the title alone for a much later film. In 1943, his *There was a Father* told a tale more acceptable to the vetting powers – a boy is drafted after marrying the daughter of his father's best friend. The father dies and the son returns to carry on the family name – though it is surprising that this rather downbeat film found any more favour than the script he was forced to abandon.

Ozu was in any case re-drafted to make propaganda films. By a curious chance he found himself in Singapore in charge of confiscated American material. He was able, quite illegally, to show himself such works as *Stagecoach*, *Fantasia* and *Citizen Kane*, none of which of course had been seen in Japan at that time.

Kurosawa was forced to make a sequel to *Sugata Sanshiro* – a blatant piece of propaganda. The hero proves that a subtle exponent of judo will always beat a hulking white boxer. This poor film was presumably a sop to the authorities so that he could make *Those Who Step on the Tiger's Tail*, his own version of the Noh drama *Ataka*. It is on the surface impeccably feudal – the fleeing Yoshitsuné, the charismatic real-life hero of the twelfth-century chronicles, is pretending to be a mere porter. When he and his group of loyal retainers reach the Ataka checkpoint on their route north, the lord in charge of the barrier smells a rat and delays the party. Yoshitsuné's servant strikes his master so as to prove he cannot possibly be who the lord suspects. Although seeing through the deception, the lord is so moved by this incredible act of devotion that he lets them pass. Thus far, the classic story is as it is known to every Japanese schoolchild. However, Kurosawa introduces a comic part, another porter, who acts as a foil rather like the Common Man in *A Man for All Seasons*, adding a sarcastic note that criticises the values offered. The film was accepted by the military government but, by an ironic twist of history, the Occupation censors banned it because it evoked Japan's feudal past. It was not shown until 1952.

The tide began turning against Japan in 1943. At Guadalcanal the Americans began their highly successful island-hopping strategy. The British regained Burma. The Asian nationalists who had welcomed the Japanese as liberators were now co-operating with the Allies to expel them. In late 1944 Russia finally declared war on Japan and by 1945 the Americans were in control of Iwo Jima and Okinawa and using them as bases for a series of devastating air attacks on the Japanese mainland. On 6 August 1945 the first atomic bomb was dropped on Hiroshima.

As Japan sued for peace, the emperor's voice was heard for the first time on the radio when he announced to a stunned nation that he was not a god. The Second World War was over, and as has been ruefully expressed more than once, "democracy was imposed on Japan". MacArthur legalised the existence of the Communist party, forbade Japan ever again to arm herself (although, by a verbal quibble, she was allowed in 1952 to begin building up her Self-Defence Forces) and set about laying the foundations for a stable and peace-loving society.

The Japanese are an adaptable people. However, fanatical devotion to emperor and fatherland had called upon all Japanese to kill themselves rather than surrender. There had been regular classes in every school and university on the correct technique for committing ritual suicide. The fact relatively few chose death rather than accept defeat says much for the flexibility of the Japanese character. Even so, the phrase "we who wrongfully survived" is a common one in the literature of the post-war years.

Dislocation and bewilderment soon gave way to the activities of rebuilding. Of war guilt there seems to have been hardly a trace. The Japanese have an amazing – and possibly enviable – capacity for forgetting, ignoring or bypassing what is unpleasant or inconvenient. Furthermore, Japanese art is traditionally oblique. The language itself resists direct statement. Ambiguities abound. The major works of Japanese literature have always impressed by their subtlety. An interior awareness is especially prized. Given this heritage it is not surprising that no major writer since 1945 has treated the war at all. Tanizaki dealt with sexual predicaments and the problems of aging in *The Key* and *Diary of a Mad Old Man* (1956 and 1962). Kawabata explored tensions between past and present in an increasingly narcissistic way until his suicide in 1972. Mishima's tetralogy *The Sea of Fertility* attempts to give a panoramic view of Japanese life over the last century but the four novels are so deliberately "poetic" and anyway written to express a bizarre theory of reincarnation that one cannot, except incidentally, see the passing of actual history. His earlier novel *Forbidden Colours* (1949) gives a picture of life under the Occupation. One of Kafû's last works is a story published in 1948, *The Scavengers*, in which he describes with bitterness the privations brought on by defeat. Two women have been scouring the countryside round Tokyo for food. The older dies, overcome by the heat. Her companion robs her corpse of the rice she has been carrying and, once over the brow of the hill, sells it at a profit to another scavenger.

Gomikawa Junpei's *Condition of Man* (1950) caters to popular taste but is nonetheless an effective anti-war novel. Noma Hiroshi's *Vacuum Zone* (1951) is a savagely realistic account of brutality in the Japanese army that has been hailed as Japan's *From Here To Eternity.* Yoshida Mitsuri wrote his *Last Hours of the Battleship Yamato* shortly after the ship was sunk in 1943 but did not publish it until 1952. The fate of this particular battleship with its proud name *Yamato* or Old Japan was naturally of geat significance. The hero of Takeyama Michio's *Harp of Burma* (1955) is a private in the Japanese army who, technically a deserter, becomes a Buddhist monk and devotes his life to burying the unknown corpses of Japanese soldiers in the jungle. This was made into a moving film by Ichikawa Kon in 1956. *Fires on the Plain* by Oka Shohei (1958) was also made into a film by this director though he altered the ending by having the hero shot. The novel shows Japanese troops in the Philippines reduced to cannibalism, and its impact was considerable in that the horrors of war are described in exceptional physical detail. Ibuse Masuji's *Black Rain* (1964) is about the dropping of the atomic bomb.

The post-war years have showed on the whole the same avid desire to absorb and master foreign artistic trends that marked the first decades after the Meiji Restoration. However, it is important to remember that Japanese itself is linguistically isolated. Even the borrowed ideographs are different in use and sound from Chinese. Any foreign word is written in a special script that stands out as an alien shape on the printed page. The Japanese are proud of their uniqueness and of their homogeneity and never really believe, despite evidence to the contrary, that foreigners can master their language or appreciate their art. This in-turning is of extreme psychological interest and explains many of the attitudes present in their fiction.

In recent years the government has sanctioned the publication of textbooks for use in schools which greatly underplay the atrocities committed by Japan. This has caused vociferous and understandable protests from China, Korea and Taiwan. But the Japanese are not a nation of breast-beaters and they seem content to look ahead to a future of increasing technological victories rather than back upon a bloodstained and ultimately futile campaign of military conquest. It is interesting that, as a legacy of those years, the average reader, cinema-goer or television-viewer still prefers two-dimensional and inaccurate accounts of Old Japan when dignity and stoicism went hand in hand with loyalty and good taste – and there were no foreigners.

## English Translations of Works Mentioned

Kawabata, Yasunari, *Snow Country*, trans. by Edward G. Seidensticker. (New York, 1955).

Mishima, Yukio. (Kimitake Hiraoka), *Forbidden Colours*, trans. by Alfred H. Marks (London, 1968).

——, *The Sea of Fertility* (Tetralogy): I *Spring Snow*, trans. by Michael Gallagher (London 1972); II *Runaway Horses*, trans. by Michael Gallagher (London, 1973); III *The Temple of Dawn*, trans. by Dale Saunders and Cecilia Segawa Seigle (London, 1974); *The Decay of the Angel*, trans. by Edward G. Seidensticker (London, 1975).

Nagai, Kafû (Sokichi Nagai), *A Strange Tale from East of the River*, trans. by Edward G. Seidensticker in *Kafû the Scribbler* (Stanford, 1965); also sep. (Tokyo, 1972).

Oka, Shohei, *Fires on the Plain*, trans. by Ivan Ira Morris (Rutland, Vermont, 1960).

Takeyama, Michio, *The Harp of Burma*, trans. by Howard Hibbett (Rutland, Vermont, 1958).

Tanizaki, Junichiro. *Some Prefer Nettles*, trans. by Edward G. Seidensticker. New York 1955.

——, *The Makioka Sisters*, trans by Edward G. Seidensticker (New York, 1957).

——, *The Key*, trans. by Howard Hibbett (London, 1961).

——, *Diary of a Mad Old Man*, trans. by Howard Hibbett. (New York, 1965).

# Notes

## Chapter 1  Britain

1. "War Books", *Horizon* 4, no. 24 (Dec. 1941) 416–37.
2. "Literature in this Global War", *College English* 4, no. 8 (May 1943) 453–9. For the maxim of 'Inter arma silent Musae' cf. also Remenyi, note 48.
3. "Why not War Writers?: a Manifesto", *Horizon* 4, no. 22 (Oct. 1941) 236–39.
4. "Have English Writers Marked Time?: a Conspectus of Prose and Poetry during Six Years of War", *The Saturday Review of Literature*, 5 Jan. 1946, pp. 2–5, 31.
5. "English Literature in Wartime", *Revue des Langues Vivantes* 11 (1946) 82–5.
6. *The Novel 1945–1950* (London, 1951) pp. 12–17.
7. "Fiction of the Second World War", *College English* 17, no. 4 (Jan. 1956) 197–204.
8. *A Reader's Guide to the Contemporary English Novel* (London, 1961, rev. edn 1972); esp. pp. 6, 15f. Cf. also e.g. Walter Allen, *Tradition and Dream: The English and American Novel from the Twenties to our Time* (London, 1964) p. 262f.
9. Esp. B.S. Oldsey, "Aspects of Combat in the Novel, 1900–1950", Ph.D. Thesis, Pennsylvania State University, 1955, (Ann Arbor: University Microfilms). Also H. Bennemann, "Der II. Weltkrieg im englischen Roman", *WZKMUL* 12 (1963) 533–7, an Abstract; it proved impossible to obtain the full text of this Leipzig Thesis. Bennemann lists earlier English and German contributions.
10. *Not Without Glory* (London, 1976), "Introduction", pp. 7–22; quotations pp. 21, 20.
11. For this see Paul Fussell's *The Great War and Modern Memory* (New York, 1975; repr. 1977).
12. *The Second World War: An Illustrated History* (London, 1975; repr. Harmondsworth 1976) p. 21.
13. "MCMXIV" in *The Whitsun Weddings*, 1964.
14. *War Begins at Home*, ed. and arr. by Tom Harrisson and Charles Madge (London, 1940) p. 35.
15. For an intensive portrait of a youngster at war one might well look at Italo Calvino, *The Path to the Nest of Spiders* (*Il Sentiero dei nidi di ragno*, 1947; transl. 1956).
16. The popularity of the subject is also shown by books recounting the production of big war films, e.g. Leonard Mosley's *Battle of Britain* (1969) and Iain Johnstone's *The Arnhem Report* (1977). Finally, there is the amazing number of reprints.

17. *The New York Times Book Review*, 17 Apr. 1949, pp. 1, 21f.
18. Cf. Mark Arnold-Forster, *The World at War* (London, 1973, repr. 1976) p. 138.
19. Quoted from: Sir Winston Churchill, *Great War Speeches* (London, 1957, repr. 1966) pp. 21; cf. p. 24.
20. *Postscripts* (London, 1940) pp. 14f.
21. To be compared with the hilarious BBC television series (1958 and later) and Norman Longmate's *The Real Dad's Army: the Story of The Home Guard* (London, 1974).
22. Cf. James Tucker, *The Novels of Anthony Powell* (London, 1976) pp. 174.
23. Esp. *The Gale of the World* (1969).
24. Its style, together with that of *Concluding*, was interestingly analysed by John Russell in *Style in Modern Fiction* (Baltimore & London, 1978) pp. 158–88.
25. *L'Armee des ombres*; written in French (1943) by Kessell (who also served in the RAF); publ. first in English transl., 1944, then in French, 1945. Quotations from the Cresset Press edn. (London, 1944, repr. 1945) p. 90.
26. *Women and Children First* (London, 1979) p. 194.
27. Quoted from: *The Songs and Ballads of World War II*, ed. Martin Page (London, 1973, repr. 1975) p. 120f.
28. Symptomatic for this is not only e.g. the crew in Lewis's *Pathfinders* but also Gibson's crew on the Dam Buster Mission, Cf. *Enemy Coast Ahead* (London, 1946) p. 19f.
29. A specific instance is brought out concisely in Martin Walker's article about El Alamein, "The Last Stand of the Old Empire", *Guardian*, 23 Oct. 1982, p. 17.
30. Stronger even than forward projections such as Arthur Wise, *Who Killed Enoch Powell?* (1972) and Sir John Hackett et al., *The Third World War* (1978).
31. *Few Eggs and No Oranges: A Diary . . .* (London, 1976) p. 473.
32. Cf. besides *The First World War in Fiction*, ed. H.M. Klein (London 1976, repr. 1979) p. 9 my "Fiction of the First World War and the Problems of Fiction" in: *Proceedings of the IXth Congress of the ICLA*, ed. Z. Konstantinovic et al., vol. 4 (Innsbruck, 1982) pp. 109–14.
33. His *Spanish Farm Trilogy* (1924–46) is one of the best Great War novels.
34. *How Dear is Life* (1954), *A Fox under my Cloak* (1955), *The Golden Virgin* (1957), *Love and the Loveless* (1958) and *A Test to Destruction* (1960).
35. Originally publ. as by "Peter Towry"; Kermode's Preface dates from 1965, repr. 1970.
36. There is one well-known example in First World War fiction: Forester's *The General* (1936).
37. Introduction to the Bodley Head edn, London, 1966.
38. Cf. *The Knights of Bushido: A Short History of Japanese War Crimes* (London, 1968, repr. 1964) pp. 179–81. A parallel to Van der Post's John Lawrence is found in Barber, *Sinister Twilight* (London, 1958, repr. 1972) p. 276.
39. Tim Carew's *The Fall of Hong Kong* (London, 1960, repr. 1963) is a conspicuous example. His motive is anger, cf. notably p. 234.
40. One of several television screenings was interestingly reviewed by David Lodge: "Dam and Blast", *London Review of Books* 4, no. 19 (21 Oct. 1982) p. 18.
41. Even from the perspective of a Personal Assistant as recorded, after C.R.

Thompson, in Gerald Pawle's *The War and Colonel Warden* (London, 1963, repr. 1965).

42. *Design and Truth in Autobiography* (London, 1960).

43. The delightful threat of a fifth and final volume, made at the end of *Mussolini*, looks like a parting joke.

44. He did revise to some extent, cf. Desmond Graham's OUP edn. (London, 1979) as opposed to the Faber edn. 1966 and the first (London: Editions Poetry, 1946). There remain aspects and details one feels he would not have left alone.

45. Quoted from: *The Terrible Rain: The War Poets 1939–1945*, ed. Brian Gardner (London, 1966, repr. 1968) p. 106f.

46. Cf. Reginald Pound, *The Lost Generation* (London, 1964). Not to be confused with the term as applied to American expatriate circles in Paris during the twenties.

47. Followed by a jump into Cold War thrillers with *Arm Me, Audacity* in 1954 – partly exploiting the earlier book.

48. Even in the States; Joseph Remenyi puts it on a par with Ibañez, Barbusse, Remarque and Steinbeck (*The Moon is Down*, 1942), though this is doubtful praise, as he berates all four for having failed to "reach the core of the problem", cf. the (problematic) article "Psychology of War Literature", *Sewanee Review* 52 (1944) 137–47.

49. The source here may emphasise the unhappy haphazardness: Hotspur, 1 *Henry IV*, 1.3.202.

50. Like e.g. Mr. Miniver in the *Mrs. Miniver* film (MGM, 1942). It shares nearly nothing with the book. Its propaganda effect was enormous.

51. This must have contributed to the success of Erskine Childers's *The Riddle of the Sands* (1903), a pre-Great War spy story, still popular today. Cf. Claude Cockburn, *Bestseller* (London, 1972) pp. 75–82.

52. How closely the experiences of 'Michael Carr' parallel those of Billany we may never know. The author, another of this war's 'Lost Generation', died mysteriously late in 1943 in or near Mantua.

53. Cf. in more detail E.C. Bufkin, *P.H. Newby* (Boston, 1975) pp. 66–79.

54. Cf. in particular *H.M. Corvette* (1942), re-publ. in *Three Corvettes* (London, 1945, repr. 1972).

55. *Unconditional Surrender* (London, 1961, repr. Harmondsworth, 1964) p. 168f.

56. *Officers and Gentlemen* (London, 1955, repr. Harmondsworth, 1964) p. 101.

57. Malcolm Bradbury first gave me the idea of connecting both works in a conversation held in 1975. I don't know how he would have developed it. A recent, interesting analysis of the trilogy is found in Andrew Rutherford, *The Literature Of War* (London, 1978) pp. 113–34.

58. *The Wind Cannot Read* (London 1947, repr. 1948) p. 59f.

59. From "Where are the War Poets?" (1943); quoted in Hewison, *Under Siege: Literary Life in London, 1939–1945* (London, 1977) p. 183.

60. Subtitled "The Fighting Man in World War II" (London 1980, repr. 1982); cf. ch. 8, pp. 314–37.

61. *The Eighth Passenger* (London, 1969, repr. 1971) p. 180.

62. For a balanced view cf. e.g. Max Hastings, *Bomber Command* (London, 1979).

63. Cf. *Enemy Coast Ahead* (note 28) p. 204f.

64. Cf. Sir Herbert Read's theses about the counter-productive impact of

painting the horrors of the Great War: "The Failure of War Books" in: *A Coat of Many Colours* (London, 1945, rev. edn, 1957) pp. 72–6; for a confirmation e.g. Philip Toynbee's Introduction to *The Distant Drum: Reflections on the Spanish Civil War* (London, 1976).

65. His reports (for the Scripps-Howard Newspapers) from Dec. 1940 to March 1941 were publ. in book form as *in England* (New York, 1941). There are of course plenty of British testimonies. For 'cheerfulness' see e.g. Donald Forbes, *Two Small Ships* (London, 1957, repr. 1959) p. 133.

## Chapter 2  France

1. Useful accounts of the Resistance include: H. Amroux, *La Grande Histoire des Français sous l'Occupation* (Paris, 1976–79); R. Kedward, *Resistance in Vichy France* (London, 1978); H. Michel, *Les Courants de pensée de la Résistance*, 2nd ed (Paris, 1958); *Vichy France: Old Guard and New Order, 1940–1944* (London, 1972).

2. *Les Collaborateurs, 1940–1945* (Paris, 1976).

3. *La Gerbe des forces* (Paris, 1937) p. 318.

4. "Vichy France, 1940–1944: The Literary Image", *French Literature and its Background* (London, 1970).

5. *Antimémoires*, vol I (Paris, 1967) p. 118.

6. G. Brée and G. Bernaure, eds., *Defeat and Beyond: An Anthology of French Wartime Writing, 1940–1945*, (New York, 1970) p. 6.

7. *La Résistance et ses poètes, I France 1940–1944* (Verviers, 1978) p. 295.

8. See E. Dunan, "La Propaganda-Abteilung de France", and "Sur la propagande allemande", *Revue d'Histoire de la deuxième guerre mondiale*, Oct. 1951 and Oct. 1966.

9. A limited amount of work has been carried out in this field: notably P.-M. Dioudonnat, *L'Argent Nazi à la conquête de la presse française* (Paris, 1981). See also H. Michel, *Paris allemande* (Paris, 1981) and *L'Affaire Grasset, documents* (Paris, 1949).

10. Paul Riche, a spokesman for Vichy, 18 Oct. 1940. Quoted in Seghers, vol. I, p. 75.

11. See H. Boterf, *La Vie parisienne sous l'occupation*, 2 vols (Paris, 1974 and 1975).

12. *Les Editions de Minuit. Historique et Bibliographie* (Paris, 1954).

13. *L'Allemagne vue par les écrivains de la Résistance* (Geneva, 1954).

14. The *Roland* and Alain Chartier's *Le Quadrilogue invectif* (clandestinely reprinted) became particularly popular during this period as statements of national greatness. The *Roland* served as a rather more European than French symbol in Graham Greene's *The Confidential Agent* (1939).

15. Quoted by J. O'Brien in "Clandestine French Literature during the Occupation", *Modern Language Journal*, Nov. 1946.

16. *Fragments d'un liber veritatis (1941–1942)*, (Paris, 1946) p. 9.

17. The question of the evolution and development of the concept of "littérature engagée", prior to Sartre's *Qu'est-ce que la Littérature?* (1947) is a complex one. Some interesting thoughts on its pre-war definition are contained in D. Schalk's *The Spectrum of Political Engagement* (Princeton, 1979).

18. Ibid., p. 5.

19. The same kind of approach is found in Kluge's *Schlachtbeschreibung* – see below Chapter 3, p. 127 f.

20. It is of course very likely that Rebatet's ideas about the inter-war years as outlined in *Les Décombres* became much firmer in his mind as a result of the war and that this is reflected in *Les Deux Etendards*.

21. Readers are referred to Chester W. Obuchowski's *Mars on Trial* (Madrid, 1978) Chs. 3–5 and to Beynon John's article (note 4).

22. Cf. Rieuneau, *op. cit.*

23. Kessel's rejection of fiction in favour of authentic lived situations is discussed with reference to the English version in Chapter 1, p. 19.

24. Such a reaction does not appear to be typical, however. A more likely response is to be found in Malraux's *L'Espoir* (Part III, ch. 4) where Manuel rejects music because it is so beautiful.

25. Ibid., p. 10.

26. Cf. Obuchowski, *op. cit.*, Chapter 4 for a detailed discussion of these two authors.

27. It is, of course, Saint-Exupéry's *Pilote de guerre* (1942) which exercises an important influence in this area. Though it stresses on dignity and French honour, the work was attacked by the Right wing for being subversive and was suppressed temporarily but it emerges from the war as both a work of commitment and a great literary work.

28. David Lodge in his *Modes of Modern Writing* (London, 1977) raises the question in a very informative way in connection with Orwell's work, notably "A Hanging", often assumed to be a "reportage" but falsely, according to Lodge.

29. For more detailed analysis of this text refer to Obuchowski, *op. cit.*, and Paulette Roy, *Jean-Louis Curtis, Romancier* (Paris, 1971).

30. Cf. Mary Green, *Louis Guilloux: An Artisan of Language* (York, South Carolina, 1980).

31. Quite apart from their satirical intentions on a social level, it is possible to see in the works of Dutourd and Aymé a literary satire at work. Both authors appear to be parodying the literature of Resistance and War. Perhaps this is more evident in Aymé for a series of footnotes to *Le Chemin des écoliers*, narrating the episodic and unlikely lives of passing characters, appear to offer an ironic comment on the narrative development of such works as Kessel's *L'Armée des ombres* and Gary's *Education européenne*. The use of coincidence in Dutourd's work points to a similar intention. There is no space to develop the argument here but it is certainly worth further attention.

32. Cf. Claude Francis, Fernande Gontier, *Les Ecrits de Simone de Beauvoir*, (Paris, 1979) p. 128 f.

33. Cf. J.E. Flower, *Roger Vailland: the Man and his Masks* (London, 1975) ch. II.

## Chapter 3  Germany

1. This catalogue is familiar not only in fiction but also from historical accounts, e.g. that of Michael Salewski in *Von der Wirklichkeit des Krieges* (Munich, 1976) p. 61, discussing the German failure to confront the past in

the immediate post-war decades. His outline can be paraphrased thus: "Business was good, criticism rare. Historians had little to say, since the relevant historical evidence was still in Allied hands. Wartime propaganda continued to prevail after the war and was accepted as gospel. Hitler was to blame for everything, and his strategic mistakes had cost Germany the war. The German soldier was the best in the world, the 'unconditional surrender' terms of the Allies had only served to unite the Germans against them, and so on. Despite the evidence of destruction all around them, the war-generation thought themselves in possession of the historical truth. Not until much later, at the end of the 60s, did doubts begin to arise."

2. Cf. Jochen Pfeifer, *Der deutsche Kriegsroman 1945–1960* (Königstein/Ts, 1981) p. 38 ff.

3. Examples are Willi Heinrich's *Das geduldige Fleisch* (1955); Manfred Gregor's *Die Brücke* (1958); Willi Berthold's *Kriegsgericht* (1959), or *Brigade Dirlewanger* (1961).

4. In this connection, I am greatly indebted to Mr Omer Bartov, of St. Antony's College Oxford, for allowing me access to a recent unpublished paper, "The Barbarisation of Warfare – German Officers and Men on the Eastern Front, 1941–1945".

5. This approach is suggested by Jochen Pfeifer, op. cit., p. 198.

6. See Dietrich Peinert, "Siegfried Lenz, *Deutschstunde*, eine Einführung", *Der Schriftsteller Siegfried Lenz*, ed. Colin Russ (Hamburg, 1973) p. 176.

7. The Nuremberg Laws of 1935 deprived Jews of their citizenship and forbade marriage with 'Germans'.

8. Compare the words of the female teacher in Horst Bienek's *Zeit ohne Glocken*: "Wir haben den Krieg nicht gewollt . . ."; "We didn't want the war, but they had us hemmed in on all sides."

9. The Russians are employing these captured German war materials against their manufacturers. The irony of self-inflicted injury is brought out also by Hermann Lenz (see p. 123, above), as well as in the outcome of Böll's *Wo warst du, Adam?*, where the hero, Feinhals, making his way home shortly before the end of hostilities, is killed by a German shell just as he reaches his parents' house.

10. The history of Gerlach's book earned it a certain notoriety when the novel first appeared. A 600-page draft was produced in Russian captivity in 1944/45, but confiscated. Gerlach was assisted by a hypnotist in his attempts to reconstruct the novel from memory after his return to Germany in 1950, and the more sensational press seized upon the story of his 'total amnesia' and of a novel supposedly 'written under hypnosis'. See "Nachwort", *Die Verratene Armee*, Heyne edition (Munich, 1978) p. 310.

11. The best-known East German war-fiction includes Franz Fühmann's novella *Kameraden*, 1955 (included in the collection *Die Elite*, Zurich, 1970); Herbert Ott's *Die Lüge* (1956); Horst Beseler's *Im Garten der Königin*, Karl Mundstock's *Bis zum letzten Mann*, Erwin Strittmatter's *Der Wundertäter* and Harry Thürk's *Die Stunde der toten Augen* (all 1957); Mundstock's *Sonne in der Mitternacht* (1959); Dieter Noll, *Die Abenteuer des Werner Holt*, (1960); and Max Walter Schulz, *Wir sind nicht Staub im Wind*, vol. 1, (1962). In other genres, there is also J.R. Becher's war drama of 1941, initially entitled *Schlacht um Moskau*, later *Winterschlacht*, and Fühmann's epic poem *Die Fahrt nach Stalingrad* (1953).

12. Andrew Rutherford, "Realism and the Heroic: Some Reflections on War Novels", *The Yearbook of English Studies*, Special Number section of vol. 12 (1982) pp. 194–207.

13. Quoted in David Luschnat, *Schriftsteller und Krieg* (Baden-Baden, 1947) p. 17.

14. Günter Grass, "Was lesen unsere Soldaten?", *Freiheit und Recht* ("Die Stimme der Widerstandskämpfer für ein freies Europa"), Jahrgang 16 (1970) Nr 4, p. 14f.

15. The need for a "clean" hero-figure was met by a best-selling tale of ultimate courage in isolation, televised in six parts and repeatedly shown on West German television: Josef Martin Bauer's compelling escape-novel, *So weit die Füße tragen* (1955), based on the real-life adventures of a German officer. The hero, Forell, escapes from POW slave-labour in the Siberian lead-mines and makes his way with enormous stamina and resourcefulness across the tundra and back to Germany. The book is a typical 1950s product, in that the stress is on the restoration of German pride; there is little reference to the recent wartime past, and a general assumption of the blamelessness of German POWs. "Why does he [a certain Dechant] always want to escape?", one POW asks another: "Well, if he's here through no fault of his own!" is the reply, to which the first counters: "We all are". This novel, too, like Kirst's *08/15* (see p. 110, above), can be seen as an anti-rhetorical and politically neutral restatement of certain pre-war and wartime values of strenuousness, self-discipline and personal redemption.

16. See also Hans Geulen, "Alfred Andersch. Probleme der dargestellten Erfahrung des 'deutschen Irrtums'", *Gegenwartsliteratur und Drittes Reich*, ed. Hans Wagener (Stuttgart, 1977) pp. 204–21.

17. *Gesammelte Werke*, Bd. 4, ed. Dieter Wellershoff (Wiesbaden, 1961) p. 94.

18. *Briefe an F.W. Oelze*, vol. I, 1932–45, ed. Harald Steinhagen and Jürgen Schröder, Frankf. a. M. 1979 (first published Wiesbaden and Munich, 1977) p. 265.

19. They could not fail to be reminded, after all, of the heady cultural discourse that represented an onslaught of *Geist* on political and social reality in the pre-Nazi Weimar Republic, and sought to legitimize anti-democratic thinking by reference to the German tradition. See Martin Swales, "In defence of Weimar", *Weimar Germany: Writers and Politics*, ed. A. Bance (Edinburgh, 1982) p. 7.

20. *Briefe an F.W. Oelze*, vol. I, p. 292. In the same letter (16 Nov. 1941) Benn enthuses over Platen's sonnets.

21. See Fritz Stern, *The Failure of Illiberalism* (London, 1972) p. 25.

22. Adorno, "Kulturkritik und Gesellschaft", *Prismen* (Frankfurt a. M. 1955), trans. Samuel and Shierry Weber as *Prisms* (London, 1967) p. 34.

23. The "reversal of values" or "world turned upside down" is of course no abstract notion but a matter of daily experience in the Third Reich where, for example, firemen *start* fires (the burning of the synagogues). Ray Bradbury's *Fahrenheit 451* shows how this particularly striking Nazi inversion of normality has entered the vocabulary of the popular imagination outside Germany.

24. These are in fact approximately the words of Oberleutnant Kreysler in Chapter 39 of Gaiser's *Die sterbende Jagd*.

25. In the East German literature, authors are ideologically bound to present

the opposite view and stress, like the title and the insistent main theme of Max Walter Schulz's novel, that "we are *not* like dust on the wind".

26. I refer to the as yet unpublished research of Mr. Omer Bartov. See Note 4, above.

27. It is at this point, among others, that serious literature runs parallel to the cheap war stories of the West German *Groschenheft* or *Landserheft* series, an analysis of which was not possible within the scope of this essay. The incidents described in these magazines frequently achieve a happy ending by presenting gallant, often successful, minor German actions and overlooking the awkward truth that the war as a whole is being lost. Other features are that officers become superman/father-figures; the enemy is heavily stereotyped (the Maquis are furtive, cowardly fighters; the Russians subhuman primitives); war is "fate", a natural catastrophe; what is condemned is the loss of the war, rather than war itself, and bad leadership at the top is to blame, etc. See Erhard Weidl, "Krieg im Groschenheft", *Basis* (Jahrbuch für deutsche Gegenwartsliteratur) Bd. 4/73, ed. Reinhold Grimm and Jost Hermand, pp. 38–47; also Heinz Brüdigam, *Der Schoß ist fruchtbar noch* (Frankfurt am Main, 1965); and Walter Nutz, "Der Krieg als Abenteuer und Idylle. Landser-Hefte und triviale Kriegsromane", *Gegenwartsliteratur und Drittes Reich*, ed. Hans Wagener, pp. 265–83.

28. Dr. Peter Hutchinson, of Selwyn College, Cambridge, has kindly supplied me with the transcript of an interesting interview he held with Heym recently in East Germany. The author claims that it was only due to the caution of his then American publishers (who were convinced that, on the experience of Remarque's *All Quiet on the Western Front*, a war novel could not succeed until ten years after the war) that *The Crusaders* did not appear before Norman Mailer's *The Naked and the Dead* and Irwin Shaw's *The Young Lions* (both 1948), to "take the cream of the trade"!

29. In e.g. Andersch's *Winterspelt*, and especially in Giordano's *Die Bertinis*, where, despite suffering all the horrors of Allied bombing, the Italian–Jewish–German Hamburg family identify so absolutely with the "enemy" that they have difficulty in regaining – as they must – a German identity at the end of the war. Cf. also Günter Kunert's remark, very close to the Bertinis' attitude, that "I knew the bombing was not directed at me, but at the 'others'. It was the just punishment that these people had undoubtedly deserved"; "Die Tortur", *Meine Schulzeit im Dritten Reich*, ed. Marcel Reich-Ranicki (Cologne, 1982) p. 198.

30. See *"Als der Krieg zu Ende war": Literarisch-politische Publizistik 1945–1950* (Eine Ausstellung des Deutschen Literaturarchivs im Schiller-Museum Marbach a. N.), ed. Bernhard Zeller (Munich, 1973) p. 86 ff.

31. Cf. Marijke Visch, "Zur Funktion von Dokumenten im historischen Roman. Eine exemplarische Untersuchung anhand von Alexander Kluges *Schlachtbeschreibung*, *Neophilologus* 64, no. 4 (Oct. 1980) pp. 564–82.

## Chapter 4     Soviet Union

1. B. Pasternak, *Doctor Zhivago*, trans. M. Hayward and M. Harari (London, 1958) p. 450.

2. A. Surkov, *Stikhotvoreniya, 1925–45, Sobranie sochinenii, Tom* I (Moscow, 1965) p. 374. All subsequent quotations from Surkov refer to the poems and prose in this publication.

3. A. Tolstoy, *Polnoe sobranie sochinenii, Tom* 14 (Moscow, 1950) p. 8.

4. A. Dovzhenko, *Ukraina v ogne* in *Literaturnoe nasledstvo, Tom* 78, *Kniga pervaya* (Moscow, 1966) p. 199. Unless otherwise indicated, all subsequent quotations from Dovzhenko refer to this work.

5. P. Vershigora, *Lyudi s chistoi sovest'yu* (Moscow, 1948) p. 105. All subsequent quotations from Vershigora refer to this work.

6. V. Nekrasov, *V okopakh Stalingrada* (Moscow, 1948) p. 20. Unless otherwise indicated, all subsequent quotations from Nekrasov refer to this publication.

7. I. Ehrenburg, *Burya* in *Sobranie sochinenii, Tom* 5 (Moscow, 1965) pp. 145–9.

8. B. Gorbatov, *Nepokorennye* in *Izbrannoe* (Moscow, 1947) p. 360. All subsequent quotations from Gorbatov refer to this work.

9. A. Solzhenitsyn, *Arkhipelag gulag, Chast'* I (Paris, 1973) p. 250.

10. Erich von Manstein, "The Development of the Red Army" in B. Liddell-Hart, ed., *The Red Army* (New York, 1956) p. 141.

11. K. Simonov, *Dni i nochi* in *Sobranie sochinenii v shesti tomakh, Tom* II (Moscow, 1967) p. 55.

12. E. Kazakevich, *Zvezda* and *Dvoe v stepi* in *Sochineniya v dvukh tomakh, Tom* II (Moscow, 1963) pp. 75, 110.

13. A. Mezhirov, Untitled poem in *Russkaya sovetskaya poeziya. Sobranie stikhov, Tom* II (Moscow, 1977) p. 500.

14. K. Simonov, "Iz biografii Saburova" in *Literaturnoe nasledstvo, Tom* 78, *Kniga pervaya* (Moscow, 1966) p. 74. Unless otherwise indicated, all subsequent quotations from Simonov refer to this work.

15. V. Inber, *Leningrad Diary*. Trans. S. Wolff and R. Grieve (London, 1971) p. 117. All subsequent quotations from Inber's prose refer to this publication.

16. M. Isakovsky, *Izbrannye stikhotvoreniya* (Moscow, 1947) pp. 7–8.

17. P. Antokol'sky *Izbrannoe* (Moscow, 1946) p. 180. All subsequent quotations from Antokol'sky refer to this publication.

18. M. Aliger, *Stikhotvoreniya i poemy v dvukh tomakh, Tom* I (Moscow, 1970) p. 148.

19. O. Berggol'ts, Untitled poem in *Sobranie sochinenii, Tom* II (Leningrad, 1973) p. 7.

20. A. Kurosheva, Untitled poem in: *Russkaya sovetskaya poeziya, Tom* II, p. 112.

21. V. Ketlinskaya, *V osade* (Leningrad, 1960) p. 528. All subsequent quotations from Ketlinskaya refer to this publication.

22. A. Fadeyev, *Molodaya gvardiya* (Moscow, 1946) p. 347.

23. A. Tolstoy, "Razgnevannaya Rossiya" in *Polnoe sobranie sochinenii, Tom* 14, p. 265.

24. S. Gudzenko, *Stikhi* (Moscow, 1961) p. 134. All subsequent quotations from Gudzenko refer to this publication.

25. M. Gershenzon, "God na voine" in *Literaturnoe nasledstvo, Tom* 78, *Kniga vtoraya*, p. 88.

26. A. Bek, *Volokolamskoe shosse, Sobranie sochinenii v chetyrekh tomakh, Tom* II (Moscow, 1975) pp. 18, 115.

27. V. Grossman, *Za pravoe delo, Novyi mir*, no. 8 (1952) p. 113. Unless otherwise indicated, all subsequent quotations from Grossman refer to the publication of the novel in *Novyi mir*, nos 7–10 (1952).

28. V. Grossman, "Iz zapisnykh knizhek voennykh let, 1941–2" in *Literaturnoe nasledstvo, Tom* 78, *Kniga vtoraya*, p. 159.
29. B. Slutsky, *V balal'one vyzdoravlivayushchikh* in *Pamyat'* (Moscow, 1969) p. 35.
30. M. Sholokhov, "Pervye frontovye ocherki" in *Literaturnoe nasledstvo, Tom* 78, *Kniga pervaya*, p. 40.
31. M. Svetlov, *Sobranie sochinenii, Tom* I (Moscow, 1974) p. 440.
32. V. Lebedev-Kumach, "Svyashchennaya voina in *Russkaya sovetskaya poeziya, Tom*, I, p. 342.
33. O. Berggol'ts, "Stikhi o vooruzhennom narode", *Sobranie sochinenii, Tom* II, p. 32.
34. A. Prokof'ev, Untitled poem in *Rossiya. Poemy i stikhi* (Moscow, 1971) p. 120.
35. A. Tvardovsky, "Zemlyaki", *Sobranie sochinenii, Tom* II (Moscow, 1959) p. 104. Unless otherwise indicated, all subsequent quotations from Tvardovsky refer to the poems in this publication.
36. N. Tikhonov, "Leninskoe znamya", *Stikhi i proza* (Moscow, 1945) p. 22.
37. I. Ehrenburg, *Voina. Aprel' 1942-Mart 1943* (Moscow, 1943) p. 22.
38. M. Aliger, "Zoya" in *Stikhotvoreniya i poemy v dvukh tomakh, Tom* I, p. 188. All subsequent quotations from Aliger refer to the poems in this publication.
39. W. Wassilewska, *Raduga* (Moscow, 1947) p. 39.
40. V. Inber, "Pulkovskii meridian", *Izbrannye proizvedeniya, Tom* I (Moscow, 1958) p. 368.
41. L. Sobolev, *Morskaya dusha. Rasskazy* (Moscow, 1943) p. 373.
42. I. Sel'vinsky, *Izbrannye proizvedeniya* (Leningrad, 1972) p. 206. All subsequent quotations from Sel'vinsky refer to the poems in this publication.
43. A. Dovzhenko, *Izbrannoe* (Moscow, 1957) p. 440.
44. Yu. Krymov, *Pis'ma s fronta, Znamya*, no. 3 (1944) p. 120.
45. "Voennyi put' E.G. Kazakevicha" in *Literaturnoe nasledstvo, Tom* 78, *Kniga vtoraya*, p. 449.
46. N. Chukovsky, *Baltiiskoe nebo, Znamya*, no. 7 (1954) p. 56.
47. A. Chakovsky, *Eto bylo v Leningrade* (Moscow, 1949) p. 46. All subsequent quotations from Chakovsky refer to this publication.
48. O. Berggol'ts, *Dnevnye zvezdy* (1959) in *Sobranie sochinenii, Tom* III, p. 309. All subsequent quotations from Berggol'ts' prose refer to this publication.
49. O. Berggol'ts, "Leningradskaya poema" in *Sobranie sochinenii, Tom* II, p. 65. All subsequent quotations from Berggol'ts' poetry refer to this publication.
50. Z. Shishova, "Blokada", *Znamya*, no. 2–3 (1943). All subsequent quotations from Shishova refer to this publication.
51. V. Inber, "Pulkovskii meridian", p. 383.
52. N. Tikhonov, *Stikhi i proza*, pp. 238, 240. All subsequent quotations from Tikhonov refer to this publication.
53. V. Grossman, *Gody voiny* (Moscow, 1946) pp. 304, 268.
54. K. Simonov, *Dni i nochi*, p. 145.
55. V. Grossman, *Gody voiny*, p. 257.
56. A. Tvardovsky, "Vasily Tyorkin" in: *Sobranie sochinenii, Tom* II, p. 221.
57. V. Vishnevsky, Entry of 6 October 1941, *Sobranie sochinenii, Tom* III (Moscow, 1956) p. 155. Entry of 17 March 1943, *Sobranie sochinenii, Tom* IV (Moscow, 1958) p. 127.
58. L. Leonov, *Vzyatie Velikoshumska, Sobranie sochinenii, Tom* VIII (Moscow, 1962) p. 9.

59. A. Nekrich, *Otreshis' ot strakha* (London, 1979) p. 22.
60. Yu. Bondarev, *Tishina, Izbrannye proizvedeniya, Tom* I (Moscow, 1977) p. 417.
61. E. Kazakevich, *Vesna na Odere* in *Sochineniya v dvukh tomakh, Tom* II, p. 478.
62. B. Okudzhava, *Proza i poeziya* (Frankfurt Main, 1968) p. 69.
63. G. Baklanov, *Iyul' 1941 goda, Novyi mir*, no. 2 (1965) p. 9.
64. K. Simonov, *Panteleev, Sobranie sochinenii v shesti tomakh, Tom* IV, p. 509.
65. S. Zlobin, *Propavshie bez vesti, Tom* I (Moscow, 1964) p. 395.
66. Yu. Bondarev, *Batal'ony prosyat ognya, Izbrannye proizvedeniya, Tom* I, p. 161.
67. G. Baklanov, *Mertvye sramu ne imut, Znamya*, no. 6 (1961) p. 58.
68. A. Kron, *Dom i korabl', Zvezda*, no. 9 (1964) pp. 18, 20.
69. V. Bykov, *Frontovaya stranitsa, Oktyabr'*, no 9 (1963) pp. 90, 103.
70. V. Bykov, *Kruglyanskii most, Novyi mir*, no. 3 (1969) pp. 32, 41.
71. A. Mezhirov, Untitled poem in: *Podkova* (Moscow, 1967) p. 3.
72. V. Nekrasov, *V rodnom gorode, Novyi mir*, no. 11 (1954) p. 162.
73. Yu. Bondarev, *Tishina*, p. 417.
74. L. Pervomaisky, *Dikii med, Oktyabr'*, no. 2 (1963) p. 25.
75. V. Grossman, *Zhizn' i sud'ba* (Lausanne 1980) p. 271.

## Chapter 5   United States

1. Louise Levita, "The *Naked* are Fanatics and the *Dead* Don't Care", *New York Star Magazine*, 22 Aug. 1948, p. 3. Quoted by Robert Solotaroff, *Down Mailer's Way* (Urbana, 1974) p. 18n.
2. Matthew J. Bruccoli, *Some Sort of Epic Grandeur: The Life of F. Scott Fitzgerald* (London, 1981) p. 86.
3. Malcolm Cowley in *The Literary Situation* (New York, 1955) p. 41, writes: "In the novels of the Second War I can find very few signs that their [American] authors have been reading French, German, or even English books."
4. Of all the extensive literature on writing on the Great War Paul Fussell's *The Great War and Modern Memory* (New York, 1975) stands out for its sensitivity and insight.
5. Captain Ralph Ingersoll, *The Battle is the Pay-Off* (Washington, 1943) p. 154.
6. Richard Tregaskis, *Guadalcanal Diary* (New York, 1943) p. 132. This feeling appears to have been widespread during the war, and after. The Welsh writer Alun Lewis wrote to his parents on 2 February 1944 from India:

> . . . although the Army is supposed to have everything it requires, I'm jiggered if I can equip my boys with the odd things they need. They give us bicycles and pumps and lamps, but no connections and bulbs. And so on. So what? We learn code after code, cipher after cipher: inevitably a new replaces the old. I think I'd prefer the 1914 type of war; it was more methodical than this one – and it ended before this one has really begun – for me.

(Alun Lewis, *In the Green Tree* [London, 1948] p. 59.) In the preface to a powerful memoir of the Vietnam war, Philip Caputo regretted the absence of clear, decisive battles in Vietnam:

Writing about this kind of warfare is not a simple task. Repeatedly, I have found myself wishing that I had been the veteran of a conventional war, with dramatic campaigns and historic battles for subject matter instead of a monotonous succession of ambushes and fire-fights. But there were no Normandies or Gettysburgs for us, no epic clashes that decided the fates of armies or nations.

(Philip Caputo, *A Rumor of War* [1977; London, 1978] p. xii.)

7. See Roger Manvell, *Films and the Second World War* (London, 1974) and Richard R. Lingeman, *Don't You Know There's a War On? The American Home Front, 1941–1945* (New York, 1971) ch. 6.
8. James Jones, *WW II* (New York, 1975) p. 150.
9. Ira Wolfert, *Battle for the Solomons* (Boston, 1943) p. 7.
10. John Gunther, *D Day* (New York, 1944) pp. 69–70.
11. John Hersey, *Into the Valley: A Skirmish of the Marines* (London, 1943) p. 43.
12. Ingersoll, *The Battle is the Pay-Off*, p. 156.
13. This debate is abundantly represented in Jack Salzman, ed., *The Survival Years: A Collection of American Writing of the 1940s* (New York, 1969) pp. 173–216.
14. John Morton Blum, *V was for Victory: Politics and American Culture During World War II* (New York, 1976) pp. 67–8, 46, 16.
15. Cowley, *The Literary Situation*, p. 27.
16. Hersey, *Into the Valley*, pp. 51–2.
17. J. Glenn Gray, *The Warriors: Reflections on Men in Battle*, with an Introduction by Hannah Arendt (New York, 1973) pp. 46–60. This is a major theme in novels of the Vietnam war. A character in one such novel, Lt. Hodges, recovering from shrapnel wounds in a hospital on Okinawa, and thinks of his old platoon:

    He missed the people in the bush, more than he had ever missed any group of people in his life. There was a purity in those relationships that could not be matched anywhere else. ... There was a common goal, and a mutual enemy.

    And, of course, Lt. Hodges turns down the chance to remain on Okinawa as Special Services Recreation Officer in order to return to what remains of his platoon. (James Webb, *Fields of Fire* [1978; London, 1981] p. 318.)

18. Ernest Hemingway, *For Whom the Bell Tolls* (1940; Harmondsworth, 1955) p. 227.
19. John Dos Passos, *USA* (Harmondsworth, 1966) p. 353. This comment was made apropos John Reed.
20. On this theme see Gray, *The Warriors*, pp. 60–9.
21. George Orwell, *Collected Essays, Journalism and Letters*, ed. Sonia Orwell and Ian Angus (London, 1968) I, p. 526.
22. Jones, *WW II*, p. 62.
23. Ira Wolfert, *American Guerrilla in the Philippines* (New York, 1945) p. 166 f.
24. See the discussion of wartime journalism in Blum, *V was for Victory*, ch. 2.

25. Philippe Ariès, *Western Attitudes toward Death: From the Middle Ages to the Present*, trans. Patricia M. Ranum (London, 1976) p. 100.

26. Tregaskis, *Guadalcanal Diary*, pp. 146–7.

27. Tregaskis, ibid., p. 69.

28. Milo Minderbender in *Catch-22*, who brings the true spirit of capitalist entrepreneurship to the conduct of war, is anticipated in detail by Corporal Soeft in Hans Hellmut Kirst's *Gunner Asch Goes to War*, trans. Robert Kee (London, 1956). Soeft is a type who would have been very much at home with the American Army in Naples (as described by John Horne Burns in *The Gallery*).

29. See *The Pentagon Papers, as published by The New York Times* (New York, 1971). In 1961 President Kennedy ordered 400 Special Forces soldiers and 100 other advisers to South Vietnam. The Joint Chiefs estimated that 40,000 US servicemen would be needed to "clean up the Vietcong threat". By 1967 the "optimum force" requested by General Westmoreland had reached 671 616.

## Chapter 6 Japan: a Perspective

1. In Japan as in Hungary the surname is placed first, the given name second.

# Select Bibliography

This bibliography is confined to material of direct relevance to the subject of the volume. Details of historical works or of critical studies of individual authors are to be found in the footnotes.

Abbé, Derek van, "Clio in the Underworld", *German Life and Letters*, 16 (1962) pp. 128–35.

Aichinger, Peter, *The American Soldiers in Fiction, 1880–1963* (Iowa State University Press, Ames, 1975).

Albright, W.P., "War and Fraternity: A Study of Some Recent American War Novels", *New Mexico Quarterly*, 21 (Winter 1952) pp. 461–74.

Aldridge, John, *After the Lost Generation: A Critical Study of the Writers of Two Wars* (Vision, London, 1957).

——, *Time to Murder and Create: The Contemporary Novel in Crisis* (Books for Libraries, New York, 1972; 1st pub. 1966).

Anderson, Rachel, *The Purple Heart Throbs: The Sub-Literature of Love* (Hodder & Stoughton, London, 1974).

[Anon], "The Novels of the Second World War", *Publisher's Weekly*, 154 (1948) pp. 1802–8.

Arnold, Heinz Ludwig, (ed.), *Deutsche Bestseller – Deutsche Ideologie: Ansätze zu einer Verbraucherpolitik* (Ernst Klett, Verlag, Stuttgart, 1975).

Baumgart, Reinhard, "Unmenschlichkeit beschreiben. Weltkrieg und Faschismus in der Literatur", *Merkur*, 19 (1965) pp. 37–50.

Belaya, G., Borev, Yu., Piskunov, V., "Literatura perioda Velikoi Otechestvennoi Voiny", *Istoriya russkoi sovetskoi Voiny, Tom* III (Moscow, 1968).

Bennemann, Heinrich, *Der II Weltkrieg im englischen Roman*, Doctoral Thesis (Leipzig University, 1963).

Bentley, Eric, "Literature of the Third Reich" (1943), repr. in *One Hundred Years of 'The Nation': A Centennial Anthology*, ed. by Henry M. Christman (The Macmillan Company, New York, 1965) pp. 234–40.

Benson, Frederick R., *Writers in Arms: The Literary Impact of the Spanish Civil War* (London University Press, 1967).

Bernstein, Walter, "Soldiers and Warbooks", *The Saturday Review of Literature*, 7 July 1945, pp. 9–11.

Bieber, Konrad, *L'Allemagne vue par les écrivains de la Résistance* (Droz, Geneva, 1954).

Blum, John Morton, *V was for Victory: Politics and Culture during World War II* (Harcourt, Brace, Jovanovich, New York, 1976).

Boisdeffre, Pierre de, *Une Histoire vivante de la littérature d'aujourd'hui, 1939–59* (Le Livre contemporain, Paris, 1959).

Brée, Germaine and Bernaver, George, *Defeat and Beyond: An Anthology of French Wartime Writing, 1940–1945* (Pantheon Books, New York, 1970).

Brüdigam, Heinz *'Der Schoß ist fruchtbar noch': Neonazistische, militaristische, nationalistische Literatur und Publizistik in der Bundesrepublik* (Röderberg-Verlag, Frankfurt a. M., 1964).

Burke, Kenneth, "War and Cultural Life", *American Journal of Sociology*, 48 (1942–3) pp. 404–10.

Byalik, B., "Podvig sovetskoi literatury", *Literaturnoe nasledstvo, Tom 78, Kniga pervaya* (Moscow, 1966).

Cadogan, Mary and Craig, Patricia, *Women and Children First: The Fiction of Two World Wars* (Gollancz, London, 1979).

Cayrol, Jean, "D'un Romanesque concentrationnaire", *Esprit*, Sept. 1949, pp. 340–57.

Cowley, Malcolm "American Literature in Wartime", *The New Republic*, 12 (Aug. 1940).

——, *The Literary Situation* (Viking, New York, 1954; André Deutsch, London, 1955).

Craig, David and Egan, Michael, *Extreme Situations: Literature and Crisis from the Great War to the Atom Bomb* (Macmillan, London, 1979).

Cysarz, Herbert, *Zur Geistesgeschichte der Weltkriege* (Verlag Herbert Lang & Cie. AG, Berne and Frankfurt a. M., 1973).

Dempsey, David, "The Novelist and the Soldier", *New York Times Book Review*, 9 Dec. 1945.

Denkler, Horst and Prümm, Karl (eds.), *Die deutsche Literatur im Dritten Reich* (Philipp Reclam jun., Stuttgart, 1976).

Debû-Bridel, Jacques (ed.), *La Résistance intellectuelle. Textes et témoignages* (Julliard, Paris, 1970).

Eisinger, Chester E., "The American War Novel: An Affirming Flame", *The Pacific Spectator*, 9 (Summer 1955) pp. 272–87.

——, *Fiction of the Forties* (University of Chicago Press, 1963).

Ellis, John, *The Sharp End of War: The Fighting Man in World War II* (David & Charles, London, 1980; Corgi Books, London, 1982).

Feigenbaum, Lawrence H., *War as Viewed by the Postwar Novelists of World Wars I and II*, Doctoral Thesis (New York University, 1950).

Field, Frank, *Three French Writers and the Great War: Studies in the Rise of Communism and Fascism* (Cambridge University Press, 1975).

Frederick, John T., "Fiction of the Second World War", *College English*, 17, no. 4 (Jan. 1956) pp. 197–204.

Fussell, Paul, *The Great War and Modern Memory* (Oxford University Press, New York and London, 1977; 1st pub. 1975).

Gieger, Klaus F. (ed.), *Kriegsromanhefte in der BRD. Inhalte und Funktionen* (Tübinger Vereinigung für Volkskunde e.V., Tübingen, 1974).

Geulen, Hans, "Alfred Andersch. Probleme der dargestellten Erfahrung des 'deutschen Irrtums'", *Gegenwartsliteratur und Drittes Reich*, (ed. Hans Wagener) pp. 205–221.

Grass, Günter, "Was lesen unsere Soldaten", *Freiheit und Recht*, 16, no. 4 (1970) pp. 14–15.

Halprin, Lee S., "American Liberalism, Literature and World War II", *Minnesota Review*, 3 (Winter 1963) pp. 179–191.

Harris, Frederick J., *Encounters with Darkness: French and German Writers on World War II* (Oxford University Press, New York, 1983).

Harrison, Tom "War Books", *Horizon*, 4, no. 24 (Dec. 1941) pp. 416–37.

Hewison, Robert, *Under Siege: Literary Life in London 1939–1945* (Weidenfeld & Nicolson, London, 1977).

Hicks, Granville, "Literature and the War", *College English*, 1, no. 3 (Dec. 1939) pp. 199–207.

——, "Literature in this Global War", *College English*, 4, no. 4 (May 1943) pp. 453–9.

Holthusen, H.E., "Reflexionen eines Deserteurs, [*Alfred Andersch*]", *Ja und Nein* (R. Piper & Co. Verlag, Munich, 1954) pp. 207–18.

John, S.B., "Vichy France, 1940–1944: The Literary Image", *French Literature and its Background* (ed. John Cruickshank), vol. 6, *The Twentieth Century* (Oxford University Press, London, 1970) pp. 205–25.

Jones, Judith R.Z., *Metamophorses of a Defeat: the 1940 Débâcle in the French Novel,* Doctoral Thesis (Stanford University, 1977).

Jones, Peter G., *War and the Novelist: Appraising the American War Novel* (Missouri University Press, Columbia and London, 1976).

Kazin, Alfred, "The Mindless Young Militants: The Hero-Victim of the American War Novels", *Commentary,* 6 (Dec. 1948) pp. 494–501.

Klein, H.M. (ed.), *The First World War in Fiction* (Macmillan, London, 1979; 1st pub. 1976).

Kuby, Erich, *Das Ende des Schreckens – Dokumente des Untergangs Januar bis Mai 1945* (Süddeutscher Verlag, Munich, 1957).

Kunnas, Tarmo, "La Littérature de guerre finnoise entre 1939 et 1963", *Études Finno-Ougriennes,* 13 (1976) pp. 40–68.

Langer, Lawrence L., *The Holocaust and the Literary Imagination* (Yale University Press, London and New York, 1975).

Lebedeva, M., *Russkaya sovetskaya literatura perioda Velikoi Otechestvennoi Voiny* (Moscow, 1964).

Lippit, Noviko Misuta, *Reality and Fiction in Modern Japanese Literature* (Macmillan, New York, 1980).

Loewy, Ernst, *Literatur unterm Hakenkreuz* (Europäische Verlagsanstalt, Frankfurt a. M., 1966).

Luschnat, David, *Schriftsteller und Krieg* (Schriftenreihe "Zwei Welten", Baden-Baden, 1947).

Manwell, Roger, *Films and the Second World War* (A.S. Barnes and Co., New York; J.M. Dent and Sons, London, 1974).

Mecklenburg, Norbert, "Faschismus und Alltag in deutscher Gegenwartsprosa. Kempowski und andere", *Gegenwartsliteratur und Drittes Reich* (ed. Hans Wagener) pp. 11–32.

Miller, Wayne C., *An Armed America: A History of the American Military Novel* (New York University Press, 1970).

Morel, Robert, *La Littérature clandestine* (Fanlac, Périgueux, 1945).

Moss, Hella, *Das Kriegserlebnis 1939–1945 im Spiegel der englischen erzählenden Literatur,* Doctoral Thesis (Marburg University, 1951).

Nahrgang, Wilbur Lee, *Attitudes Toward War in German Prose Literature of the Second World War, 1945–1960* (University of Kansas Press, 1966).

Newby, P.H., *The Novel 1945–1950* (Longmans, Green & Co. for The British Council, London, 1951).

Nutz, Walter, "Der Krieg als Abenteuer und Idylle. Landser-

Hefte und triviale Kriegsromane", *Gegenwartsliteratur und Drittes Reich* (ed. Hans Wagener) pp. 265–83.

O'Brien, J., "Clandestine French Literature during the Occupation", *Modern Language Journal*, 30, no. 7 (Nov. 1946) pp. 441–8.

Obuchowski, Chester W., *Mars on Trial. War as Seen by French Writers of the Twentieth Century* (Studia Humanitatis, Madrid, 1978).

Oldsey, Bernard S., *Aspects of Combat in the Novel, 1900–1950*, Doctoral Thesis (Pennsylvania State University, 1955).

Pfeifer, Jochen, *Der deutsche Kriegsroman 1945–1960: Ein Versuch zur Vermittlung von Literatur und Sozialgeschichte*, Scriptor, Königstein/Ts., 1981).

Plotkin, L., *Literatura i voina* (Moscow and Leningrad, 1967).

Prümm, Karl, "Das Erbe der Front. Der antidemokratische Kriegsroman der Weimarer Republik und seine nationalsozialistische Fortsetzung", *Die deutsche Literatur im Dritten Reich*, (ed. Horst Denkler and Karl Prümm) pp. 138–64.

Rappmannberger, Franz J., "Zur belletrististischen Literatur des 2. Weltkrieges", *Wehrukunde*, 6 (1957) pp. 661–6.

Remenyi, Joseph, "Psychology of War Literature", *Sewanee Review*, 52 (Winter 1944) pp. 137–47.

Rieuneau, Maurice, *Guerre et révolution dans le roman français de 1919 à 1939* (Klincksieck, Paris, 1974).

Ritchie, J.M.H., *German Literature under National Socialism* (Croom Helm, London, 1983).

Russ, Colin (ed.), *Der Schriftsteller Siegfried Lenz* (Hoffmann und Campe, Hamburg, 1973).

Rutherford, Andrew, *The Literature of War: Five Studies in Heroic Virtue* (Macmillan, London, 1978).

——, "Realism and the Heroic: Some Reflections on War Novels", *The Yearbook of English Studies*, Special Number section of vol. 12 (1982) pp. 194–207.

Rymer, J. Thomas, *Modern Japanese Fiction and its Tradition* (Princeton University Press, 1978).

Salewski, Michael, *Von der Wirklichkeit des Krieges: Analysen und Kontroversen zu Buchheims 'Boot'* (dtv) (Munich, 1976).

Scannell, Vernon, *Not Without Glory: Poets of the Second World War* (Woburn Press, London, 1976).

Schütz, W.W., *Pens under the Swastika: A Study in Recent German Writing* (SCM Press, London, 1946).

Schwartz, Delmore, "New Writing in Wartime", *The Nation*, 12

Aug. 1944.

Schwarz, Wilhelm J., *War and the Mind of Germany*, (European University Papers no. 117) (Verlag Herbert Lang & Cie. AG, Berne and Frankfurt a. M., 1975).

Simmons, E., "The Organisation Writer (1934–46)", *Literature and Revolution in Soviet Russia 1917–1962* (ed. M. Hayward and L. Labedz), (Cambridge University Press, London, 1963).

Sinyavsky, A., "Literatura perioda Velikoi Otechestvennoi Voiny", *Istoriya russkoi sovetskoi literatury*, Tom III (Moscow, 1961).

Smith, Myron J. Jnr. *War Story Guide: An Annotated Bibliography of Military Fiction*, (The Scarecrow Press Inc., Metuchen, New Jersey and London, 1980).

Smith, W.J., "The War Novel", *Commonweal*, 64 (11 May 1956) pp. 146–9.

Struve, G., *Soviet Russian Literature, 1917–1950* (University of Oklahoma Press, Norman, 1951).

Sutherland, John, *Bestsellers: Popular Fiction of the 1970s*, (Routledge & Kegan Paul, London, 1981).

Trilling, Diana, *Reviewing the Forties* (Harcourt, Brace, Jovanovich, New York, 1978).

Vincent, Melvin J., "Fiction Mirrors the War", *Sociology and Social Research*, Nov. 1945, pp. 101–11.

Visch, Marijke, "Zur Funktion von Dokumenten im historischen Roman. Eine exemplarische Untersuchung anhand von Alexander Kluges 'Schlachtbeschreibung'", *Neophilologus*, 44, no. 4 (Oct. 1980) pp. 564–82.

Vondung, Klaus (ed.), *Kriegserlebnis: Der Erste Weltkrieg in der literarischen Gestaltung und symbolischen Deutung der Nationen* (Vandenhoeck & Ruprecht, Göttingen, 1980).

Wagener, Hans, "Soldaten zwischen Gehorsam und Gewissen. Kriegsromane und tagebücher", *Gegenwartsliteratur und Drittes Reich*, (ed. Hans Wagener) pp. 241–64.

——, *Gegenwartsliteratur und Drittes Reich: Deutsche Autoren in der Auseinandersetzung mit der Vergangenheit* (Philipp Reclam Jun., Stuttgart, 1977).

Waldmeir, Joseph J., *American Novels of the Second World War* (Mouton, The Hague, 1969).

Wehdeking, V.C., *Der Nullpunkt: Uber die Konstituierung der deutschen Nachkriegsliteratur (1945–1948) in den amerikanischen Kriegsgefangenenlagern* (J.B. Metzler, Stuttgart, 1971).

Weidl, Erhard, "Krieg im Groschenheft", *Basis*, 4 (1973) pp. 38–47.

Wolle, Francis, "Novels of Two World Wars", *Western Humanities Review*, 5 (1951) pp. 270–90.

Zeller, Bernhard (ed.), *"Als der Krieg zu Ende war": Literarisch-politische Publizistik 1945–1950. Eine Ausstelluug* ... Kösel-Verlag, Munich, for the Deutsches Literaturardiv am Schiller – National Museum Marbach, 1973).

# Name Index

239

# Subject Index